# GREAT
# GAME ON

# GREAT GAME ON

## THE CONTEST FOR CENTRAL ASIA AND GLOBAL SUPREMACY

## GEOFF RABY

MELBOURNE
UNIVERSITY
PRESS

Melbourne University Publishing acknowledges the traditional owners of the unceded land on which we work, learn and live: the Wurundjeri Woiwurrung peoples of the Kulin Nation. We pay respect to elders past, present and future, and acknowledge the importance of Indigenous knowledge.

MELBOURNE UNIVERSITY PRESS
An imprint of Melbourne University Publishing Limited
Level 1, 715 Swanston Street, Carlton, Victoria 3053, Australia
mup-contact@unimelb.edu.au
www.mup.com.au

**f** X 🔘

First published 2024
Reprinted 2025
Text © Geoff Raby, 2024
Maps © Guy Holt, 2024
Design and typography © Melbourne University Publishing Limited, 2024

Cover design by Peter Long
Typeset by Megan Ellis
Cover images by Alamy (Jochen Eckel/Süddeutsche Zeitung Photo) (Vladimir Putin) and Shutterstock (Xi Jinping)
Printed in Australia by McPherson's Printing Group

NATIONAL LIBRARY OF AUSTRALIA    A catalogue record for this book is available from the National Library of Australia

9780522879667 (paperback)
9780522879674 (ebook)

*For Susan Bolvenkel-Prior, who has lived with this book in our lives longer, and more intrusively, than one could reasonably expect.*

# CONTENTS

# ACKNOWLEDGEMENTS

This book would not have happened without the encouragement, support and guidance of Professor James Curran. I am also deeply grateful to Nathan Hollier, who originally commissioned the work and commented on early drafts; to Syd Hickman and Ralph Hillman for reading and correcting the entire draft, and for their incisive comments; to Lucinda Holdforth for inspiration and practical encouragement to write; to Sarina Rowell for her masterful and sympathetic detailed editing; and to many friends and colleagues in Beijing, among the foreign and local think tank, business, media and public commentariat communities, who will know who they are. I am also thankful to two anonymous referees; and to my editor and publisher, Foong Ling Kong at Melbourne University Publishing, who patiently helped me land this work. I would especially like to thank Cathy Smith, Senior Editor at Melbourne University Publishing, for her close attention to the manuscript at every stage. As ever, all mistakes belong to me.

# PREFACE

My thinking about this book began soon after the US and North Atlantic Treaty Organization (NATO) forces fled Afghanistan in 2021. It might have been the parallels with the fall of Saigon that captured my attention: the US's messy retreat in the face of what was a significantly weaker enemy in terms of resources and brute firepower. In the reporting of the shambolic turn of events returning the Taliban to power after twenty years of insurgency, the thought seemed to be lost that this was the Western powers' last hurrah in Central Asia. The long-contested field had suddenly been left to Russia and China.

This was a momentous event in global history but was treated more as a local incident in public discussion in the West. Afghanistan's place in the stability of the Eurasian order and, from there, the global order was scarcely appreciated. There seemed to be a good opening for a survey of the subject to help inform public discussion on the future of Eurasia and what it means for the world order. As I was living in Australia, from where Eurasia feels so distant, this was to be a boutique endeavour.

Having been a diplomat and senior civil servant for twenty-seven years, I understand how senior policy makers and politicians usually form their views, and ultimately formulate and implement policies—sometimes fatally, as with the US's failed interventions in Vietnam, Iraq and Afghanistan. I had only recently published my book on China's grand strategy and what it might mean for Australian foreign policy. A book on Eurasia minus the West seemed like a relatively straightforward extension of my previous book. I had also been intrigued by how little, until the First Opium War (1839–42), China's maritime frontiers had mattered to its sense of security.

When my thinking about the book was well underway, two further events suddenly seemed to make the task much more substantial, and therefore challenging and protracted. The presidents of China and Russia announced a pact of bilateral cooperation based on their asserted 'friendship without limits'. Western media, amplified by politicians and their modern camp followers of think-tank analysts, saw this as an 'axis of autocracies' and declared there was now just one theatre of security: the West versus the rest. But this seemed to neglect the long and complicated history of China and Russia, and how, because of geography and experience, they view their security differently. The second event was Putin's invasion of Ukraine, and what this meant for Russia's relations with China and Central Asia. China's ambivalent response—little different from that of India and many other countries—attracted the most opprobrium from the usual group of suspects in Western media and governments. The task I had set myself was now, to my mind, a much greater challenge than when I began. Hence, discussion of China and Russia in the past, present and future now accounts for a big part of this book.

With the US and NATO's retreat from Afghanistan, Putin's invasion of Ukraine, and China's inexorable economic, military and diplomatic ascendency, a new Great Game in Eurasia is in play, within a new context. The stage is the same, but the pieces have changed, and some new actors are engaged, while the European imperial powers have gone. But this Great Game, unlike its predecessor, will profoundly affect the global order. This book attempts to understand the forces shaping what may end up being epochal changes. Unusually for a work by a Western analyst, it is written from the perspective of China's ancient quest for security in Eurasia, which ultimately determines its moves on the board. As someone who has lived in Beijing, as I have, for almost twenty years in total, as a senior diplomat, businessman and analyst, the world of geostrategy and security looks very different when viewed from there than it does from Washington or, say, Canberra.

This book is written for a non-specialist, lay audience, in the hope it will better inform public discussion about these issues and hence better inform policy decisions. It is geopolitics from the ground up. My own travel stories are woven into the places, histories and politics covered by this study. It is hoped that this will make for an approachable and interesting introduction to what is otherwise a vast and complex subject.

# A NOTE ON EURASIA

The definition of Eurasia is a bit like variable geometry: it can define a place by different reference points at different times depending on the purpose. One is reminded of Alice chatting gaily with Humpty Dumpty in Lewis Carroll's *Alice in Wonderland*. When she asks how many meanings a word can have, Humpty Dumpty replies, 'When I use a word, it means just what I choose it to mean, neither more nor less.' At its most expansive, the definition of Eurasia can stretch from China's eastern littoral west to some distinctive geographical point in Europe, such as the Vistula River in Poland, and southwest to the Caspian Sea and Iran. More usually, it is used to describe an area from China through Central Asia to the Caucasus Mountains, between the Caspian Sea and Black Sea. This is the meaning used in this book. But, more importantly for the present study, is the subset of Core Eurasia. For simplicity, this is the five Central Asian states (Kazakhstan, Uzbekistan, Turkmenistan, Tajikistan and Kyrgyzstan), Afghanistan, Mongolia and China. Something of a novelty in this book is that China's Xinjiang is treated as a stand-alone territory— not because it is being suggested it is not part of the People's Republic of China, which it patently is, but to draw attention to its historically deep ethnic, religious, cultural and linguistic connections with much of Central Asia to the west. Well after work on this study commenced, I became aware that Central Asia scholar Adeeb Khalid had done the same in his book.[1] And one last point on geography: Central Asia is divided by the north–south Tian Shan mountains, which mark China's western frontier. On the west side is Turkestan, or West Turkestan; on the east is East Turkestan.

# A NOTE ON NAMES AND PLACES

In most academic studies of the history and geopolitics of the lands and peoples covered in these pages are detailed explanations of different spellings and usages of proper nouns over the centuries. In writing this book, I have sought both simplicity and familiarity by adopting what I hope are the most recognisable contemporary usages. Sometimes, this will involve inconsistencies; for example, while current Chinese *pinyin* transliteration is used throughout, Kuomingtang, abbreviated as KMT, from the older Wade–Giles spelling, is used; rather than Guomingdang, abbreviated as GMD, from *pinyin*. Sometimes, older English names are used for places whose historical significance occurred during colonial occupation: such as the use of Port Arthur, rather than Lvshun, when referring to the deep warm-water port in China at the terminus of the Trans-Manchurian Railway. Where a place is also of recent significance, its current name is used as well: for example, Port Arthur (Lvshun) and the Upper Oxus (Amu Darya) river. Far too many instances of spelling variations exist to list all of them here, but frequently occurring in this book are Khotan, rather than Hotan, for the southwest Xinjiang oasis; and Dzungar, rather than Zunghar or Junggar, for the ancient Central Asian Mongolian khanate. It is hoped sufficient context is provided for the persons and places to be readily recognised.

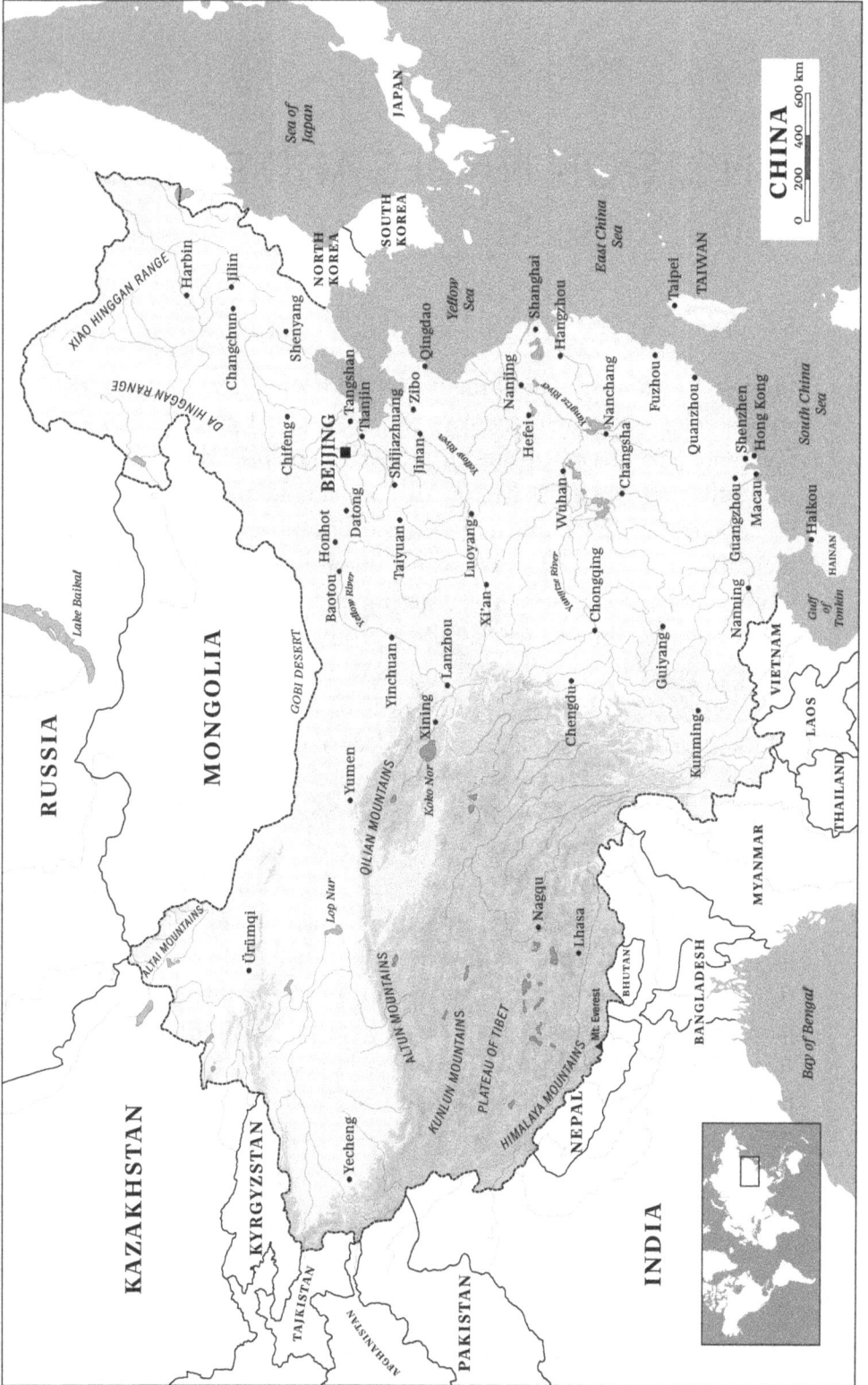

AMUR RIVER

0 100 200 300 km

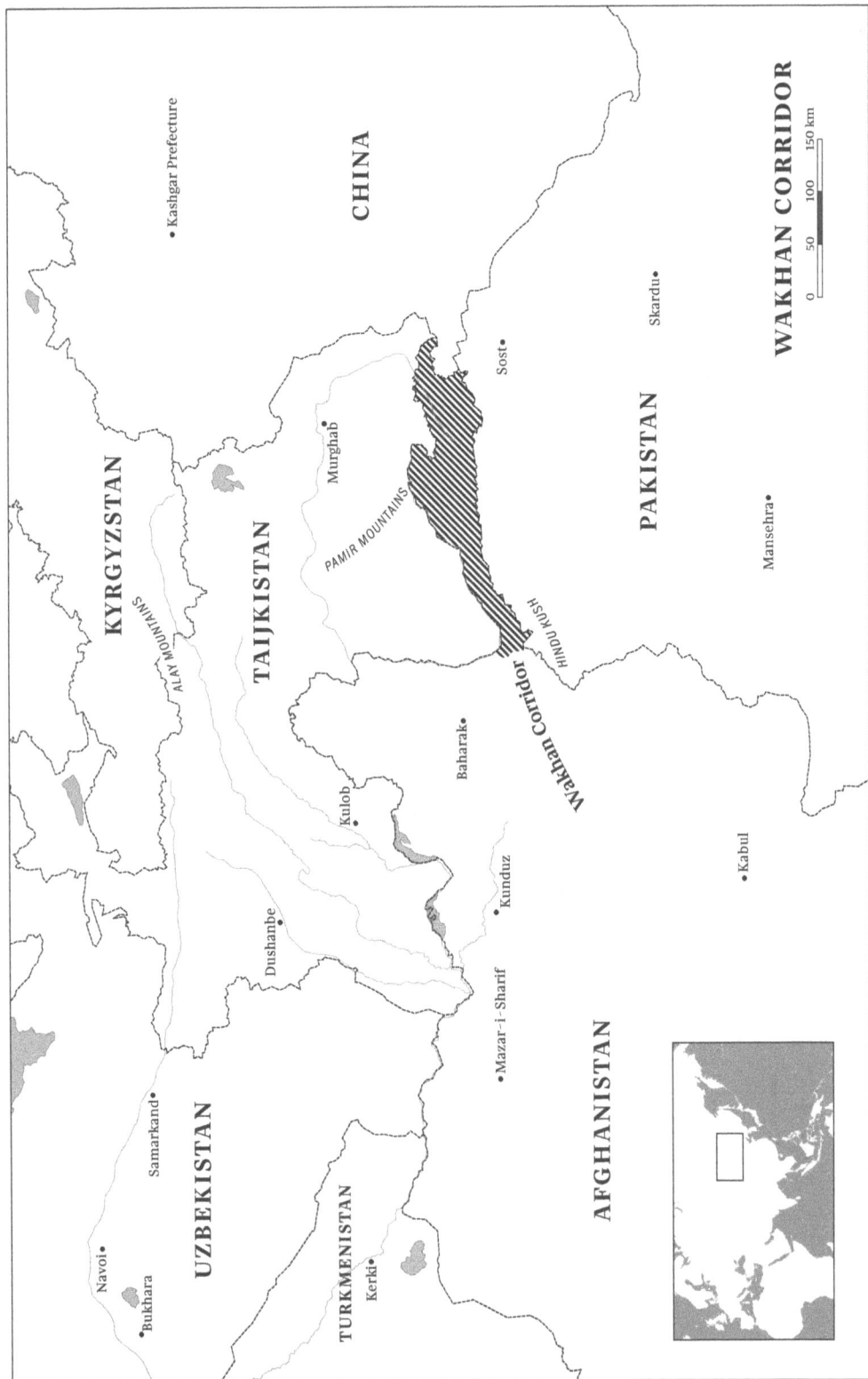

WAKHAN CORRIDOR

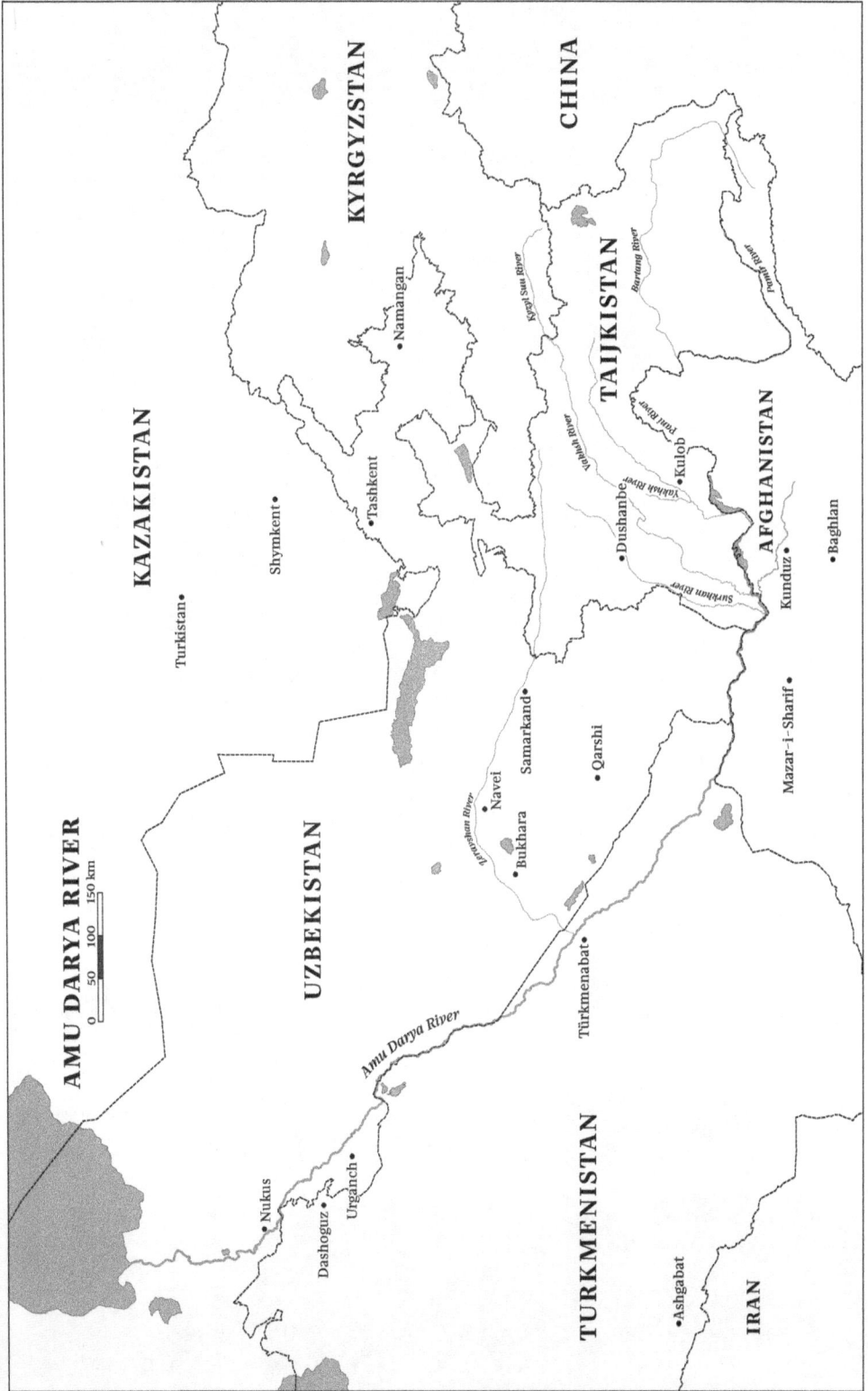

KYRGYZSTAN

CHINA

KAZAKISTAN

•Namangan

TAIJKISTAN

Naryn Suu River

Bartang River

•Tashkent

Panj River

•Shymkent

Vakhsh River

Panj River

AFGHANISTAN

•Dushanbe

•Kulob

Yakhsh River

•Turkistan

•Baghlan

Surkhan River

•Kunduz

Zeravshan River

•Samarkand

•Navei

•Qarshi

•Bukhara

•Mazar-i-Sharif

UZBEKISTAN

AMU DARYA RIVER

0   50  100   150 km

Türkmenabat•

Amu Darya River

•Nukus

•Urganch

Dashoguz •

TURKMENISTAN

•Ashgabat

IRAN

# CHAPTER 1

# EURASIAN HINGE OF THE GLOBAL ORDER

*'… a place like Kashgar might usually be associated with back-of-beyond travel writing. But, in fact, it could be the centre of the world geopolitical order.'*[1]

On 15 August 2021, the US fled Afghanistan, just as all past invading empires have done. The US and its allies' 20-year occupation of Afghanistan was the longest in modern history. Like all the others, it was utterly unsuccessful. It was not just the way the US left: chaotic scenes at the airport; bodies of desperate Afghanis dropping from a transport plane as it took off; a flood of refugees seeking safe passage out of their homeland; and officials prevaricating and, sometimes, lying about which loyal Afghan local support staff for diplomatic missions would receive documents to enable them to leave.

Images of mayhem, panic and widespread despair instantly filled online reports and multiple tweets globally. The world was riveted by this mess. *So, this is how the End of Empire looks?* Some of us who were from an older generation had seen it all before. We had waited expectantly for the nightly black-and-white television broadcasts of the collapse of Saigon in South Vietnam. Seared into our memories were grainy images of US military helicopters lifting diplomats and local staff off the roof of the American embassy—an embassy to a country that no longer existed. In 2021, apart from the fact that we were watching the retreat from Kabul on our smart phones, it was eerily familiar.

It was not just the dramatic pictures: it was that both occupations, so costly in blood and treasure, were ultimately about a vague idea based on little understanding of the historical and political conditions at play in the countries invaded. In Vietnam, it was saving the country from 'communism' and, beyond that, defeating a non-existent threat of Chinese communism taking over South-East Asia. In Afghanistan, it was ridding the country of Islamic-inspired jihadist terrorism and building a secular liberal democratic state in the heart of Central Asia, where none had ever existed.

In an earlier geopolitical contest—which came to be popularly known as the Great Game—played out between Great Britain and Imperial Russia for control of Central Asia and India between 1842 and 1907, Russia's designs on British India existed mainly in the minds of London officials and bellicose media. By the start of the twentieth century, the moniker 'Great Game' had become shorthand for British and Russian imperial competition in Eurasia. At the time, it was a widely accepted phenomenon but of limited historical validity. With strong resonance for today's China Threat, Britain's imperial strategists, politicians and the popular media believed it posed an existential challenge to British rule in India. That Russia sought to acquire British India was deemed to be true by definition. It was a revealed truth; in much the same way that today's China Threat has become. Demonstration that this was in fact Russia's intention was not required. Never mind if a yawning gap existed between whatever the tsar's real intentions may have been towards India and Russia's actual capacity to achieve them. Chapter 2 of this book discusses the supposed threat having been more imagined than real.[2]

Similarly, the public justification for US and allied involvement in the Vietnam War was based on China's purported designs on South-East Asia. As with their forwardist, or hawkish, colleagues in London a hundred years earlier, the threats in the case of Vietnam were also mainly in the minds of Washington think-tank analysts, military strategists, Pentagon planners and media cheerleaders for war.

## Crucibles of Instability—Afghanistan and Xinjiang

The Western retreat from Afghanistan saw the return of the Taliban. After twenty years, nothing was achieved. Afghanistan in the heart of Central Asia is again run by a terrorist organisation. It will again be free to nurture and promote Islamic militantism beyond its borders. The liberal experiments of educating girls, respecting women's rights and abandoning a theocratic state have ended. Western financial sanctions pile on more misery for the people and, most likely, strengthen hardliners in government.

The consequences of the West's failure in Afghanistan are profound. Central Asia is now a more dangerous and potentially unstable region than it has been for the past twenty years, with a heightened threat of Islamic militantism reaching from the Caucuses through Central Asia to Xinjiang. The age-old dream, held by Islamic fundamentalists, of the region becoming a caliphate may no longer be something to be dismissed out of hand.

Both Russia and China would have been sorry to see the US leave Afghanistan, despite being uncomfortable with its substantial military presence in Central Asia.[3] Both will eventually need to find accommodation with the government in Kabul, and seek to persuade, bribe or cajole it not to sponsor terrorism beyond its borders. The chances of doing so, however, are slim. As explained in Chapter 3, even if the Kabul government were itself willing to assist in limiting the spread of fundamentalism across Afghanistan's borders, it is already under challenge from various radical strains of Islamic fundamentalism within Afghanistan. Meanwhile, Afghanistan-based terrorist groups are seeking to destabilise Pakistan, an erstwhile Taliban supporter.[4]

Potential radicalisation of Xinjiang and the stirring of an East Turkestan independence movement have long been of concern to Beijing.[5] Since 2017, its heavy-handed policies in Xinjiang to 'strike hard' against Islamic fundamentalism and separatism are likely to contribute to bringing about what it is seeking to avoid: namely, further radicalisation of Xinjiang's Islamic populations. Some Uyghur militants have received training with the Taliban. Afghan-based Uyghur militants can be expected to become an even more important source of instability in Xinjiang in future.[6]

China was the first country to meet with the new Taliban leadership. The meeting occurred in Tianjin with foreign minister Wang Yi, just weeks before the Taliban took control of Kabul.[7] China has been active in organising regional partners to support Afghanistan and, unilaterally, via the Belt and Road Initiative (BRI), has proposed extending the China-Pakistan Economic Corridor (CPEC) from Peshawar through the Khyber Pass into Afghanistan.[8] Speculation abounds that Beijing intends to build rail and road links between Kabul and Kashgar via the Wakhan Corridor.[9]

While most of Xinjiang was not actively contested during the Great Game, the southwest city of Kashgar, at the intersection of ancient Silk Road routes between Central Asia, India and China, was a major theatre of the Great Game: from the late nineteenth century, the British and Russian consulates there were heavily involved as direct participants. But Xinjiang as a whole has also been a long-standing part of the geopolitical contest between Russia and China. In both Imperial and Soviet periods, Moscow viewed Xinjiang as the missing part of its Central Asia domain. It is closely bound to other parts of central Asia through language, religion, culture and identity. At times, Russia had come close to absorbing Xinjiang into the empire, or as a Soviet republic. Chapter 4 analyses why China's central rulers, over long periods, have been obsessively fixated on stability in Xinjiang and security along its western frontier. Beijing can be expected to pour more resources into Xinjiang to promote both its economic development and stability. Xinjiang already absorbs a disproportionate share of all China's expenditure on security.[10]

At the same time, Beijing seeks to have malleable client states on its borders. Historically, the main threats to China have come from Central Asia, the Russian steppes and Mongolia. For the past twenty years, Beijing has sought to draw Central Asia into its sphere of influence while, at the same time, trying to avoid antagonising Russia, which sees Central Asia as its natural constituency after centuries of imperial domination. Culturally, these states are much more Russian than they are Chinese, underpinned by a 'relationship of trust between the political elites' and their ties to the Kremlin.[11]

## Invasion of Ukraine, and Central Asian Echoes

Putin's invasion of Ukraine may well have been one of the unintended consequences of the US's withdrawal from Afghanistan. The speed of the collapse, and the general sense of public relief in the West that it was all over, may have encouraged Putin to think that he could invade Ukraine with impunity, as the West no longer had the stomach for confrontation. The strength and unity of the Western response would most likely have caught him out, as it would have China's president, Xi Jinping.[12]

In addition to unifying the West against Russia, and expanding NATO to include Finland and Sweden, the failure of the invasion to achieve early capitulation by Ukraine, and the protracted battle that has ensued, has weakened Russia's standing in, and influence over, Central Asia. During the first two years of what Putin intended to be a short campaign, its military's capacity was shown to be wanting, its leadership and planning poor, and the training, loyalty and morale among the troops lacking. Learning by doing, however, Russia has more recently managed to hold on to its initial gains in what is increasingly becoming for both sides a war of attrition.

The invasion also alerted Central Asian states to an emerging Putin Doctrine, akin to the Brezhnev Doctrine. The Soviet Union's invasion of Czechoslovakia in 1968, ordered by party general secretary Leonid Brezhnev, was justified on the basis of the Brezhnev Doctrine, which allowed military intervention if there was a threat to any socialist state: a threat to one was a threat to all. The Soviet invasion of Afghanistan was likewise justified by the Brezhnev Doctrine. The Putin Doctrine is based on the concept of the 'Russian World' and is focused on the conditions of the 25 million Russians left outside Russia when the Soviet Union collapsed. It is a concept that can be stretched to cover all former Soviet republics, including in Central Asia. This makes Central Asian leaders nervous and the populations suspicious.[13]

China, of course, is watching Russia's Ukrainian war closely, for, among other things, what it can learn about its own, untested, military capabilities. Unlike the People's Liberation Army (PLA), the Russian military is already considerably battle hardened from campaigns in

Syria and operations in Africa. Putin's invasion also holds important lessons for Beijing as it contemplates its military options for Taiwan's absorption into the People's Republic of China (PRC). These are ever diminishing, as Ukraine amply demonstrates.[14]

Russia's weakness after its failure to achieve a decisive, rapid victory in Ukraine has left Central Asia more open to China exercising greater influence over the former Soviet republics. Through the BRI, and regional institution building, such as with the Shanghai Cooperation Organisation (SCO), China had already been expanding its influence considerably in the region, but Central Asian states have been cautious about China's embrace and Russia watchful of its activities.

In February 2022, to the shock of the US-led West, Xi Jinping and Vladimir Putin issued a joint statement in Beijing, saying that the bilateral relationship between China and Russia was so close that it was a friendship 'without limits'. Two years later, the phrase is largely buried on the Chinese side and neither includes it in official propaganda. At the time, I described it as a 'Concert of Convenience' with an inevitably limited shelf life.[15] Beijing and Moscow share a common objective to balance US and Western influence in global affairs. But in view of their competing security interests, long-standing historical animosity, lengthy and vexed borders, and underlying racial fears of the 'Other', there is little hope for structural stability in the relationship: competition rather than cooperation prevails. This relationship will never be an easy one.

Russian Central Asia expert Arkady Dubnov wrote in 2018 that the 'point at which Russia and China's interests may diverge still appears to be far in the future'.[16] But this reflects something of the wishful thinking of Kremlin supporters of Putin's pivot to Asia. The question is whether Putin's invasion of Ukraine and China's continuing expansion of influence in Central Asia have brought that time nearer. This book concludes that they have, and that China is already well on its way to becoming the pre-eminent power in Core Eurasia.[17]

**Chussia Anxiety**

The Putin-Xi joint statement, released on the eve of the Beijing Winter Olympics, and just twenty days before Russia's invasion of Ukraine, would seem to lend credence to the view that a new era of inter-state relations between Russia and China has begun. Russia's invasion of Ukraine, however, may have instead stoked fires of mistrust and suspicion on Beijing's side. China was clearly unprepared for the invasion.[18] It was also not the first time that Putin had embarrassed China during the hosting of an Olympic Games and deprived the Communist Party of China (CPC) of their propaganda value. In August 2008, Putin attended the opening ceremony of the Summer Olympics. Later that evening he returned to Moscow, and the next day Russia invaded Georgia, pushing the games to the margins of international front pages.

More substantially, however, the invasion flouted a fundamental principle of China's foreign policy: non-interference in another country's internal affairs, according to Article 2(7) of the United Nations Charter. It also put Beijing in a most awkward diplomatic squeeze between fidelity to the newly minted relationship with Russia and possible sanctions from the West. The invasion tested Western resolve to resist the autocracies, and the West rose to the occasion.[19] Domestically, in China it raised a systemic question: does China see itself and its future as being part of a rump of renegade states or as a respected, influential member of the international community?[20]

In time, the Putin-Xi declaration may come to be viewed like the Molotov–Ribbentrop pact of 23 August 1939 that cleared the way for Hitler to invade Poland. Two years later, Nazi Germany invaded the Soviet Union. The pact had, however, served the interests of both Hitler and Stalin. For Stalin, it gave the Soviet Union two more years to prepare for what he knew would be an inevitable war with Germany.[21]

Since the February 2022 statement, Western commentary and strategic thinking have been consumed by the notion of an 'alliance of autocracies' or an 'axis of authoritarian states', and similar metaphors dredged up from World War II. I term this the 'Chussia

Anxiety'—the fear of China and Russia forming a coherent anti-Western alliance, in an effort to reshape the international order to make it more congenial for dictators. All of this, however, ignores the deep historical, cultural and security differences between the two.[22] These are explored at length in Chapters 5 to 7, and their geostrategic implications examined.

All along their common borders, Russians and Chinese harbour deep historical animosities and suspicions. Colin Thubron, in writing of his slow travels along the Amur River, which forms the border between Russia and China in China's northeast, documents—town by town on his journey—ancient injustices that today are nurtured both as fresh grudges and scores to be settled.[23]

## Geopolitics of Core Eurasia

No doubt Putin and Xi would want to wish away the deep historical divisions and resultant popular antipathy of their people towards each other, at least in the borderlands: their extant territorial antagonisms that derive, in China's view, from 'unequal treaties' left over from the nineteenth century; their incompatible approaches to how to achieve their respective security; their unequal power and growth trajectories; and the vastly different extent to which they engage with, and integrate into, the broader international system. When viewed from these perspectives, as in Chapter 8, Chussia can be seen to have feet of clay. The reality is that it is more a Western-created phantom than a geostrategic phenomenon.

Whereas China had been mindful of Russia's sensitivities towards Central Asia as its primary sphere of influence, it has shown greater preparedness to assert its influence since Putin's invasion of Ukraine. In May 2023, Xi Jinping's convening without Russia's participation a summit with the five Central Asian states, and establishing a permanent C+C5 mechanism and China-based secretariat, was a clear statement of China's newly acquired authority over the region. So too was the formal diplomatic recognition in January 2024 of the Taliban government in Kabul, stealing a march on Russia and the rest of the international community.[24] Chapter 9 discusses China's ascendency over Central Asia.

While China's economy is complementary with the resource-rich economies of Central Asia, Russia's is largely competitive. Both Russia and some Central Asian states are rich in mineral resources and energy, while China is a major importer of these commodities. Moreover, China faces dangerous strategic bottlenecks, as most of its key commodity imports come through the Strait of Malacca, which the US could blockade in the event of a conflict; perhaps one over Taiwan.[25] So, beyond peripheral security provided by drawing Central Asia into its sphere of influence, the resource- and energy-rich countries of the region are a major strategic incentive for China to become the dominant power.

As China establishes its pre-eminence in Central Asia, Russia will look at ways to reassert itself. It is unlikely to accept that the region is to be part of Beijing's sphere of influence. But, given its depletion from the war in Ukraine and continuing Chinese economic growth, Russia may not be able to reassert itself effectively. Its deep links across Central Asia will remain in place and, with these, its influence in the region will still be considerable. If Putin fails in Ukraine, Russia's regional standing will be harmed, militarily it will be weaker, and it will have caused long-term damage to its economy and demoralised the population, all of which happened following its failed war in Afghanistan.[26]

## Mackinder and Spykman Return

The Eurasian 'heartland' was first identified over a century ago, by British geostrategic realist Halford John Mackinder, as the world's geopolitical pivot. Mackinder argued that whichever state controlled Central Asia—with its resources and strategically critical geography, which he called the 'heartland'—would be the dominant world power: 'who rules the heartland, commands the world'.[27]

Mackinder's 'heartland' analysis has, to some extent, been revived by China's BRI. It has been taken up with gusto by geopolitical realists such as Robert Kaplan, in his best-selling books *The Revenge of Geography* and *The Return of Marco Polo's World*, and by many other analysts who regard it as providing a model for the BRI.[28] Mackinder's thesis—albeit 'aimed badly, argued illogically, but startling enough to expose what few had yet seen'—drew attention to the fact that transcontinental railways had effectively made Europe and Asia a single continent, which might cause Britain, which had controlled the seas for centuries, to be eclipsed by a new power with distinctly different forms of government and ways of life. Mackinder and those following his approach have been criticised for elevating maps over analysis.[29] The subtitle of Kaplan's *Revenge of Geography* says it all: 'What the map tells us about coming conflicts and the battle against fate'.

In the early 1940s, with the direction of World War II starting to turn in favour of the Allies, and with the demonstration of the advantages of sea power, Nicholas Spykman, a Yale University professor of international relations, turned Mackinder on his head, arguing that who controls the 'rimland'—the densely populated maritime littoral states around Eurasia—will also control the heartland and become the dominant global power. He maintained that the rimland states were more important than the heartland because of their access to the oceans and trade. Spykman's rimland included Japan, South Korea, South-East Asia, the Indian Ocean and the Middle East; all areas of US strategic interest and generally characterised by a dominant American influence since World War II.

For both the Mackinder and Spykman schools of geostrategy, geography is the most important factor in geopolitics because it is the most permanent. But both should not be read without acknowledging their historical and political context: Mackinder's perspective derived from the end of the Great Game and British rivalry with Russia; Spykman sought to elevate naval power over land power.[30] Spykman was also building on the late nineteenth century theoretical and historical studies by Alfred Thayer Mahan of the relationship between naval strength and geopolitical power.[31]

Maritime primacy underpinned Britain's global dominance from the eighteenth century. Then again, in the twentieth century, maritime power, not land power, prevailed; accordingly, the US has been the global pre-eminent power. Unlike Britain, however, the US has commanded a privileged position not available to any other power: it has a secure continental base and no hostile borders.

As China becomes secure in its continental power, it turns to develop its maritime power; a project on which it has been increasingly engaged for the past two decades.

Spykman's thesis gained currency during the Cold War.[32] Together with US diplomat George Kennan's policy prescriptions, it is sometimes credited with providing the Cold War geopolitical foundations of containment of the Soviet Union.[33] Strategic analyst Mohammad Soliman has argued that Japanese prime minister Shinzo Abe's geopolitical innovation, first proposed in 2007, promoting the concept of the 'Indo-Pacific', drew on Spykman's theories of geopolitics. The Indo-Pacific concept, derived from the rimland theory, has led to specific policy initiatives such as the Quad, and various minilateral security arrangements, such as the Japan–South Korea–US, and Japan–Philippines–US, security arrangements.[34] AUKUS, the arrangement by which Australia is assisted by the UK and US to acquire nuclear-powered submarine capacity, sits squarely in Spykman's geostrategic frame. For this reason, AUKUS aims to sustain US geopolitical primacy into the distant future. Spykman's theories not only help us to understand the Indo-Pacific concept, the Quad and AUKUS but also the rising tensions in the South China Sea and East China Sea. They also implicitly recognise that China, as it achieves dominance over the heartland, will then turn its attention to the rimland. China's massive naval build-up of recent years could therefore have been anticipated.

With the West effectively out of the contest for the 'world island'—the landmass consisting of Europe and Asia—primacy in Central Asia will ultimately depend on the relative strengths of Russia and China, and domestic political stability within both great powers.[35] On current trends, China would, in Mackinder's—albeit contested—terms, then control the Eurasian heartland and become the dominant global power. Carter administration national security adviser and renowned strategic analyst Zbigniew Brzezinski warned of this potential threat to US global hegemony; but while he thought China could be a potential rival one day, in the mid-1990s the possibility seemed to him to be remote.[36]

## China's Grand Strategy

In perhaps the closest work to the present study, Raffaello Pantucci and Alexandros Petersen contend that China's growing influence in Central Asia is not part of a grand strategy but an ad hoc response to domestic needs within China. Hence, according to their account, trade and investment are the main drivers of China's engagement in Central Asia. Its geopolitical approach to Central Asia is presented as being transactional rather than strategic. In their view, China has not set out to become the dominant power and it 'shirks the responsibility' of that role.[37]

But, as argued in my 2020 book, *China's Grand Strategy and Australia's Future in the New Global Order*, China's security concerns have long been focused on frontier stability within Eurasia, with Xinjiang of paramount importance to Beijing's own sense of its security. Until the First Opium War with Britain, threats to China's security and of invasions had come from the interior of Asia.[38] As Peter Perdue persuasively contends, the Qing incorporation of Xinjiang had nothing to do with any sense of Xinjiang 'belonging' to China, and hence the creation of a unified people (*minzu* 民族) as defined by later nationalist ideology, but everything to do with peripheral security.[39]

The West's retreat from Afghanistan has raised the stakes regarding China's engagement in the region. But Beijing had been laying the foundations for the past thirty years, through the SCO, Asian Infrastructure Investment Bank (AIIB), the BRI and the New Development Bank (NDB) and many other China-led initiatives. China's expanding role and influence in Central Asia are therefore critical to its grand strategy—it may be incremental and piecemeal, but it is deliberate.

Paradoxically, China's grand strategy is based on weakness not strength. When the CPC prevailed over the Kuomintang (KMT) in 1949, it did not take over a state or a functioning political entity but, rather, shards of territory. It was, and had long been, beset by enemies from across the sweeping Eurasian land mass. These historical conditions have fed Beijing's contemporary deep sense of insecurity and vulnerability as to its frontier borders.[40]

As argued here, it would be a mistake to assume that the current cordiality in Russia–China relations will be a permanent state of affairs. Pantucci and Petersen, while acknowledging one central theme of this book that the region finds itself 'obliged to choose between Moscow and Beijing', opt to set this latent strategic competition to one side. Instead, they see the current concert of convenience between Russia and China to be enduring, for:

> while Moscow may worry about its loss of influence in Central Asia, ultimately both the Kremlin and Zhongnanhai are too focussed on their geostrategic positioning together on the international stage against the West to let themselves be torn apart by Central Asia.[41]

This, however, conflates avoiding confrontation with Russia, for tactical reasons, with indifference to exercising influence over its traditional areas of security concern. Chinese strategic planners will be aware of the risks of having to manage increasingly fraught relations on two fronts: one with the US and one with Russia. Confrontation with the US is believed to be inevitable, with China's rise and the resulting challenge to the US-dominated order. Avoiding confrontation with Russia is a policy choice, which, for the time being, China has chosen to exercise.

Historically, China has sought its security through building dominant relationships with its neighbours, or tributary states. Security is achieved by the existence of pliant states that accept China's pre-eminence and a transactional relationship. Russia's security has been through occupying and controlling peripheral states, and 'civilising' the inhabitants to be Russians. It fears land-based invasions and consequently seeks to have a zone of buffer states around its borders, including against China. This has created, and will continue to create, tensions across the region.

## World of Bounded Orders
The final chapter of this book makes some policy observations on how the West might respond to China's pre-eminence in Eurasia.

We are living through the second great power shift in the past forty years. The first shift was from the US to China; the second is from Russia to China. How then to respond to an immensely powerful China that no longer needs to fear for its security due to threats from Eurasia, when, for the first time in its long history, it is the dominant power in Eurasia? Having finally settled its security in Eurasia, China will be free to focus its strengths and assets on becoming the dominant global power, if it so chooses. The analogy here is with the US, which, having secured its borders and established primacy over the Western Hemisphere, was able to assert its power globally.

With China dominant in Eurasia, a world order comprising two bounded orders, one led by the US and one by China, is likely to be how international relations between states will be arranged. This will be an order of both competition and cooperation. Global issues such as climate change, Islamic fundamentalism, asymmetrical security threats and transnational crime will require global responses. Equally, competition over access to technologies and markets—and, especially, values—will be heightened. China will want to make the world safe for the CPC and protect the security of its borders, while the US order will resist efforts at interference in domestic politics, and seek to defend and promote pluralist, competitive models of political and social organisation.

The shape of this world order is already apparent. The Biden administration's doctrine of 'latticework' security alliances—where countries participate in a variable geometry of groupings joined by the common objective of pushing back against China and, where possible, containing her—is the shape of things to come. So are the multiple arrangements, led by China, among the loosely defined 'Global South'. Other regionally powerful states—India, Russia, Turkey, Iran, Brazil—will arrange themselves according to perceived threats to their interests and security. It is likely to be an order that is both less global and multilateral than the post–World War II order and one that is much more transactional. Whether it will be more violent will depend on a return to a more explicitly Westphalian system, which can balance power among competing states.

The long Great Game in Central Asia is drawing to a close. Putin's invasion of Ukraine has allowed China to establish its primacy in Core Eurasia. Having achieved security within Eurasia, China can turn to project its prodigious power globally. This book concludes that it is now game on between China and the US-led West for global pre-eminence, and that Eurasia is the hinge of the global order.

# CHAPTER 2

# ORIGINAL GREAT GAME

*'A great deal of misapprehension arises from a popular use of maps on a small scale … If the noble lord would use a larger map, he would find that the distance between Russia and British India was to be measured not by the finger and thumb, but by a rule.'*

Lord Salisbury, secretary of state for India (1874–78)

The Turpan local bus depot on the outside of town was buzzing with travellers, hunting for their bus, clamouring to get on, thrusting luggage through open windows to reserve seats. Much yelling and gesturing added to the chaos. It was hard to keep my footing on the frozen ground cracking underneath my boots. Weak yellow shards of light from the rising sun still had not penetrated the icy mist.

In February 1989, I was the Australian embassy's economic counsellor in Beijing, and already experienced in travelling in some of Asia's more remote regions at that time, including Nepal and Tibet. A friend and I were joining the trickle of foreigners using local transport to traverse Xinjiang to reach the ancient fabled Silk Road oasis of Kashgar. Xinjiang was just being opened to individual foreign travellers. I wanted to be among those foreigners, so as to experience, firsthand, Uyghur culture, which had largely been preserved, despite half a century of communism in China. Travelling over four days along the northern arm of the vast, talcum-powder-like, Taklamakan Desert would enrich the experience, albeit at considerable personal discomfort. Luckily, at the time, I did not know how much it would hurt. But then, in those days, the option was either unreliable and infrequent commercial aircraft or those unreliable, infrequent, shabby local buses. For an inveterate adventurer like me, the choice was obvious.

Kashgar had also been the focal point of the Great Game, where the competitors—Britain and Russia—had consulates that coordinated networks of spies and informants across Central Asia to monitor their opponents' activities. From here, London and St Petersburg would be advised on the next moves to make. From 1842 to 1907, they engaged in shadowboxing, feints and complicated maneouvers.[1]

At the start of the twentieth century, Rudyard Kipling captured the imagination of readers throughout the British Empire and beyond with his story of Kim, a young English boy growing up in British India, caught up in a great game of grand strategy unfolding between Britain and Russia in Central Asia. Famously, Kipling has Kim say his farewell thus: 'Now I shall go far and far into the North, playing the Great Game.'[2]

Alarmed at Russia's continuing expansion of its territory across Central Asia in the second half of the nineteenth century, Britain came to believe that St Peterburg was greedily eyeing British India itself. For over sixty years, the two empires jockeyed for position in Central Asia, while a third empire, China, under the declining Qing dynasty, was often no more than a bystander. Russia's nineteenth century expansion into Central Asia, however, had next to nothing to do with dastardly designs by St Petersburg on British India, and everything to do with its need to be recognised as a Great Imperial Power by being part of the European 'civilising' colonial enterprises of the nineteenth century.[3] The Great Game still exerts much fascination, for its caricature of nineteenth century Victorian and Imperial Russian actors and intrigue. It involves a cast of adventurers, spies, bounders and scoundrels—with lashings of ambition, ego and naivety—each of them in the service of their imperial realms.

Turpan on that February morning was bitterly cold. It is the third-lowest point on earth and surrounded by snow-covered peaks. In 1989, it was also one of the most isolated cities on earth, in remote Xinjiang province. The Berlin Wall still stood fast, despite gradual and perceptible weakening of the Soviet Union's vice-like grip on Eastern Europe. The general secretary of the Soviet Union's ruling Communist Party, Mikhail Gorbachev, had begun to experiment with political (*glasnost*) and economic (*perestroika*) reforms, in part influenced by the reform and open-door policies seeping across China, under the guidance of paramount leader Deng Xiaoping.

Although all borders and points of land entry were officially shut, the vastness of this region of high mountains to the north, east and south, and deserts that have challenged travellers for millennia, meant that, despite the best efforts of modern states to control their borders, they were inevitably porous. In 1987, Beijing had begun to ease slightly the formal border restrictions that had been in place for much of the previous thirty years. By 1989, Uzbeki traders were openly selling Astrakhan fur coats and hats in Urumqi's markets, carried from the far western edge of the Aral Sea in the Soviet Union.

We eventually set off, an hour or so late, in the smoky grey light that blanketed Turpan. Before reaching the edge of the city, the packed and cramped bus had its first breakdown. It was to be one of many. On some days, we bounced and banged our way across the northern edge of the desert for twenty hours, after repair stops, and toilet and food breaks, only to crash out, exhausted, in some dank concrete roadside stop. The sheets in the damp, cold beds looked like the Shroud of Turin. You could see the images of the previous occupants in them.

On day four, we reached Kashgar. Courtesy of a protracted break-down in the late afternoon, we arrived on the outskirts after the city was closed for the day. A dusk-to-dawn curfew was in place. At that time of year, those arriving after 6 p.m. had to stay the night outside the city limits, where accommodation was meagre. Undeterred by what was, no doubt, a common experience, our driver beckoned us to remain on the bus while he went off to discuss the situation with the police. After half an hour, he returned and began collecting money from the passengers to pay a bribe. He refused my contribution. After some more stressful waiting, a happy bus finally headed off into the old city of Kashgar, and the promise of good rooms and some decent food. Being February and bitterly cold, meals along the Taklamakan had consisted of grey noodles with smelly mutton and chilli, three times a day.

Kashgar was everything it had promised to be: vibrant, exotic; with every Central Asian nationality represented, from Kazakhs,

Tajiks, Persians, Uzbeks, Kyrgyz, Afghans and Pakistanis, to a small smattering of Han Chinese, in Central Asia's melting pot. Kashgar even then felt like the geopolitical centre of Central Asia. As Robert Kaplan, the realist strategist who emphasises the role of geography in China's geopolitical strategy, observed in 2018, 'a place like Kashgar might normally be associated with back-of-beyond travel writing. But, in fact, it could be the centre of the world geopolitical order.'[4]

Bedding down that evening—in a warm, comfortable room in the Seman Hotel in Kashgar—the old Russian consulate, with its pitched tiled roof, was next door, and European chimney stacks and a façade of yellow fired bricks were just visible from the bedroom window. Opened in 1890, the consulate formalised Imperial Russia's presence in Kashgar and far western China. It also marked the furtherest extent of Russia's eastward expansion into Central Asia. For the next ninety years, until the current period of Russia–China comity, Russia pressed at different times its territorial and political interests in Xinjiang, along China's soft underbelly.

### Where Empires Meet

In 1872, reflecting St Petersburg's growing interest in the region, Russia had struck trade deals with the powerful Yaqub Beg, the Muslim ruler of Kashgaria, offering Beg full diplomatic recognition in return for opening his markets to Russia. Beg was a military commander from Kokand in the Fergana region of today's eastern Uzbekistan. In 1865, he crossed the Tian Shan mountains to take advantage of violent Muslim uprisings against Manchu rule that were breaking out across Xinjiang in the 1860s. With a small army, he was able to establish himself as the ruler of the region centred on Kashgar, which he named Kashgaria.[5]

For an unsophisticated ruler of a Central Asian khanate, Beg was surprisingly adept at managing great power relations. He played off Russia and Great Britain against each other: first allowing Russia to establish a diplomatic presence in Kashgar; then inviting, in 1873, a 350-strong British trade mission to visit. With this, Britain sought to expand its presence in Central Asia, out from Kashgar, and begin to push back against Russian advances. As Peter Hopkirk writes:

Britain's policy of masterly inactivity in Central Asia, condemned
by its hawkish critics as craven surrender to Russia's designs, was
at last coming to an end.[6]

The policy of muscling up to Russia appeared to produce some
early, welcome geopolitical results for London. In 1873, after years of
dispute, St Petersburg suddenly acknowledged long-standing British
demands that the region of Wakhan, which included the Upper Oxus
(Amu Darya) river, was in the domain of the emir of Afghanistan,
rather than the emir of Bukhara, who was loyal to St Petersburg.

With this, Russia conceded that eastern Afghanistan lay within
Britain's sphere of influence and outside its own. Wakhan was valued
by Britain as a buffer between it and Russia. The British felt that
they had secured a major concession from Russia and a significant
diplomatic success. Russia's 'concession' was itself actually a pragmatic
recognition of the geographical, and hence military, difficulties of
extending its influence over Wakhan to the border with British India.[7]

Just as the British were congratulating themselves over this,
Russia's relentless march to expand its control across Central Asia was
about to continue. Despite assurances from St Petersburg to London
that no further conquests were planned for Central Asia, three major
expeditionary forces were being assembled to take over the Khiva
Khanate.[8] In May 1873, the khan fled, and Russia occupied the
ancient, mudbrick Silk Road city of Khiva. This was a major strategic
victory, giving Russia control of the Lower Oxus river and the
Caspian Sea's eastern shore. It also closed a gap on Russia's Central
Asian southern flank, and brought her within 1000 kilometres of
Herat in Afghanistan, 'India's ancient strategic gateway'.[9] Britain's
ambassador in St Petersburg warned the foreign office that, with the
conquest of Khiva, the Russians 'had secured a base from which they
could "menace" the independence of Persia and Afghanistan, and
thereby become a standing danger to our Indian Empire'.[10] Russia
continued to absorb territory by coopting local khans who knew
they could not match its military strength.

During this time, Peking moved against Yaqub Beg, to reassert
control over Xinjiang. In 1877, three Qing armies advanced on

Kashgar. Beg initially sought to resist and then fled, dying sometime later. The accounts of this are contested, but by 1878 Peking was again in control of Kashgar. Over the next decade, beyond the borders of Xinjiang, through skilful diplomacy, subterfuge, lying and abundant military assets, Russia annexed a territory that was about half the size of the US. Short of going to war, Britain could do nothing about it. Russia was now within only 320 kilometres of Kashgar. Although it was separated by the high Tian Shan mountain range, British military planners were increasingly alarmed by Russia's advances.[11]

Playing catch-up with Russia, the British legation in Peking was instructed to seek accreditation for a British India political officer, Ney Elias, to travel to Kashgar from Leh, today the Himalayan capital of India's Ladakh province, to commence the process of opening a diplomatic mission. Elias had spent seven years in the remote high-altitude town of Leh, near the border with Tibet, collecting intelligence on the passes in the region to Xinjiang, and on the trading centres of Kashgar and Yarkand, and reporting back to London.[12] At the time, the main Silk Road route from China to India connected Yarkand in Xinjiang with Leh. It went over the Karakoram mountains, crossing the dizzying Karakoram Pass at 5540 metres. Leh had become an important Silk Road terminus and distribution centre in the high Himalaya and, unsurprisingly, an important place for intelligence gathering.[13]

Britain's request to open a consulate in Kashgar was rejected by the Qing court. Ostensibly, the reason was that trade between the region and British India was insufficient to justify a permanent diplomatic mission there. Other reasons may have been in play, including Britain's earlier efforts to curry favour with Yaqub Beg against the Qing, or backroom interference by the newly settled official Russian representative, Nikolai Petrovsky.[14]

In November 1891, ten years after Russia had been permitted by the Qing under the 1881 Treaty of St Petersburg to open its consulate, Francis Younghusband and George Macartney, who would eventually become Britain's long-serving consul general in Kashgar, diverted from their intelligence gathering in the high Pamirs to winter in Kashgar. Relations between Peking and London had improved over this time and the Qing governor of the region permitted both men to stay over winter. He also allocated them accommodation at a residence called Chini-Bagh ('Chinese Garden' in Uygur). This was to become the permanent British consulate in Kashgar, but was not formally recognised as such until 1908; it was upgraded to a consulate general only in 1911.[15] Macartney served in Kashgar for a total of twenty-eight years over two postings. By the close of his tenure, the Great Game had come to an end as the empires turned their attention to more pressing matters far from Kashgar. By the 1920s, the British had gone from Central Asia. For the next fifty years, Xinjiang was a theatre of competition between China and Russia.

_____

In February 1989, exploring Kashgar's largely intact medieval mudbrick old town, the sense of time having stood still was palpable. Streets specialised in certain types of products—in one, all the little stalls sold only brushes; others, cooking utensils; in another, silverware vendors sat cross-legged on carpets behind rickety small scales, as items such as bracelets were sold by weight. Shops lined another laneway, selling knives with elaborate inlaid semiprecious stone handles in all sizes, which were prized decorative items; other narrow, twisting alleys offered musical instruments, copper utensils and decorations; others, jade and semiprecious stones; and, of course, others hosted carpet shops in great numbers.

Before Kashgar was a tourist destination for Chinese and foreigners, the weekly Sunday market was like a scene from a blockbuster epic movie set somewhere in the Middle East at the time of ancient empires. Waking early on Sunday, the streets around the Seman Hotel were clogged with small donkey carts, piled high with produce; drivers caning their animals to canter ahead of others, to secure favourable spots in the market to display their wares. Men in long fur-lined coats and knee-high boots, with black felt-lined hats pulled down over shaggy grey hair, shading aquiline noses protruding from wispy beards, were followed closely by women in chocolate brown burkas with mesh grates across their eyes and nose. It was as if the whole of Central Asia was compressed into this cramped, dusty, noisy space.

Animals too were representative of the diversity of the region and Kashgar's historic role as an ancient magnet that drew the particles of Central Asia together. Sheep of all kinds were prolific, as were goats, including high-alpine specimens such as the 'blue goat'; cows; bulls; Bactrian camels in big numbers; poultry; wild birds; and, sadly, skins of endangered species, notably the snow leopard. Regional fruits, nuts, honey, yoghurt and meats were abundant. These scenes would not have changed over the centuries.

In 1989, Chini-Bagh still had its magnificent garden intact, as planted by Lady Macartney when she accompanied her husband on his first posting to the consulate in 1908. The long driveway gently curved under huge elm trees towards the official residence. Flowerbeds lined the pathways, but nothing was in bloom in February. The residence was located on a small escarpment; from the top floor, the entire mudbrick city could be seen below. The building had two crenellated square towers over the entrance, and Romanesque windows around the second floor. It might be described as romantic colonial desert architecture; also as like something from a movie, this time about the French Foreign Legion.

The British and Russian consulate buildings, which are of great historical significance, were largely in their original condition and had been reasonably well maintained. They were being used as various types of restaurants and snack shops. When I returned in the mid-2000s, both were dilapidated. Tragically, Lady Macartney's garden had gone, having been replaced by an ugly high-rise hotel development in the 1990s. On subsequent visits, it was obvious that these sites had been allowed to deteriorate further. It is as if the Chinese government can't make up its mind about them. Recognising their historic importance, it won't allow their demolition, notwithstanding how valuable the land is now. The buildings are, however, physical reminders of what many Chinese would see as a shameful period of the nation's history, where the Qing were onlookers to the great historical contest playing out on Chinese soil, and so the government is unwilling to preserve them. They stand today as sad relics of a time when Kashgar was at the centre of the world's greatest imperial rivalry, in the late nineteenth and early twentieth centuries.

## Great Game

The first use of the term 'Great Game' to describe the mid-nineteenth century strategic rivalry growing between imperial Britain and Russia was by Captain Arthur Conolly of the British East India Company. He coined the phrase in 1840, when Russia supported the siege of Herat by Shah Qajar of Persia. The Emirate of Herat was backed by both the Bukhara Emirate and Khiva Khanate. In response, Britain sent forces into the Persian Gulf. Russia withdrew its support for Persia.[16] While other dates are sometimes mentioned as being the start of the Great Game, 1842 is usually chosen, marked as it was by a tragic twist of fate. In June 1842, Captain Conolly and a fellow East India Company officer, Colonel Charles Stoddart, were executed together in the main square of central Bukhara, on the orders of the emir of Bukhara, by then a Russian puppet ruler. Stoddart had been sent by the British East India company to meet with the emir, to negotiate an alliance against the Russians. Instead, he was imprisoned and held in squalid conditions for many months. Conolly had volunteered to find out what had happened to Stoddart and he himself was also imprisoned.[17]

The Great Game ended in 1907, with the signing of the Anglo-Russian Convention, which settled the borders of Afghanistan. This included formal agreement on the Wakhan Corridor being a buffer zone between the powers. By that time, both Russia's and Britain's strategic priorities had moved on from Central Asia, as the powers were challenged by other threats to empire. For Britain, they came from the Middle East, and the rise of Germany in Europe; while Russia had been humiliated by Japan in the Russo-Japanese War of 1904–05 (fought on Chinese soil and water near today's port city of Dalian, at Lvshun) and was also concerned by Germany's growing strength. British historian and leading authority on the region Alexander Morrison observed that:

[t]he relative ease with which these long-standing disagreements were apparently resolved took the Germans by surprise ... The priority for both empires by [1907] lay in Europe with their common fear of Germany.[18]

Defeated in the Crimean War (1853–56), Russia was insecure about what it regarded as its natural sphere of influence. In the face of British and other allied opposition to its expansion into its western and southwestern contiguous regions, St Petersburg—having first absorbed the steppe (Siberia)—looked to Central Asia and beyond, to the Far East. Expansion into Central Asia extended dramatically Russia's sphere of influence. It was certainly active, diplomatically— through intelligence gathering, cultivating local emirs in its favour against Britain—as well as militarily and commercially. It has also been argued by Russian scholars that St Petersburg had a 'civilising mission' to bring Christianity and modernity to the disparate Muslim khanates and emirates that made up Central Asia.[19]

Russia sought to create for itself a Eurasian empire at the time of empire building around the world by European maritime powers. In doing so, it would also strengthen its security against historical threats from Central Asia and Mongolia. It seems unlikely Russia's imperial ambitions would have extended to it being a real threat against British India. Distance from supply bases, vertiginous mountain passes, and the logistical and physical challenges for man and animal alike at the time would have made a Russian military expedition into British India almost impossible.

From the Russian perspective, the major strategic concern was an expansion of British India into Central Asia through Afghanistan, which opened into Russian Turkestan. St Petersburg had watched with unease British expansion west from Bengal towards Afghanistan. Afghanistan had long suffered from foreign invasions, and from foreign designs on it, because of its strategic location between India and Central Asia. In the nineteenth century, Britain, anxious about its empire, saw it as the route through which Russia might invade India. Similarly, Russia saw it as the corridor through which Britain would inevitably expand its influence and presence in Central Asia, into Russia's self-proclaimed sphere of influence.

The tsars wanted to prevent Britain from establishing a permanent presence in Afghanistan and turning it into a British protectorate.[20] Mutual suspicions fed off each other.

The high passes of the Himalaya, Kun Lun and Karakoram mountains would have prevented the sort of large-scale military invasion required for Russia ever to threaten British India seriously. It would have been suicidal for an invasion force of the size that would have been necessary to take India to attempt such a crossing. The Pamirs had passes that conceivably might have provided routes into the Hunza Valley for an invading Russian army, but, again, most of these were treacherous and at high altitude. Whether St Petersburg seriously contemplated a military advance into India is contested, but certainly it was concerned about British expansion into Central Asia. Britain was clearly the superior military power, although its defeat in Afghanistan in the First Anglo-Afghan War (1838–42) would have encouraged St Petersburg to wonder if this was still true in Central Asia. The view that the Great Game was, however, a 'proto–Cold War' between these empires is disputed by Russian historian Evgeny Sergeev, who, drawing extensively on both Russian and English sources, emphasises the importance of other regional actors with whom the great powers had to engage and coopt to advance their interests.[21] It was a much more complex strategic game than just St Petersburg versus London, as it is often presented.

Scant evidence exists to suggest that the objective of Russia's activities in the area was motivated by having designs on India and capturing it from Britain. The only time Russia showed any intention to seize India from the British was in 1801, when mad Tsar Paul I sent a force of 20,000 Cossacks off to take India; luckily for them, this 'hair-brained enterprise' was halted before getting far.[22] In 1843, Tsar Nicholas's advisers had presented plans for an invasion of India, but these seem to have been more in the form of scoping out options, for they were never acted on. No invasion or attempted invasion ever occurred.[23] As it has been throughout its history, India was effectively isolated from Central Asia and China by some of the world's highest mountains and spindly precipitous passes. It is only tangentially connected with the Eurasian security system.

The hawks on both sides were known as the 'forward school' or 'forwardists'. They advocated policies to confront the other militarily and resist expansion, especially towards Afghanistan and the strategically important Khiva Khanate, in today's Uzbekistan. The lack of trust, and misunderstanding and anxiety, on both sides as to the other's motivation did at times prompt actions that led to misadventure and conflict that may not have occurred otherwise, such as Younghusband's invasion of Tibet in 1903–04.

In a recent major study of Russian imperial expansion into Central Asia, Morrison rejects out of hand any idea of a Great Game in Central Asia aimed at wresting control of India from Britain. He describes the Great Game as having:

> an enduring hold ... on the way English-speakers view Central Asia and its history ... [it is] the most potent of historical cliches ... [that] has spawned a whole school of historical writing ... consisting largely of a series of anecdotes of adventure and derring-do by heavily moustachioed officers and explorers against a picturesque but badly drawn Central Asian backdrop.[24]

At the end of his book on the Great Game, Hopkirk himself opens up for debate the question whether in fact there was ever a Russian threat to India. Although he is in no doubt that his cast of forwardists in London and St Petersburg were swept along by convenient beliefs and shibboleths, and competitive euphoria, he leaves it open as to whether the target of imperial competition was ever India. He concludes that:

> [w]ith the benefit of hindsight, modern historians may question whether there was ever any real Russian threat to India, so immense were the obstacles that an invasion force would first have had to overcome.[25]

As a final judgement, it is telling. Geopolitical strategists are good at coming up with worst-case scenarios, which politicians sometimes eagerly grab onto to give themselves an agenda with which to promote their public standing. Careers were made due to the Great Game. Many lives were also lost due to reckless policies. The real test for strategic analysts is to ascribe probabilities to possible events. Everything, more or less, is possible, but how likely is an event to occur? Once probabilities are considered, the range of possibilities falls away sharply.

Often, however, there is little scrutiny and critical analysis of how realistic are such 'threats'. Ascribing the worst motives to an opponent does not mean that they will be realised. The gap between intention and capacity, and between the façade and reality, can be vast. This is more so when the location of a potential threat is remote and, as it was in the Great Game, in territories that are little more than blanks on the map for most people.

## Russia Anxiety

Britain, as the dominant global power at the time, felt threatened by Russian expansion into Central Asia. It saw it as a direct challenge to its pre-eminence, just as the US sees China's economic resurgence and geopolitical rise today. Rather than being a proto–Cold War, the Great Game may have been more of a Thucydides Trap, where the dominant power sees everywhere threats to its position, causing it to react and overreact even where the menace does not exist.

Mark Smith, a leading British expert on Russia, argues that the Great Game was a manifestation of 'The Russia Anxiety' in Europe and Great Britain, rather than an existential threat to British India.[26] As Smith observes, with relevance to today's China Threat:

> One reason the Russia Anxiety can be so virulent but also so fleeting is that it represents an accumulation of Russophobic rhetoric rather than real conflict. This was not a clash of civilisations in any strategic or substantive sense, though the language of British politics often placed Russia outside the boundaries of civilisation.[27]

Smith also notes that during this period, Russia was not at war more often than the other great powers, not least Britain itself.[28]

But despite, or because of, Britain's dominant position, the fear of Russsia's ambitions was ever present. It shaped strategic thinking, and hence defence planning, even in Britain's remote antipodean dominions.[29] In Australia, the coast of the southern state of Victoria today hosts as tourist attractions late-nineteenth-century gun batteries at places like Queenscliff, overlooking the entrance to Port Phillip Bay; and at Port Fairy, in the remote westerly reaches of the state. Fort Denison in Sydney Harbour was a product of the Crimean War, with work on its fortifications commencing in 1855. Russia remained the abiding threat to Britain's Australian dominions throughout the nineteenth century.

In 1864, the London *Times* warned that a Russian invasion of Australian colonies was imminent.[30] When the Russian-led coalition of Bulgaria, Romania, Serbia and Montenegro prevailed over Turkey in the Russo-Turkish War (1877–78), Whitehall saw this as a further step towards India by the Russian Empire. Consequently, the Australian colonies were warned of the coming Russia threat to Australia's security.[31] During the 1880s, Sydney's coastal and harbour defences were progressively strengthened in the face of an imagined Russian invasion.[32]

Following several unannounced port calls by Russian naval vessels and an excitable media's scare about Russia's 'true' intentions, Britain's secretary of state for the colonies, John Wodehouse, felt compelled to write a calming memorandum, advising colonial governors that relations between Britain and Russia were cordial at the time. Nevertheless, in 1885, Fort Scratchley was built at Newcastle, New South Wales.[33] In 1885, Britain moved troops from the Sudan to defend the northwest frontier of India against 'the designs of the "Unspeakable Russian Bear" in Afghanistan'.[34] Some of these may have included Australian volunteers who had signed up to serve with Britain in Sudan.[35]

By the time Imperial Russia had completed its expansion across Central Asia, the 'Russia Threat' had become a staple of strategic thinking throughout the British colonial world. Even in Australia, fear of invasion from Russia produced an 'invasion literature'. *The Invasion* by WH Walker (1877) had Russian troops fanning out across Sydney's eastern suburbs and the city engaged in hand-to-hand combat, with gallant local resistance fighters eventually driving the enemy into the sea.[36]

Kipling's novel *Kim* (1901) was also part of Britain's Russian threat literature. India's northwest frontier, and possible Russian incursions into India, became the setting for fictional adventure stories. Supposed incursions by Russian spies into Chitral in the northern Khyber Pakhtunkhwa formed the basis of Kipling's story, and, at the same time, that of another Russian invasion novel, *The Half-Hearted* (1900), by John Buchan. The plot was based on an event in 1890, when three European travellers crossed the Baroghil Pass into Chitral. The ruler of Chitral, who by then was on Britain's payroll, identified them as Russians, and promptly had them arrested and despatched to Shimla, where they were interviewed by the viceroy, Lord Dufferin.[37]

According to Hopkirk, to 'everyone's relief' they were not Russian spies at all but the well-known French explorer Gabriel Bonvalot and his team—evidently not so well known to the Anglophones in Chitral. Contrary to Hopkirk's statement that there had been a sense of relief, one would have thought that it may have been to everyone's shame that the men were not Russian. Bonvalot surely would not have been amused at being transported the gruelling 720 kilometres, across high mountain passes, to be interviewed by the viceroy in his summer retreat.

### Geopolitics and Geostrategy of the Great Game

Throughout the period, strategic trust between Britain and Russia was absent, and there seems to have been little diplomatic effort on either side to build it. Just as with today's response by the US, Australia and other liberal Western capitals to the China Threat, calmer alternative interpretations of Russia's strategic ambitions could be found but seldom resonated among the popular press and hence in the halls of Westminster. Hopkirk observes that, in addition to those professionally engaged in the Great Game:

a host of amateur strategists followed it from the sidelines, giving freely of their advice in a torrent of books, articles, impassioned pamphlets, and letters to the newspapers.[38]

Lord Salisbury, secretary of state for India (1874–78), who was also afflicted with the Russia Anxiety, tried at times to exercise some restraint, reminding his fellow 'forwardists' that the geography of Central Asia and the distances involved put certain obstacles before any Russian advance.[39]

Russia had its own 'forwardists', alarmists and populist tacticians and strategists. St Petersburg's first disastrous attempt to occupy Khiva was based on a false rumour of a detachment of British troops having entered the ancient city. In 1839, alarmed that the British were about to take Khiva—of great strategic importance to Russia in terms of its control of the Lower Oxus and hence the Caspian Sea—Tsar Nicholas ordered a lightning strike, which was repelled by Khiva regulars. Russia did not return to Khiva for another thirty-four years, when it finally prevailed.[40] This was not a checking move in the Great Game but, rather, part of Russia's wider geopolitical strategy to extend its influence in, and dominance over, Central Asia.

On 27 June 1865, Russian troops attacked and captured Tashkent, which was the richest and most populous city in the Khanate of Kokand (from where the eventual khan of Kashgaria, Yaqub Beg, had launched his successful assult on Kashgar). In 1867, after subduing the Khanate of Kokand, Tsar Alexander II named Tashkent the capital of Turkistan—to be administered by a governor-general, Konstantin Petrovich von Kaufmann, of whom it was said that the only thing German about him was his name. In 1871, Tashkent would be the home of the first Orthodox church in Turkistan, as the region was to be named. Along with Kashgar, Tashkent became a centre of Great Game intrigue and espionage. More importantly, it was the key military base for conducting Russia's campaigns to conquer the rest of Central Asia.[41] Russia's successes in Khiva and Tashkent shocked British policy makers into a fundamental rethink of Central Asian strategic policy. At the time, the forwardists accused the British government of having been lulled into complacency, uncertain whether it should be concerned about Russian conquests in Central Asia.[42] The Russia Anxiety was heightened, and the defence of India again became a pressing concern.

In 1868, the tsar incorporated the Emirate of Bukhara into Turkistan as a protectorate. Then, in 1873, the Khanate of Khiva underwent the same fate. It was a tremendous psychological boost for Russia after its complete humiliation in its last attempt to take Khiva, enhancing its prestige and reputation for military invincibility. That Khiva was of enormous strategic and emotional value in and of itself for Russia was ignored by the forwardists in London and the foreign office. They could see only that it brought Russia within 1000 kilometres from Herat.[43]

The remaining area of Central Asia, known as Transcaspia (the land of Turkmen), fell into Russia's hands in 1881. With that, Russia completed gaining control of Central Asia up to the Chinese border in the east and Afghanistan to the south. It had established itself as the dominant power, achieving its strategic and security objectives. It had no need of Indian adventures. Russia went on to easily absorb Merv on Afghanistan's frontier, providing ready access to Kandahar and beyond to the Kyber Pass.[44] If an invasion of India were ever a strategic objective, Russia had the approach to the country that it needed. The option was never exercised.

Sergeev has suggested that the reality of Russia's dominance in Central Asia gradually opened a new phase of strategic competition between it and Britain. From the late 1880s, 'fragile equilibrium' emerged, where competition shifted to bilateral negotiations over boundaries, made more urgent for Britain because of Russia's successes in establishing pre-eminence in the region. Other theatres of strategic significance for Britain also started to press for attention. By the late nineteenth century, and following another humiliating defeat in Afghanistan in the Second Anglo-Afghan War (1878–80), Britain was feeling the pain of imperial overreach.[45]

## Legacy of the Great Game

Britain's tacit acceptance of Russia's dominance over Central Asia saw strategic competition shift to the Pamirs, which were contested by Britain, Russia, China and Afghanistan. Russia was also interested in Tibet because it was concerned that Lamaism, which reached as far as Siberia, Altai and Mongolia, could be manipulated by the British against it. Apart from three Tibetan delegations visiting St Peterburg, Russia made no move to establish control or exercise influence there. By the time of Colonel Francis Younghusband's invasion of Tibet, as will be discussed in Chapter 4, London was losing interest in the Great Game and Tibet's value was seen merely as it being one more trade route to China.

By the turn of the twentieth century, the global order was in flux. In East Asia, Japan was ascendent, having defeated China in the Sino-Japanese War (1894–95) and then having had the climactic shock of defeating Russia in the Russo-Japanese War (1904–05), with support from Britain. The Anglo-Japanese Alliance of 1902, and again in 1905, threatened Russia. At the same time, Germany led a failed attempt to form a German, Franco and Russo alliance against Britain. Events internal to Central Asia, and, more so, events external to the region, brought Britain and Russia into negotiations; in 1907, this resulted in three Anglo-Russia agreements, which settled border issues involving Persia, Afghanistan and Tibet. It was the Afghanistan Treaty establishing permanently the Wakhan Corridor—a buffer zone between Russia and British India—that eventually brought the Great Game to an end.[46]

For over sixty years, Britain and Russia shadowboxed over different strategic objectives. Britain, fed by the Russia Anxiety and concern about any challenge to its global pre-eminence, sought to deny Russia what Britain believed to be the ultimate prize, British India. Russia, having perhaps considered this prize and concluded it was out of reach, looked elsewhere to build an empire like other European great powers had and, in doing so, to advance its interests and security. Expansion across Central Asia was achieved without Russia ever having to confront militarily its great power rival. Russia extended its borders, its influence and its economic advantage in Central Asia. By the turn of the twentieth century, Britain was stretched in many directions. It turned to diplomacy and negotiated settled arrangements with Russia that protected its core interests in India, acknowledged Russia as the dominant Eurasia power and put its forwardists back in their boxes. In short, Britain found, by necessity, a way of accommodating the rising power of Russia. The catastrophes of subsequent decades did not arise because Russia was accommodated.

While the Great Game was an event mainly confined to the minds of populist politicians on both sides and embedded in the public imagination, it left a lasting legacy for modern statecraft. Buffer zones, scientific borders (delineated by natural geographical features), spheres of influence, interests and corridors of neutral territory were popularised, and became commonplace in the media and public discussion of the Great Game. Concepts such as 'détente' and 'entente' also came into diplomatic use during it.

The end of the Great Game also provides an insight into the evolving relationship between great powers as their relative balance of power changes over time, with different economic performance, the pace of technological change, and territorial conquest. In the end, Russia and Great Britain found an accommodation: Britain provided strategic space in Central Asia for an ascendent Russia, and Russia did not threaten Britain's core interests in India. The ideologists, boosters and propagandists who comprised the forwardists on each side were quietened, and foreign policy was ultimately made by the empires on the basis of their interests. Dale C Copeland suggests that it was not uncommon for great powers to find middle ways that rejected zero-sum outcomes.[47] This notion of 'dynamic realism'—changing behaviour as circumstances and interests change—could also apply to the China Threat of today. For at the beginning of the twentieth century, the dominant power, Britain, eventually and peacefully accommodated both the ascendant powers of Russia and the US.

# CHAPTER 3

# GRAVEYARD OF EMPIRES

*'Afghanistan is more than the "graveyard of empires". It's the mother of vicious circles.'*
Maureen Dowd, US public intellectual, columnist

*'Afghanistan—where empires go to die.'*
Unknown

Afghanistan has always been a key to Eurasian security and stability. Its geostrategic location links Persia in the west, Central Asia in the north, and Pakistan/India and China in the east and northeast. It is the geopolitical hub of Eurasia. Its importance is such that, over the past 200 years, it has been invaded on seven occasions by great powers. On each occasion, the invaders beat humiliating retreats: the 'Graveyard of Empires'.[1]

Afghanistan has been almost continuously part of the Eurasian geopolitical contest since the Arab caliphates extended their control over Central Asia during the seventh to ninth centuries. More recently, in the nineteenth and twentieth centuries, it was at the heart of the British–Russian imperial contest—the Great Game. Britain invaded and was defeated on three occasions (1838–42, 1878–80, 1919); Russia and the Soviet Union also on three occasions (1829, 1930, 1979–91); and US/NATO defeated once (2001–21). With the US retreat from Afghanistan, the West has effectively abandoned having influence in Central Asia. Where, for centuries, three empires contested power and prestige, now only two remain.

The Great Game ended when the question of Afghanistan was settled. In 1907, the Wakhan Corridor buffer zone between British and Russian interests was officially created, Afghanistan's eastern border was recognised by all parties, and strategic competition in Core Eurasia between Britain and Russia subsided. External factors had also brought Britain and Russia to the negotiating table, but settlement of Afghanistan's position was central to the achievement of stability and *entente cordiale* between Britain and Russia. After that, great power competition in Eurasia involving Western actors was in abeyance until the Soviet invasion of Afghanistan in 1979.

## Soviet Invasion

For a generation growing up in the 1960s and 1970s, Afghanistan was a sleepy backwater on the hippy overland trail between Australia and Europe. The people were friendly, it was ridiculously cheap even for down-and-out hippies, marijuana was abundant, and harder drugs were not too difficult to find. Music, dance, cuisine and language connected this remote landlocked country with the Middle East and North Africa. Backpackers would often hole up there for extended periods, charmed by the lifestyle and enchanted by Afghanistan's natural beauty. Islam was non-intrusive and welcoming. But it wasn't all fun. Illness and drug overdoses were common. Unfortunate British hippy backpackers were laid to rest by their consular officials in Kabul's main cemetery, next to soldiers of a similar age who had died in the British defeats in Afghanistan in the nineteenth century.[2]

Few of those smoking joints in Kabul or Herat tea shops would have had any knowledge of the country's centuries-long pivotal role in global affairs. None could have imagined that by 1979 the Soviet Red Army would have invaded, shutting the country and severing the hippy trail across Asia. European hippies were stranded in India, in large numbers. In 1981, as a hippy backpacker myself, I was recovering from serious hepatitis in a New Delhi tourist camp, under a heavy army canvas tent in sweltering late April heat. Dozens of European hippies, who had hoped to travel cheaply home across Afghanistan, had been stuck there for more than a year. With little money and no prospect of getting home, they somehow managed to sustain their various addictions, mainly heroin.

The Soviet invasion followed a period of political instability and came at the request of Hafizullah Amin, the leader of the Marxist

Saur Revolution. The Saur Revolution overthrew the despotic autocrat Mohammad Daoud Khan and instituted a series of reforms, including highly unpopular land redistribution. Following Moscow's intervention with a 'special operations force', Amin and his close advisers were assassinated by the Soviet military and replaced by the more moderate Babrak Karmal, head of the Parcham faction. Babrak was also unable to establish control across the country, and ongoing instability alerted his Moscow backers that Afghanistan was primed for US intervention. A full-scale military invasion then ensued.

By late December 1979, regular troops were rolling across the Friendship Bridge from Tajikistan into Afghanistan, near the Tajik town of Termez. The bridge was then the only structure capable of supporting heavy vehicles crossing the Amu Darya river. And so began the Soviet Union's Vietnam: a war against motivated, tenacious guerrillas, with tenuous local political support, long and vulnerable supply lines, and poorly defined strategic objectives.

The Amu Darya carves a wide valley through this desert region. On the Tajikistan side, the mountains are set back from the river, permitting relatively flat paved roads to be built, following its course. The hills rise more steeply on the Afghanistan side. When I was visiting in October 2017, on an old men's road trip around Central Asia, we noticed, at several places along the Amu Darya upstream from the Friendship Bridge, white UN vehicles parked on the Afghan side, clearing landmines, a lasting legacy of the Soviet occupation.[3] Each of the main protagonists—the Soviet Union, the Mujahideen and the Taliban—extensively mined the terrain, to prevent or restrict the movement of opponents. Afghanistan was once one of the three most heavily landmined countries in the world, Egypt and Iran being the others.[4]

It is likely that imperial Britain's military disasters and early Russian experiences there weighed heavily on the Communist Party leadership's collective mind. The Brezhnev Doctrine, however, called for military intervention when a Soviet client state was threatened by political upheaval that could change a pro-Moscow government. Moscow claimed that the Kabul government requested Soviet intervention because the CIA was working against it within the country; and, to the east, pro-US Pakistan was actively supporting insurgencies across their common land border. After the Iranian Revolution, Iran was also encouraging Islamic subversion across the western border.[5]

Mark Smith has argued that at the time of Moscow's decision to invade, when détente between the US and the Soviet Union was tenuous:

> [t]he Politburo made one of its greatest errors, ordering the invasion of Afghanistan, supporting a local communist regime against what would in time be defined as Islamist insurgents.[6]

It was seen as a new and serious escalation of the Cold War. The Carter administration responded to the invasion by intensifying its anti-Soviet campaign. In addition to increasing the supply of arms and training to groups of Mujahideen, the US targeted its elevated propaganda campaign towards Islamic groups within and outside Afghanistan. The US also specifically targeted Muslim populations across Central Asia, with its criticisms of the Soviet system. As Indian analyst Dilip Hiro has observed:

> Washington's lead was followed by Saudi Arabia, which combined propaganda broadcasts with courses on the Quran and Islamic law; and later by Egypt … Kuwait, and Qatar.[7]

The invasion also alarmed Islamabad. The US threatened a military response if the Soviet Union invaded Pakistan. In Washington, President Carter's national security adviser, Zbigniew Brzezinski, said the US was willing to use force if necessary to defend it. Carter also said he intended speeding up military aid to Pakistan.[8]

Once more, these far-off shocks rippled to the political surface in distant places and, once more, the Russian threat loomed large over Australian politics. The prime minister, Malcolm Fraser, despite contrary advice from his own intelligence agency, the Office of National Assessments (ONA), told the Australian parliament that the Soviet Union was thrusting towards the Arabian Gulf, to take control of global crude oil supplies.[9] The Soviet's Afghan War gave Fraser, a strident Cold War warrior, the chance to confirm his deep-seated suspicions of Moscow's global ambitions.

In echoes of the Great Game, Fraser conjured up a Soviet threat where this time the prize was crude oil, not India, but where the practical obstacles to getting it were no less formidable and the strategic calculus no less forgiving. Still, it was enough to assert a threat from the Soviet Union; establishing if it was practicable and achievable was not necessary. The Russia Anxiety—as during the Great Game, and as often today, with the China Threat—led to a suspension of critical faculties. The media lapped it up. The Melbourne *Age*—in those days, usually balanced—headlined its story about Fraser's response: 'Fraser hits Soviets, Afghanistan moves "risk peace"'.[10]

Some months later, addressing the country about the Soviet invasion of Afghanistan, Fraser said that:

Undeniably, Afghanistan is important to Australia, not only as a test case for Soviet behaviour in the 1980s; but also because of its geographical location in a region of major strategic significance to the Western World, the oil producing countries of the Persian Gulf and Arabian Peninsula.[11]

But Fraser had a bigger objective. He opposed détente and wanted nothing less than the complete defeat of the Soviet Union in the Cold War. Fraser saw an opportunity to help push it over, with the spectre of a Soviet existential threat to the West's crude oil lifelines. A year later, with the election of Ronald Reagan, détente was dead.

Fraser's assertion, and the readiness with which it was taken up by the media, reflects the extent of ignorance in Australia about Russia's security interests and priorities within Central Asia. Speaking in a debate in parliament, the opposition's John Dawkins, referring to a leaked ONA assessment, said:

[the government position] is entirely inconsistent with that of the Office of National Assessments. It is entirely out of touch with the views of the ONA which does not agree with [Fraser's] position at all.[12]

In August 1980, in another major debate on Afghanistan in the Australian parliament, the then leader of the opposition, Bill Hayden, gave a long, considered and insightful analysis of the invasion, based on a detailed briefing from the ONA, which was sharply at odds with the Fraser government's position. As an example of lucid analytical reasoning, it is worth quoting at length. Hayden said:

> The Soviet invasion is much too important to look at in terms of the Prime Minister's fantasies … The justification the Russians advance for their action is transparently false … But this leaves us with this question: Why did the Soviet Union behave as it did? A sober and realistic answer is essential if the right lessons are to be drawn. Some of the analysis we have heard … is based on ideas of the 19th century.
>
> By the middle of 1979, Afghanistan was slowly coming apart … The Soviet Union, always paranoiac about instability on its borders, saw both Iran and Afghanistan in turmoil. It also saw a Marxist government on the verge of falling to Islamic, anti-Soviet rebels. It decided to arrogate to itself, as it did in Czechoslovakia and Hungary, the right to decide the destiny of another sovereign nation. Soviet aggression then seems to have been a result of a perceived weakness to the south, rather than a confident step in a steady expansionist drive.[13]

Hayden rejected Soviet expansionism as a motive for its invasion of Afghanistan and attributed it instead to peripheral security, and Moscow's own sense of insecurity along its borders. He mocked Fraser's assertions about Soviet designs on Middle East oil supplies. His references to nineteenth-century thinking were a direct rebuke to the modern 'forwardists' at the time. Today, we have our own for-wardists regarding China.

In the event, the Soviet Union's invasion of Afghanistan was a disaster for all participants. Having failed to secure its objectives, unable to secure control of the country, and exhausted financially and in terms of military capacity, Moscow unilaterally withdrew, leaving a shattered country behind. For ten long years, Moscow wasted blood and treasure in a futile effort, fighting an insurgency to stabilise the country. Having become Russia's Vietnam, it contributed substantially to the collapse of the Soviet Union in 1991.

## Enter the US

During the Soviet–Afghan War, the US intensified its arming and training of Islamic resistance groups, some of which eventually emerged as the Taliban. In its proxy war with the Soviet Union in Afghanistan, the US created the forces that would eventually turn on it at the beginning of this century. The CIA's role was carefully documented in George Crile's 2003 book, *Charlie Wilson's War*, subsequently made into an award-winning humorous movie of the same name, featuring Tom Hanks. The book was based on interviews with key participants in the 13-year covert operation, which cost hundreds of millions of dollars.[14]

During the decade after the Soviet departure, the Mujahideen's scattered factions fought among themselves, and with more radical anti-Western groups, such as al-Qaeda offshoots. In time, the Taliban prevailed. This success in taking control of much of the country provided a settled refuge for al-Qaeda from which to organise attacks on prestige US targets, culminating in 9/11.

Operation Enduring Freedom, the US-led NATO retaliation for the 9/11 attacks, began in October 2001. A 'coalition of the willing' was formed, in a moment of international cooperation caused by disgust at the terrorist attacks and a growing number of related and unrelated incidents around the world. The invasion of Afghanistan, with the specific and well-defined goal of routing al-Qaeda, was widely popular, especially as success came quickly. Evening news showing US bombers pounding al-Qaeda hideouts in deep bunkers in the Tora Tora mountains reinforced the sense of the West's seemingly invincible power.

After initial startling victories against the Taliban and al-Qaeda, which forced them to flee in large numbers into Pakistan's border areas, such as Balochistan in the southwest, and the Pashtun tribal areas in Pakistan's northwest, the US objectives switched. Now it was the age-old challenge of securing Afghanistan for one set of imperial interests over another— in this case, the US-led West against Islamic fundamentalism.

It was the zenith of the US-led unipolar moment. Even Russia and China backed the US-led war on terror, and used it to justify their own internal repression of Islamic minorities.[15] But, once more, an imperial power was drawn into Afghanistan and, once more, well-defined initial objectives became lost in the frustration of fighting a protracted insurgency. Afghanistan was to become America's second Vietnam.

Twenty years of costly and deadly military intervention in Afghanistan has left the Taliban back in charge, as it had been when the conflict started. While many more women have been educated over that period, and the seeds of a more liberal society planted, the Taliban seems as determined today as ever to plough up the field of a free society and destroy the green shoots of modernity.

## Taliban Between Beijing and Moscow

It could be expected that this is the end of a long history of imperial misadventures in Afghanistan. One would think that lessons may have been learned, but this should not be assumed. Afghanistan remains a major source of instability in Central Asia and so will continue to attract the interest of the great powers. Once again, under Taliban rule, it risks becoming an incubator for various strands of Islamic fundamentalism to spread throughout Muslim Central Asian states; the Caucasus; and, especially and most destabilisingly for the region, Xinjiang province in China. With Beijing's ever-harder authoritarian approach to governing Xinjiang and suppressing dissent, it is likely to create for itself the very problem it is seeking to avoid. It gravely risks radicalising the Uyghur and Kazakh Muslim populations further.[16] These in turn are likely to become increasingly susceptible to radical influences emanating from Afghanistan and elsewhere in the region.

Over the decade before the US withdrawal, China had begun to work with Kabul more actively, through aid programs and other forms of assistance. While preferring to manage relations with countries bilaterally, from 2016 Beijing participated in the Quadrilateral Coordination Group (US, Afghanistan, Pakistan and China). This sought to find a peaceful settlement, mainly by trying to bridge gaps, and to reduce mutual animosity and suspicion between the coalition-backed Afghan government and Pakistan, and throughout Pakistan with the Taliban. Beijing had also sought to strengthen directly its ties with the Taliban. In 2015, it hosted discussions between the Taliban and the Afghan government in Urumqi. On 28 July 2021, just eighteen days before the US withdrawal commenced and anticipating the imminent collapse of the republican government, the Chinese foreign minister hosted a meeting with the Taliban leadership, in Tianjin.[17]

While China was regarded as having an outsized influence over the Afghanistan peace process because of its special relationship with Pakistan, and Pakistan being the most important foreign partner for the Taliban, little was achieved. Moreover, although a long-standing supporter of the Taliban, Pakistan's influence over its actions is also limited in certain respects.[18] Following the 2016 US drone assassination of the Taliban's leader, Mullah Akhtar Mohammad Mansour, for example, the Taliban refused to engage in the Quadrilateral peace process, despite Pakistan's urging. Islamabad also resisted Beijing's pressure to assume a more accommodating position towards the republican government.[19]

China had been consistently upping its engagement with the Afghan republican government. It worked with Kabul to shut down bases established by Uyghur terrorist groups on the Afghan border. It continued to expand its economic aid and provided support with Covid-19 vaccines. It expanded its engagement with Western powers until their retreat.[20] The impact of all this was, however, limited by what was acceptable to the informal international consensus on dealing with the Taliban government. But, in December 2023, Beijing and Kabul exchanged ambassadors. This was followed, on 30 January 2024, by President Xi Jinping formally accepting the credentials of the ambassador of Afghanistan appointed by the Taliban, along with forty-one other ambassadors, at a regular credentials ceremony in Beijing. While China's foreign ministry is reluctant to confirm unequivocally that this amounts to full diplomatic recognition of the interim government in Kabul, for all intents and purposes China has broken with the international understanding that the Taliban be denied formal diplomatic recognition.[21]

Until the most recent move on diplomatic recognition, China had aligned itself with the international community in calling on the Taliban to implement reforms, work with all ethnic groups, and give women education and work opportunities. At the same time, it provided aid, and called on the West to lift sanctions and unfreeze assets. In return, it seeks Taliban support for China's security concerns over Uyghur 'separatism', radicalism and border security. Its strategy was to be close to and supportive of the regime, to advance its own interests, but to stop short of 'mothering' it.[22] China will not want to shoulder the burden of rebuilding Afghanistan alone, but it will be alert to doing what is necessary to prevent others from doing so. China has now reassessed its strategy, and believes the Taliban regime has sufficient control over the country to maintain political stability and ensure security, especially for Chinese enterprises wanting to invest there.

Earlier, China had made it clear that it intended to step up progressively its support for the Taliban regime. On 25 July 2022, at a conference on Afghanistan held in Tashkent, China's special representative on Afghanistan, Yue Xiaoyong, announced that Beijing would help fund a transnational railway across Uzbekistan, through Afghanistan, and on to ports in Pakistan.[23] China has also been active in international forums, encouraging greater accommodation of the new regime in Kabul. More acutely than most, China sees the threats to its own security from instability in Afghanistan, and has sought to encourage the Taliban to disavow terrorism and oppose terrorist groups, especially the East Turkestan Independence Movement (ETIM) and the Islamic State–Khorasan (IS-K), a Central Asian offshoot of the Islamic State; and to work with it to prevent cross-border terrorism and the spread of radicalism into Xinjiang.[24]

During the September 2022 meeting of the SCO in Samarkand, Uzbekistan, Beijing announced that it would provide Afghanistan with duty-free trade for 98 per cent of its products under a new bilateral trade agreement. Although this was more of a gesture of goodwill, as China's imports from Afghanistan are minimal, in announcing the new agreement Wang Yi called on Afghanistan to crack down on all terrorists on Afghan soil, including the ETIM/Turkestan Islamic Party (TIP), and curtail the illicit trade in drugs.[25]

Beijing has several related strategic objectives regarding Afghanistan. The first is to secure its western frontiers, namely Xinjiang, from Islamic fundamentalists who could promote separatism. Beijing regards the 'three evils'—separatism, terrorism and religious fundamentalism—as major threats to its security.[26] The second is to provide security for BRI projects in Afghanistan and Pakistan, and make the country safe for Chinese investment, especially in the resources sector. The third is geostrategic. As with the Great Game, Afghanistan remains central to Core Eurasian geopolitics.[27]

The collapse of the US-led ambition to build a politically stable state that could resist terrorism has brought China's and Russia's worst fears to the fore. Both would have preferred for NATO, and allies like Australia, to continue to spend blood and treasure in Afghanistan to fight the appeal and resist the spread of fundamentalism in Central Asia.

With the West's withdrawl from Afghanistan, Zhongnanhai would have been confirmed in its policy from 2017 of striking hard against Uyghur and other Muslim minorities in Xinjiang. Western NGO and government accusations of Beijing engaging in 'genocide', ethnic cleansing, Islamophobia and so on have obscured the brutal great power reality that Central Asia, of which Xinjiang is a big and resource-rich part, is inherently unstable and potentially prone to Islamic fundamentalist insurrection. That reality came much closer with the Taliban's victory.

## Afghanistan and China's Terrorist Threats

It is commonplace among Western analysts to be dismissive of China's concerns about the terrorist threats it faces from radical Islamist groups operating from inside Afghanistan. The Western narrative has been that, at most, these concerns are exaggerated, and used to justify increasingly harsh repression of the Uyghurs and Kazakhs in Xinjiang, based on ethnic and religious grounds, or because they are a deviation from Marxist principles that see organised religion as a threat to state power, justified by Marx's assertion that religion was the 'opium of the masses'. Essentially, Beijing's concerns are presented as being Han chauvinism and ideologically motivated.[28]

The ETIM/TIP is a predominately Uyghur group to which Beijing has attributed terrorist attacks over many years. TIP seeks to extricate Uyghurs from Han Chinese control and establish an independent Emirate of East Turkestan. It is part of an al-Qaeda-led transnational jihadi group that sees Beijing as an enemy of Islam for its treatment of the Uyghurs. It supported the Taliban in the field as it moved against the republican government, and so can expect a certain degree of support and comfort in its aims against China. At the same time, the Taliban government has been careful to reassure the international community, especially China, that Afghanistan will not be allowed to be used again as a base to export militant Islamic terrorism.[29]

In July 2022, the UN Security Council reported that TIP had, following the US withdrawal, rebuilt militant bases in Afghanistan's Badakhshan province and purchased weapons. Badakhshan's location on the border with Tajikistan includes the Wakhan Corridor, which touches the border with China. The area has been contested by various terrorist groups and was also a past stronghold of the republican government–aligned Northern Alliance. That there have not been any recent reported terrorist attacks is attributed to the Taliban's restraining influence. It is suggested that while the Taliban will not repatriate foreign terrorists, it will take 'quiet measures to restrict or neutralise their activities'.[30]

The Afghanistan-based IS-K has increased its activities against Pakistan and elsewhere in Central Asia since the fall of the republican government. In the 2010s, it declared China to be an enemy and has targeted it since. Following the US's withdrawal, IS-K's influence has increased, and it has been recruiting from other militant groups, including the Taliban and, worryingly for China, TIP. IS-K has been actively targeting Uyghur militants with its recruitment propaganda inside China.[31] While the numbers involved are believed still to be small, Beijing is alarmed by this recent development in Uyghur militancy. Other Taliban and ethno-separatist groups operating in Pakistan have also continued to attack Chinese targets. TIP has, meanwhile, been strengthening its ties to those groups.[32]

Western commentators have expressed surprise and concern that China, with so much at stake in Afghanistan, has not shown greater leadership and been more active in encouraging the Taliban regime to moderate its polices, despite having called for it to do so. Kabul would seem to be doing what Beijing hoped it might, although perhaps not with the anticipated level of enthusiasm. Until 2024, Beijing had not made any concessions to Kabul, holding out to see how determined it was to restrict the spread of terrorism and re-establish internal security.[33] Granting formal diplomatic recognition to the regime in Kabul was, therefore, a big step. It showed that Beijing was satisfied with both its strategy and Kabul's behaviour regarding the spread of terrorism across its borders, believing it deserved further encouragement.

Beijing's behaviour should not surprise anyone. It is consistent with what Afghanistan means to China. It is principally about peripheral security, and particularly Xinjiang. When Chinese security is viewed from the perspective of Beijing, it can be seen to be based on a deep sense of strategic vulnerability. China's interests in security, in terms of how Beijing perceives it, will, of course, trump all other considerations.[34]

## Taliban and Uyghurs

The relationship between the Taliban and Uyghurs is nuanced. They have common beliefs and religious practices, which derive from the Hanafi sect of Sunni Muslims. But the Taliban is a multi-ethnic political movement, while the Uyghurs are an ethnic group, so their identities are different, and they understand and practise their faith differently. Uyghurs are ethnically Turkic, which they share with the peoples of some neighbouring Central Asian states. Uyghurs are comparatively liberal in their attitude towards women's and children's rights, and they value education highly. Most Uyghurs would view the Taliban as extremists. Herein is the historic lost opportunity caused by Beijing's heavy-handed repressive response to its security fears.[35] It should have been relatively straightforward for it to accommodate Uyghur and Kazakh quests to maintain their cultural, religious and linguistic identities while remaining firmly within the Chinese state. Instead, Beijing chose hard-edged repression derived from a reflexive understanding of how to respond to its insecurities.

Having travelled extensively on seven occasions—as both Australia's ambassador to China, and privately as a tourist—to Xinjiang, and as someone who has Uyghur friends and attended special events, such as weddings, fundamentalism does not begin to come to mind while there. In urban areas, veils and the chador, and especially the burka, are these days uncommon. Most Muslim women cover their head with a scarf, if at all. Of course, this also reflects the influence of secular guidance and some regulations imposed by the party/state. Women and men mix openly and freely in the streets, and in markets, restaurants and entertainment venues. What one sees on the streets in Kashgar, Khotan or Yarkand is quite different from what one sees in Peshawar, Pakistan, near the Afghan border, for example. There, most men are dressed in the traditional conservative shalwar kameez, sporting long beards, while fully veiled women scurry to the shops and then quickly return home. Nonetheless, Islamic fundamentalism is more prevalent and apparent in social behaviour in these three southern oasis towns of Xinjiang.

## Uneasy Accommodation between China and the Taliban

Until early 2024, it seemed that China would likely move in lockstep with the broader international community on formal diplomatic recognition of the Taliban interim government. Instead, Beijing has stolen a march on the rest of the international community, and especially Russia. China's BRI will become the principal vehicle through which deeper economic integration with Afghanistan will be advanced: investment by Chinese state-owned enterprises will increase substantially. Afghanistan is rich in some mineral resources of great interest to China, such as copper and lithium, which are vital components in the transition to green energy. China will become the dominant economic power within Afghanistan.

Previously, China has been content to block acquisitions of mining rights to prevent others making moves, but not to develop the deposits. In 2019, an official survey of Afghanistan's mineral reserves estimated deposits of 2.3 billion tonnes of iron ore, 30 million tonnes of copper and 1.4 million tonnes of rare earth materials. In addition, its lithium reserves are thought to be of global significance, perhaps comparable to those of Bolivia, which has the world's largest proven reserves.[36] While some of these numbers may already seem eye-watering, actual reserves could be expected to be much greater when surveyed adequately, using advanced geological techniques. The iron ore figure, for example, looks to be enormous, but each year China already imports over 1 billion tonnes of iron ore.

In 2008, Jiangxi Copper and China Metallurgical Group Corporation (MCC) jointly acquired the rights to develop a massive copper mine at Mes Aynak, in central Logar province. Located some 40 kilometres southeast from Kabul, it is reportedly the world's second-biggest copper deposit. The project would include a processing plant and rail infrastructure, incorporating lines to Pakistan, connecting to the CPEC, and from there to Gwadar Port on the Arabian Sea. To date, it has not progressed.[37] The Taliban regime is keen to see the mine proceed, but establishing infrastructure and security is still a formidable obstacle. If a reasonable degree of political stability and security could be put in place, the project would still be attractive to MCC. Ironically, the Taliban, which prevented its development for over a decade, is now pushing for construction to begin, but MCC is still non-committal.[38]

It remains to be seen how China will come to view Afghanistan in time. The Taliban's commitment to preventing militant Islam from spreading across its borders remains uncertain. Security, more than business, will condition Beijing's policies for quite a while. Mutual trust between Beijing and Kabul will, for a long period, be a work in progress. Over time, Beijing may come to treat it as another 'tributary' state, useful for resource extraction. It may also see

Afghanistan as a helpful ally in its geopolitical imperatives, such as by contributing to an anti-Western alliance. These outcomes, of course, are not mutually exclusive. Most likely, China will insist—explicitly or implicitly—that Afghanistan is in its sphere of influence. Russia, quite legitimately, will have other views. Once more, the age-old geopolitical competition over Afghanistan resumes.

## Russia and Afghanistan

With the waning of Moscow's influence across Central Asia, as will be discussed in Chapter 9, Russia is likely to seek to try to expand its influence in Afghanistan, as a key relationship underpinning its influence in Central Asia. Russia's relations with the Taliban have until recently mainly mirrored Beijing's. Its primary concern is to prevent the spread of Islamic terrorism beyond Afghanistan. Like China, it has maintained its embassy in Kabul, but unlike China, has not formally recognised the Taliban government. It sees Afghanistan as a potentially important market for its oil and gas, especially considering Western sanctions. For its part, cash-strapped Kabul sees Russia as a source of cheap oil and gas. It has not criticised Russia's invasion of Ukraine but, rather, has called for restraint on both sides.[39]

Russia's strategy for dealing with Afghanistan under Taliban rule has been described as a 'synthesis of diplomacy and deterrence'.[40] Its intention is to maintain cordial relations with the Taliban regime, while not unsettling Central Asian states by accommodating Afghan fundamentalists. In 2018, however, Russia was accused by the Afghan republican government of providing military assistance to the Taliban. Moscow strenuously denied the allegations, but it would have been in its interests to prolong the war in Afghanistan.[41]

Beijing and Moscow share a deep concern about the potential for terrorism to spread throughout Central Asia and the Caucuses. Moscow has adopted a three-pronged response. First, in competition with China, it is strengthening its engagement with Pakistan, which it sees as an indispensable back channel to the Taliban regime. Second, it is expanding its security cooperation with India. It shares India's concerns that terrorism from Afghanistan may spill over into Kashmir and Central Asia. If anything, it has complicated its balancing

act by ramping up its cooperation—both economic and miliary—
with India after its invasion of Ukraine. Third, it is increasing its
engagement with Central Asian partners regarding security threats
from Afghanistan. Its capacity to do so, however, is hampered by its
war in Ukraine and the drain it imposes on resources.[42]

In response, IS-K has elevated its propaganda against Russia,
declaring it to be a 'crusader government', the 'Crusader East' and
an 'enemy of Islam', and is calling on supporters to attack Russian
targets. On 5 September 2022, the Russian embassy in Kabul was
attacked by a suicide bomber. It was the first such attack on a foreign
target since the Taliban took over in August 2021.[43] This successful
attack followed two earlier ones, in Uzbekistan in April and in
Tajikistan in May 2021.[44] On 22 March 2024, Tajiki IS-K killed 130
and maimed many more in an audacious attack on the Crocus City
Hall in central Moscow. The Islamic terrorist threat against Russia
from Afghanistan is a real and ever-present danger.[45]

The Islamic State has long targeted Russia as a priority enemy,
along with the US. The grievances are historical—Russian occupation of Islamic lands in Central Asia, the crushing of the Chechen
Muslims, and intervention in Syria in support of President Bashar al-
Assad. The attitude is also tactical: to create difficulties for the Taliban
regime and to perpetuate the international isolation of Afghanistan.
Its Central Asian subsidiary, IS-K, has declared that it will attack
foreign infrastructure projects, commercial activities and foreign
humanitarian organisations, to make life as difficult as possible for
the Taliban regime.[46]

**The Impact on Afghanistan of Russia's Invasion of Ukraine**
The war in Ukraine harms Afghanistan, as it diverts resources, attention
and sympathy from it. The Taliban itself may be reluctant to move
closer to Russia, in view of its newly acquired pariah-state status.
For practical reasons, the Taliban seeks international recognition. It
has presented an international face of responsibility by calling for a
resolution of the crisis through 'dialogue and peaceful means'. The
Russian invasion of Ukraine is also deeply troubling for the Taliban
due to its similarities to the Russian invasion of Afghanistan. It has

been suggested that the invasion of Ukraine may assist the Taliban regime by deflecting international attention from its own abuses of power and its gross human rights violations. This seems unlikely, as governments can focus on multiple issues simultaneously, chewing gum and walking at the same time.[47]

If any player is a winner from Putin's invasion of Ukraine, it is China. Central Asian states have been equivocal about Russia's invasion, have not supported it, and are concerned about Russia's potential threat to them. This resonates with the Brezhnev Doctrine. With international attention reset towards Ukraine, China is working to stabilise politics in Afghanistan to advance its interests.[48]

## Afghanistan and Pakistan

The relationship between the Taliban and Islamabad has long been a key element in the former's survival and eventual triumph over the US/NATO forces in Afghanistan. China certainly regards its close relations with Pakistan as a major asset in its calculations regarding Afghanistan and how to influence events there.

After the October 2001 US invasion of Afghanistan, al-Qaeda activists that fled across the border into Pakistan, along with the Taliban, regrouped and organised insurgency operations into Afghanistan across Pakistan's western border. To the utter frustration and chagrin of the US and its Western partners fighting the war in Afghanistan, Pakistan continued to arm and support the Taliban throughout the conflict and harbour other Islamic fundamentalist leaders—such as Osama bin Laden, until his assassination in 2011 by US forces in his Abbottabad compound near Islamabad.

Since the fall of Kabul in 2021, however, tensions along the Pakistan–Afghanistan border have increased substantially. Pakistan is now engaged in its own war on terror along sections of its border with Afghanistan. To prevent the movement across the border of other radical Islamist groups from Afghanistan, Islamabad has begun fencing the entire 2640-kilometre section of the border that was the Durand Line.

In 1893, the Durand Line had been agreed between the British India government and the Emirate of Afghanistan to define the border, and demarcate the Wakhan Corridor as a buffer zone between British India and Imperial Russia. It divided the Pashtuns between Afghanistan and what is now Pakistan, and many still live on both sides of the border. It is seen, reasonably, as a colonial relic that splits the Pashtun people. Fencing it also disrupts traditional movements across the border and disrupts commerce, including the drug trade that helped sustain the Taliban during twenty years of war. The fence is deeply resented by Kabul.

As if to highlight the swirling complexity of radical Islam in Afghanistan after August 2021, Islamabad has ignored protests from Kabul because it fears the activities of an anti-Pakistan Taliban terrorist group operating from Afghanistan. The Tehrik-i-Taliban (TTP) aims to create a mini–Islamic emirate inside Pakistan along the Durand Line, and so extend the territories of the Taliban's Islamic Emirate of Afghanistan.

Initially, Islamabad embraced the Taliban's victory, with the then prime minister, Imran Khan, declaring that the Taliban had finally broken the 'chains of slavery'.[49] The euphoria has been short-lived, however, as the Taliban has consistently refused to constrain the TTP, despite it having agreed, at the time of signing the Doha Agreement in February 2020, to prevent Afghanistan from being used as a base to export terrorism. Kabul wants Islamabad to stop building the Durand Line fence, and to help it win international support and recognition. It is using the TTP to put pressure on Islamabad to these ends. In response, Islamabad has postponed extending formal diplomatic recognition to the Taliban government in Kabul.

Islamabad is also alarmed by the growing links between the TTP and the even more radical IS-K, which is intent on spreading instability within Pakistan itself. Kabul, however, sees the TTP–IS-K relationship as further leverage against Islamabad. Islamabad is also increasingly isolated by the US and the West, and is likely to turn more to China to help it balance Kabul—especially to prevent Afghanistan from becoming an international terrorist base again. In this, Islamabad's and Beijing's objectives are closely aligned, particularly as IS-K seeks to establish an emirate in Xinjiang.[50]

The networks of terrorist groups that ultimately threaten Xinjiang will encourage Beijing to deepen its involvement with, and influence over, the Islamic Emirate of Afghanistan, and seek to cultivate factions within the Taliban that will restrain the export of radical Islam into Central Asia and Xinjiang. The locus of the contest will move decisively to Xinjiang and Central Asia. A major theatre of the Great Game—the border areas of Pakistan, Afghanistan and China—is likely to see increasing armed conflict and terror.

China's moving ahead of the international community to recognise the Taliban interim government in Kabul should have come as no surprise. Beijing's objectives in doing so are to: restrict the spread of Islamic fundamentalism into Xinjiang and neighbouring Islamic Central Asia states; capture substantial investment opportunities, especially in natural resource–based industries; and, geopolitically, advance Beijing's ambitions to become the dominant power in Core Eurasia. The major risk to China's ambitions is the spread of Islamic fundamentalism to Xinjiang. Since the Qing expansion into these lands in the eighteenth century, the challenge of how to integrate and pacify Xinjiang has persisted to this day.

# CHAPTER 4

# FRAGILE FRONTIER

*'[T]he story of Chinese policy in Xinjiang is filled with unintended consequences.'*[1]

In June 1904, during what was to be the last hurrah of the Great Game, Colonel Francis Edward Younghusband set out from British Shimla to invade Tibet. Although London authorised it merely as a punitive expedition to right perceived slights against Britain from Tibetan border transgressions, the men on the ground determined it would be a full-scale invasion. Britain's viceroy to India, Lord Curzon, had in Younghusband a wilful, ambitious, introverted but highly capable military commander and explorer, who shared his belief that the Tibetans were already in cahoots with the Russians. Nothing short of a full occupation of Tibet by Britain could ensure that this Great Game prize would not be lost to Russia.[2]

Curzon and Younghusband knew a Tibetan mission to St Petersburg had been feted by the Russian Imperial court. A Russian subject from Buryatia, Agvan Dorzhiev, was living in Lhasa and was thought by British intelligence to be a close confidant of the Dalai Llama. They believed that Dorzhiev had drawn up a Russo-Tibetan Treaty, that Russia was supplying Lhasa with modern arms, and that a Cossack detachment had been pledged to come to its aid should Tibet feel threatened by Britain. Military intervention was deemed imperative by Curzon and Younghusband.[3]

Far removed from the self-serving and self-interested myopia of these two, Britain and Russia had finally settled the contentious India–Afghanistan border in the north, which in 1907 would become the Wakhan Corridor. Meanwhile, Russia's humiliation at the hands of the Imperial Japanese Armed Forces in Port Arthur (Lvshun) at the tip of China's Liaoning Province was of greater consequence to St Petersburg than any potential adventurism in the far-flung, isolated, high-altitude deserts of Tibet.

Younghusband's invasion of Tibet was a brutal, bloody campaign. Far from being armed with modern Russian weapons, its defenders were equipped with ancient muskets, sticks and stones. They had no Russian support, intelligence or training.

While Curzon explained to London that the expedition was intended to open a trade route from Shimla to Tibet, and beyond to China, more likely it was due to sheer frontier adventurism driven by his and Younghusband's egos. Alas for them, things had moved on. Both London's and St Petersburg's imperial assessments had changed. Rather than being a career-making adventure for Younghusband, the expedition was disowned by London. John Keay, a leading authority on the Himalaya, observes: 'Younghusband fades from Imperial history at this point'.[4]

In 1961, Peter Fleming published the seminal account of Younghusband's expedition, *Bayonets to Lhasa*. He was the elder brother of famous novelist Ian Fleming, the creator of the James Bond phenomenon. Peter Fleming was an accredited journalist with the *Times* of London, a writer and adventurer. He travelled widely in China in the 1930s, during the period of Nationalist government.

In 1936, he published his account of the long trip he made from Beijing to Kashmir, via Xinjiang, as *News from Tartary*. He was accompanied by the brilliant Swiss photographer Ella Maillart. Fleming's account, however, makes no mention of her, nor of her contribution to the expedition's success. Maillart wrote her own account of the trip, published as *Forbidden Journey*.[5] Including many of her photos, it was a much more rigorous account of the people they encountered and lands across which they travelled than Fleming's swashbuckling memoir. However, in the 1980s, *News from Tartary* had a resurgence in popularity, as China began opening up and independent travel to Xinjiang became possible again.[6]

## Escape from Tartary

Fleming's book was a big influence on my decision to travel, in February 1989, by land from Beijing to Kashgar. With my intended route being to the north of his, it was not meant to be a reconstruction of his bold journey. But, in the end, *News from Tartary* was an unexpectedly most helpful guide to what such a trip may throw up by way of challenges. Unlike Fleming, though, my travel was by train and bus. His was by any mode of transport available at that time. And although much had changed in the intervening fifty years, much had stayed the same—despite seismic changes wrought by war and revolution—especially when it came to China's officialdom.

The first leg was a 30-hour train ride from Beijing to Lanzhou, the capital of Gansu province. The diesel engine was a relatively recent innovation for China's railways. Only in the 1980s did they begin to replace steam engines. The world's last commercial steam train factory was in Datong, Shanxi province, past which our train clattered four hours after leaving Beijing's only railway station. (The factory would stop manufacturing steam locomotives in 2002.) From there, the route largely followed the vast, eroding loess soils of the Yellow River. So much of China's history has been shaped by the meanderings of this river from deep within its interior.

At the time of my trip west, China was going through one of its periods of political and social liberalisation, accompanied by an intensely charged political atmosphere. The tragedy of the Tiananmen Square military crackdown was some four months off. Amid great controversy, China's first avant-garde art exhibition opened in February at the National Art Museum. A television series that had become a sensation was riling conservatives. The lines of the coming clash were getting clearer.

The 1988 six-part *River Elegy* series, screened by one of the government's CCTV stations, looked at events in China's history when its potential was never realised because, according to the program, its conservative, authoritarian Confucius culture intervened and thwarted progress. It described China's culture as 'yellow', being inward looking and backward. To develop and achieve its potential, the program argued, China needed to become more 'blue'—open, outward looking, engaged with the world. After the military attack on the demonstrators in Tiananmen Square on 4 June that year, *River Elegy* became a strictly taboo film, never to be heard of again, in China.[7]

Lanzhou was traditionally the entry point to the Silk Road after traders and adventurers left Xi'an. In February 1989, it was cold, heavily polluted and remote. Over three days there, the surrounding mountains were glimpsed in brief snatches through the smog and mist. Lanzhou was famous for its ingenious irrigation system, involving a network of large water wheels, and its hand-pulled beef noodles. The water wheel system dated from the Ming dynasty and was developed to bring water from the rapidly flowing Yellow River to irrigate the fields surrounding the city. In 1952, some 250 wheels were still in operation. Today, twelve or so of these 15–18-metre-high structures remain, strung along the southern bank of the Yellow River.

After thirty hours sharing a compartment with four others and extracting every last intelligible utterance from my almost non-existent Chinese, we finally arrived and somehow found our hotel. This had not been my first overnight railway adventure in China. I had done 24-hour trips from Beijing to Wuhan and Shanghai and, on several occasions, from Beijing to Datong. In the 1980s, Datong was a particularly popular getaway for foreigners visiting Beijing, as it was one of the nearer cities that was open to them at a time when many were officially closed. It also had extraordinary Tang dynasty Buddhist sculptures on the walls of concealed grottos not far from town.

The Lanzhou Hotel was one of two options for foreigners at the time. It was a 20-minute walk from the railway station to this Soviet-era cavernous building. The arrival of a pair of foreigners was itself a big novelty, and soon half-a-dozen or so staff had attached themselves to the check-in counter, observing every aspect of the process. Then, as now, registering guests was a serious and pro-tracted process, involving much examination of passports, and made all the more difficult by the clerk's inability to speak any language other than Mandarin or the local dialect.

My companion's registration proceeded smoothly enough, and she was handed back her passport. Mine seemed to be creating some difficulties. I had expected as much, as I was travelling on a diplomatic passport, which must then have been a rare sight in those places. After some time, a couple of more senior managers joined the swelling group of onlookers and helpers. As my irritation at the whole thing was rising, I waved my red diplomatic registration card, which, in more advanced places in China, such as Shanghai and Guangzhou, was all I usually needed to complete registration. After more discussion among themselves, the check-in clerk, looking sullen and reluctant, completed the registration and finally we had our room key.

Although it seemed that the red diplomatic registration card had again done the trick, I was uneasy. Something seemed to be wrong with my passport, which had caused the extensive discussion and hesitation over checking me in. Never mind—we stayed three days, mainly to purchase the ticket for the next stage of the trip, and wandered around the city of nearly a million people, eating our way through quantities of Lanzhou beef noodles. In those days, it was not possible to buy a ticket from Beijing to Urumqi, only to Lanzhou. It was also not possible to buy return tickets anywhere. The usual routine on arrival at one's destination was to go immediately to the station ticket office and, if it was open, purchase the return ticket. No trains existed past Urumqi. It was literally the end of the line for all of China. Our tickets were purchased and check-out completed without further incident.

The train from Lanzhou to Urumqi was to be the fabled Iron Rooster. It was a steam-powered locomotive, which Paul Theroux had only recently written about in his travel book *Riding the Iron Rooster*. Published in 1988, it was the hottest China-travel book at that time. Urumqi was then regarded as one of the most isolated cities on the planet, with all the surrounding borders to the former Soviet republics tightly closed.[8] Urumqi is located near the continental pole: that is, the furtherest place on earth from open water. It lies 2645 kilometres from the nearest ocean.[9]

The trip took nearly forty hours. North of Lanzhou, the train chugged uphill through the 1000-kilometre Hexi Corridor in Gansu province; a long, narrow neck of land, and the key artery of the Silk Road, connecting its western reaches with central China and the eastern littoral. Heading north, the land became drier and desert started encroaching. By late afternoon, we were passing the most western end of the Great Wall at Jiayuguan, in bitter cold but brilliant sunlight. Jiayuguan fort was built in 1372, during the Ming dynasty, and was regarded as the furthest western limit of the Ming empire. Beyond that lay the barbarian lands.

Since the Han dynasty (202 BC – 9 AD, 25–220 AD), this part of Gansu had marked the edge of civilisation. The nearby Buddhist grotto cave paintings of Dunhuang owed their existence to tributes paid by wealthy merchants, to receive divine protection as they ventured west on one of the many arms of the Silk Road, or to give thanks for their safe return to civilisation. Outside Dunhuang is Yu Men Guan (Jade Pass Gate), through which merchants passed; and further on, marking the western frontier, are the ruins of the Han dynasty garrison storehouse and watchtowers of Hecang Cheng.

Protected by imperial troops, based at these isolated fortified outposts, from nomadic invasions coming from the expansive deserts and steppe to the west and northwest, Dunhuang flourished as a centre of Gandharan Buddhist art, especially during the Tang dynasty (618–907 AD). In the 1980s, it was only just being rediscovered in the West as a destination for archaeological research and tourism. In August 1988, Noboru Takeshita was the first Japanese prime minister to visit Dunhuang, wishing to emphasise the ancient cultural links between China and Japan. The visit caused a sensation in Japan, for it suggested to nationalists that Takeshita was acknowledging that its cherished culture was essentially derived from China's.[10]

Eighty years earlier, the British explorer Aurel Stein brought the Dunhuang caves to the attention of Western scholars and treasure hunters, with his discovery there of the secret Buddhist library.[11] In 1907, on one of his several trips along the ancient caravan routes of western China, Stein came to Dunhuang, looking for sacred artefacts. An itinerant monk opened what has become known as Cave 17, to reveal to Stein a vast stash of ancient scrolls, paintings and silk banners that had been lying there for more than 1500 years, undisturbed, and preserved by the bone-dry atmosphere of the area.[12]

According to Stein, he helped himself to some 'twenty-four cases, heavy with manuscripts, and five more filled with carefully packed paintings, embroideries and similar art relics'.[13] These treasures were packed and sorted in Khotan, in southern Xinjiang, and eventually found their way to London, where the Stein Collection resides in the British Library, and also to Delhi and Srinagar. In time, these foreign-held collections will become burning sores in the bilateral relations between China and the UK, just as the Elgin Marbles from Greece remain. Still, as recently as 2021, the Dunhuang Museum display was almost silent on these looted treasures.

From Jiayuguan, night fell and the sound of the steam engine rose against the darkness. As morning broke, the horizon to the north and east supported the Altai Mountains. This range of about 2000 kilometres in length runs northwest to southeast and lies across China, Mongolia and Russia. The three countries meet at the Friendship Peak, the highest in the Altai, at 4374 metres. It had been cold since leaving Lanzhou, but now the temperature penetrated with stinging lashes each crack in the carriage and along the corridors. Another long, rattling day lay ahead before reaching Urumqi.

When we arrived, the cold of Urumqi was a shock, even after having been cold for days. Checking into the Kunlun Guest House, it was already pitch dark outside. We were advised that the time for dinner had already been and gone, and the kitchen would close soon.[14] Whatever was being served, we knew it had to be better than the train food of the past two days; we were anxious to sit down to eat before it was too late. But, again, the problem with my passport came up. Once more, a swelling crowd was gathering and, with no common language, we had no idea what was going on. My red diplomatic card didn't instantly do the trick here either. At immediate risk was our dinner, as the city's few restaurants were all about to shut their doors. Eventually, with an ample demonstration of great reluctance, we were given our key and shown to our room in time to catch the last serving of dinner. I clearly had a problem, and the hassle with checking in was likely to be repeated throughout Xinjiang. Worse, we might be sent back to Beijing, or I might even find myself in gaol as a foreign spy. It was a restless night.

Next morning, at around nine, someone was rapping on the door. Opening it, I saw that there stood a tallish, lean young man, with blue eyes and an aquiline nose. I guessed that he was of Kazakh heritage, Kazakh being the third-largest ethnic group, behind Uyghur and Han, mainly located north of Urumqi. He spoke excellent English and identified himself as being from the local public security bureau. My heart sank; prison beckoned. He asked to see my passport. With a quick flick through it, he advised me that I was travelling in China illegally. He was not interested in my red diplomatic card. He said that I did not have a valid visa to be in China, let alone to be going so far west. He reminded me that Xinjiang was a sensitive area for a foreigner to be travelling in and that I could well be in a serious fix. He said I should leave immediately and return to Beijing, to avoid trouble. My stomach tightened, gloom and despair engulfing me at the thought of turning back now, after days of uncomfortable, tiring train travel—so close, but still so far from realising my dream of visiting the ancient mudbrick Silk Road oasis of Kashgar.

He invited himself into our room, which was in the Soviet style: excessively big and overfilled with heavy furnishings. He and I sat next to each other, in large armchairs with the ubiquitous lace antimacassars on the back and arms. Between us was a just-opened carton of Dunhill cigarettes. I tried to encourage my guest to contact the local branch of the foreign ministry. I was certain that they would smartly sort things out in my favour. Or, failing that, I asked him to let me ring the foreign ministry in Beijing. In desperation, I even invoked the name Liu Huaqiu, the vice foreign minister responsible for the Americas and Oceania department, whom I knew well. All of this drew uncomprehending, distant looks and a silent gaze. Knowing how siloed Chinese government departments were, and that this matter was one for the public security bureau, the futility of what I was saying to get myself off the hook was, even in those circumstances, embarrassing. I felt that we had reached the end of the road of this much-anticipated trip.

I offered the young man a cigarette, and it was quickly accepted. I had noticed him eyeing off the open carton between us. We sat and smoked; my situation was discussed back and forth. I explained about our forward-travel plans and that the real purpose of the trip was to visit Kashgar. I emphasised that, although I was a senior diplomat, on this trip I was just a tourist. We smoked and smoked, but always ended up at the same point: I would have to return to Beijing immediately. It was then that I recalled Peter Fleming's *News from Tartary*, and how he and Ella Maillart had travelled from Beijing to Kashgar, were detained for not having the correct papers, held for a period and then sent on to their next destination. Could this now be happening to me?

After yet more time and many cigarettes later, our visitor got up and said that he would help me by taking my case to someone at a more senior level. He said there were no guarantees. He asked if he could take a couple of packs of cigarettes from the carton, but they were nearly in his overcoat pocket before I could say yes. He left, and my companion and I sat, waiting anxiously, for several hours. During that time, we tried to review my options but, of course, no information about flight schedules was available. In any event, we doubted if I could buy a ticket without the correct papers. The sense of hopelessness hung heavily in the now-overheated room.

When our visitor returned, he knocked and walked straight in, sat down and helped himself to a Dunhill. My heart sank again when he began by saying that he had been away for so long because he was looking for his superior but could not find him. Seemingly fascinated by his exhaled smoke, he said that he would make a decision himself, but that his superior might overturn it later. If we left Urumqi immediately, we would be permitted to travel on to our next destination, the ancient oasis town of Turpan, rather than needing to return to Beijing. Elated by this news, we also found it nearly hilarious that what had happened was straight out of the 50-year-old pages of *News from Tartary*. Local officials did not want the responsibility and hassle of having detained a foreigner. At some point, they were going to send Fleming and Maillart on to their next destination, just as we were off to Turpan.

I also knew that there was no way someone like our visitor would be able to 'make a decision' on his own. It would have had to be approved by his superior. In any case, although we would be sorry to miss the museums of Urumqi, and especially the well-preserved Caucasoid corpses from 1800–200 BC in the Xinjiang Regional Museum, we were, like Fleming and Maillart, on our way again.[15] Our visitor readily accepted the rest of the cigarettes in the carton and would help us with our bus tickets. As we set off, not only was Fleming's example reassuring us that we might reach Kashgar as he had done, but his book became something of a guide to how our trip across the sparsely populated reaches of Xinjiang would unfold.

The rest of the trip to Kashgar went similarly. I would have trouble checking into hotels and then, eventually, be moved on by local officials. In Kashgar, as with everything there, the check-in was more relaxed than it was elsewhere. After some days, when we wanted to leave, the next challenge came when we tried to buy air tickets to Shanghai. Somehow, though, with a quick shuffling of my passport and my companion's passport, and a flash of my red diplomatic pass, two tickets to Shanghai were being laboriously written out by hand by the obliging young female assistant. It was a case of the 'art of confusion' prevailing.

In Kashgar, officialdom felt remote. This was not so when we had to transit in Urumqi for the Shanghai flight. Although our onward tickets seemed all that we needed to check into a room at the airport hotel—where a speaker without any controls, high up on the wall, announced the departure of flights throughout the night—to board my flight I still needed my passport. When it was discovered I did not have the required visa, I was marched out of the mad crush trying to board. My passport was thumbed at a glacial pace, with each foreign visa read and re-read again, even though it was doubtful any of it was comprehensible to the officer. The situation looked bad for me. I was starting to panic that this was where I would be taken away and interrogated for spying. And then, after what seemed an eternity, my ticket was closely examined once more and, without comment, I was returned to the pushing, shoving, heaving mob trying to board the Shanghai-bound flight.

The vastness, remoteness and political sensitivity of Xinjiang—both due to internal risks and its borders—makes travelling there still challenging if done in any way other than a fully organised official tour. Xinjiang is the periphery of empire, and its conquest, security and loyalty have long bedevilled Beijing. Its wealth of resources has attracted covetous neighbouring states, especially Russia, and made it a prize that Beijing would never let be lost. For centuries, Xinjiang has held the utmost strategic importance for Beijing.

**Frontier without Borders**
After the fall of the Tang dynasty (618–907 AD), for almost 900 years the lands that were to become known as Xinjiang lay beyond the reach of China. It was consolidated into China only in the second half of the eighteenth century by the Qing dynasty (1644–1911).

Xinjiang's geopolitical sensitivity is readily seen due to its neighbourhood. It is some 1.7 million square kilometres, which is about four times the area of California and one sixth of China's total area. In the far north, the Altai Mountains separate it from Russia and Mongolia; to the west, the Tian Shan mountains separate it from Kazakhstan and Kyrgyzstan; and to the south, the Kunlun, Karakoram and Pamir mountains separate it from India, Tajikistan, Pakistan and Afghanistan.

Prior to the Qing conquests, Xinjiang comprised two regions, divided by the Tian Shan mountains, which were distinct geographically, ethnically and historically. In the north was Dzungaria, with fertile pastureland and forests, and a mix of settled and nomadic populations. The Dzungars were of Mongol descent and the Buddhist faith. In the south is the Tarim Basin, which holds the massive Taklamakan Desert, with widely distributed, fertile settled oases along its northern and southern boundaries. The people there were of mixed Turkic ethnicity, from Central Asia; mainly Buddhist but later Muslim. Although much of the south is desert, it is rich in oil and many minerals, and the fertile areas around the desert oases are highly productive in terms of crops, horticulture and livestock husbandry. Autumn in Xinjiang offers a cornucopia of delicious peaches, apricots, walnuts, sweet melons and grapes. The ancient Silk

Road's northern and southern arms skirted the Taklamakan Desert, following the oases.

Before the Qing conquests, these oases were independent Central Asian kingdoms. Kucha, on the northern route of the Silk Road around the Taklamakan Desert, for example, was a major Buddhist centre until the Muslim expansion in the eleventh century. The first substantial translation of Buddhist texts into Chinese was initiated by a monk from Kucha, Kumarajiva (344–413 AD), whose father had migrated from India to Kucha, to devote his life to the study of Buddhist scripture. Kumarajiva relocated to Chang'an, the capital of the Tang dynasty, now Xi'an, where he established a translation bureau in 401 AD. It was responsible for hundreds of translations of Buddhist texts from Tibetan into Chinese, some of which are still read today.[16]

The Tang dynasty initially extended Chinese rule into Xinjiang from Gansu, along the Hexi Corridor to Dunhuang, and as far as Turpan, on the edge of the Taklamakan Desert, eventually drawing Central Asia together with China in a pan-regional administrative area. As Harvard historian and expert on Central Asia Valerie Hansen writes:

> [t]he people of the Tang Dynasty lived in a culturally mixed world filled with foreign art, music, and fashions. They also lived in a world governed by regulations … The Tang rulers were able to sustain an extraordinary degree of control throughout their empire.[17]

By the eleventh century, the Islamification of Xinjiang had commenced, and was largely complete by the end of the sixteenth century. From the fourteenth century, with the decline of the Mongol Empire, the Tarim Basin and Dzungaria were also occupied by successive waves of tribal and nomadic people from Tibet and Central Asia. Consequently, although Islam had established itself as the major religion across the region by the time of the Qing, Buddhism and Shamanism also continued to be ubiquitous.

US Central Asian scholar James Millward has argued recently that Islam was a powerful force drawing Xinjiang towards Persia and

Turkic lands in the west. Islam connected Xinjiang 'culturally to the west, the broad zone of Central and South Asia whose high culture was in Persian or Chagatai Turkic'.[18] Xinjiang was also at the intersection of the various Silk Roads, linking Cathay in the east with Mediterranean states in the west. Commercial and familial associations and networks often joined the people of Xinjiang to places far away from the Tarim Basin oases and nomadic pastoralists. By the sixteenth century, as the ethnic and religious landscape came to resemble that of more modern times, and the surrounding empires of China, India, Persia and Russia began to take shape, loyalties to these 'distant dynasties and their imperial metropoles' emerged.[19] Xinjiang existed on the fringes of these empires, itself as a 'shadow empire' without any single ruling authority, until the Qing conquests.[20]

The Qing empire was the largest in Chinese history. Once the Qing emperor Kangxi established his rule over the Ming's territory in 1683, he turned his attention to Mongolia, Manchuria, Tibet and Xinjiang. Hansen notes that:

> Because the claims of the People's Republic of China to these regions often hinge on the past, this … history is one of the most contentious in all Chinese history. Utterly different accounts coexist in and outside of China, and it is not always possible to check the original sources, some of which remain locked away even today.[21]

Han Chinese have long referred to this area as *Xiyu* (western region), or *Huijing* (Muslim territory). The Qing adopted the name *Xinjiang* (new frontier) only in the 1750s, following their victories over the Dzungars and the consolidation of the region into the empire.[22] Prior to 1759's defining Qing conquest of the Dzungars, which saw their genocide under the orders of Emperor Qianlong, Xinjiang was a region without political borders, central control or administration, and with multiple linguistic and ethnic affinities. When the Qing had regained most of these territories, they began to expand Chinese control further to the southwest and west into Central Asia.[23]

By 1760, Emperor Qianlong was in control of most of what is Xinjiang today.[24] Perdue, in his monumental study of the Qing's westward expansion, argues that the closing of the last Eurasian frontier with the Qing's conquest of Xinjiang marked a watershed moment in global history, similar in importance to the closing of the American frontier.[25]

David Brophy, in his history of the creation of the Uyghur 'nation', argued that for the early Qing, Xinjiang's borders were viewed less as territory to defend than as a series of tributary states like any other in continental inland Asia, with an easy ebb and flow of people across their vastness. It was not until later in the nineteenth century, over a hundred years after the Qing's final conquest, that formal demarcation of borders began to matter.[26]

By the eighteenth century, the British Raj and Imperial Russia were beginning to press on Xinjiang. This brought it into 'unprecedented contact with a wider world'.[27] Squeezed between the expanding Russian Empire and British India, Xinjiang increasingly came to be seen in the imperial metropolitan capitals as a buffer zone. Brophy puts it thus:

> As Russian Turkistan became Russian, and all of India became British, each of these neighbours drew Xinjiang into a colonial periphery of its own. The Qing court's ability to maintain its authority in Xinjiang depended on the disposition of these two Great Game rivals, who eyed each other across a space they treated not so much as inalienable Qing territory but as a buffer zone of ambiguous territory.[28]

The Qing rulers were preternaturally adaptive, and well versed in the different cultures of their subjects. They devised specific policies for each of the regions brought under their control. The Qing honoured the Dalai Lama, for example, and sought to fulfil the ideal of the *chakravartin*, a ruler who worked for the Buddhist order without ever becoming a monk.[29] Later, treating these conquered territories as if they were colonial entities, the Qing administered them through a separate bureaucracy created especially for the purpose: the *Lifan Yuan* or Court of Colonial Affairs.[30]

Under the Qing, Xinjiang was governed from Yili in the northern pastoral areas, where armies could raise horses and generally support themselves. This region was organised more like a military base, with 'fifteen to twenty thousand soldiers, accompanied by some hundred thousand family members, in garrisons located mainly in the northern grass lands'. This was occurring at great cost to the central government and far exceeded taxes received.[31] For the first century, the Qing did not interfere much with the local Islamic governments in the Tarim Basin's oases, permitting Islamic law and religious practices to continue undisturbed. At the same time, it consolidated administration and ruled the Tarim Basin oases as part of a centralised empire based on the Qing's own bureaucratic methods.[32]

Political control and public administration in Xinjiang (as in Mongolia, Manchuria and Qinghai) were based on the Qing banner system, which created an 'overarching administration that saw to the needs of military personnel and supervised local government by indigenous elites'.[33] It comprised military units tasked with conducting administration and that answered directly to the emperor. It was, however, a complex and multi-layered system, with local arrangements for day-to-day matters, while the bannermen held a monopoly over military force and finance.

Initially, the Qing tightly restricted Han Chinese migration to the Tarim Basin. Until 1830, imperial Qing had not attempted 'sinicization', or assimilation of the local population. It preferred to allow local indigenous rulers the status of khans—or in Xinjiang, that of begs—but under the banner system and hence with some constraints on their power. Han Chinese were prohibited from settling permanently in the Tarim Basin, and were restricted mainly to Urumqi and the fertile valleys in the north. Migration policy changed in 1830, as the court came to see a strategic advantage in populating the Tarim Basin with Han Chinese, but few were attracted to it.[34]

Despite sporadic jihads against Qing outposts in the Tarim Basin, Xinjiang under Qing rule was largely stable throughout the early nineteenth century.[35] However, pressure began to build mid-century, as Qing finances were increasingly depleted by instability elsewhere in China—especially in the case of the Taiping Rebellion (1850–64) in the Yangtze River region of eastern China.[36] The Taiping Rebellion was in essence an ethnic Han uprising against a foreign occupying power: the Manchu. Its disruption of global cotton production also made it a worldwide geopolitical event that consequently saw the British intervening on the side of the corrupt, failing Qing dynasty.[37]

### Kashgaria and the Great Game

The shortage of silver from Beijing to fund the Xinjiang garrison led local officials to resort to punitive taxation, the sale of official positions, bribery and 'general decrepitude', including development of opium addictions. Economic malaise and endemic misrule provided the underlying conditions for widespread rebellions, which broke out from 1864. The Tungans (Hui Chinese, who were Muslims) had been migrating in their tens of thousands to Xinjiang. Tensions between them and the Han Chinese had been building when a rumour circulated in June 1864 that the Qing Tongzhi emperor had ordered a pre-emptive massacre of thousands of Tungans. Across towns and cities in Xinjiang, from the north to the southwest, Tungans revolted against the failing Qing administration.[38]

With the collapse of Qing power in the Tarim Basin, some khanates west of the Pamirs mobilised to take advantage of the situation. In 1865, Yaqub Beg—we met him earlier in the Great Game—was sent by the khan of Khoqand, in the Fergana Valley in eastern Uzbekistan, to join with Kyrghiz forces that had plundered Kashgar. Assisted by local Tungans, he then captured the Qing fort at Kashgar. A bloody massacre of Han Chinese ensued, during which the remaining Manchu officials blew themselves up in a gunpowder store. Having vanquished the Han Chinese, he then turned on the Kyrgyz fighters, and drove them out of Kashgar and had himself proclaimed beg. Secure in Kashgar, he next conquered Khotan, after a battle that led to many local Uyghur deaths of those defending the city. In 1867, he attacked Kucha, which quickly fell. By 1871, Yaqub Beg controlled all southern Xinjiang from Kashgar to Turpan, including Urumqi.[39]

With an army of some 40,000 comprising mainly Khoqandis and Uyghurs, Yaqub Beg's khanate, Kashgaria, was based on fundamentalist Islamic principles and values, including sharia law, and survived until the Qing reconquest of Xinjiang in 1877. His rule, however, was characterised by economic failure, mainly due to Kashgaria's isolation from China, excessive taxation to support his military, and oppressive violent rule from despised Khoqandi governors and officials who filled the top governing positions. But as the empires of Russia and Britain jockeyed with each other over Kashgar as the Great Game progressed, Yaqub Beg briefly enjoyed recognition and some prestige in far-flung places.

In the 1850s and 1860s, Russia had conquered Transoxiana (Turkestan), including parts of Khoqand; and, in 1871, annexed the Yili Valley in northern Xinjiang. The return of the Qing, however, remained the principal threat. Yaqub Beg's policy therefore sought friendly relations with both Russia in the north and Britain in the south. In 1872, he signed a trade agreement with Russia. In 1873–74, he welcomed British envoys, hosted a 350-member trade delegation led by East India Company commissioner Thomas Douglas Forsyth, and signed a commercial treaty with Britain. Forsyth also delivered a personal letter from Queen Victoria to Yaqub Beg.[40] In response, Beg posted an ambassador to London. Beg's khanate was accorded full diplomatic recognition, some international support, and covert supplies of arms to be used against the Russians, if needed. The British had hoped that Kashgaria might act as a buffer against further Russian eastern and southern expansion in Turkestan.

Yaqub Beg was also recognised by the Ottoman sultan Abdulaziz, who bestowed on him the status of emir, and supplied arms and military training, underlining the Ottoman Empire's growing interest in Central Asia. Brophy argues that this was not so much an expression of pan-Islamic solidarity as it was an expedient gesture to deflect criticism of the sultan for not having protected the Muslims of Bukhara from the Russian invasion in 1868. News of a new sunni

khanate arising in the deserts of Central Asia stirred some excitement
in Istanbul. It was seen as an opportunity for the Ottomans to assert
influence in a distant place at a time when their territories were
coming under increasing pressure closer to home, from Britain
and Russia, and without provoking a reaction from these imperial
powers. A Muslim state in China would enable the Ottomans to
burnish their claim to be the spiritual leaders of the Muslim world.
They had no relations with the Qing, and, being in East Turkistan,
their claims would not antagonise the British or the Russians, who
were suspicious of Ottoman intentions towards their own Muslim
colonial subjects.[41]

Sultan Abdulaziz sent his own nephew as a special envoy to Yaqub
Beg's court. He in turn sent to Istanbul an envoy, who returned with
an imperial letter, a medal for Yaqub Beg, and a gift of rifles and
cannons, together with training officers—and the sultan's sword, to
be used in a ceremony in which allegiance to the sultan was sworn.
For the remainder of the Kashgar Emirate, its coinage and Friday
prayers proclaimed the sovereignty of Sultan Abdulaziz.[42]

Central Asian historian Adeeb Khalid argues that accepting the
Ottoman caliph as a suzerain did not restrict Yaqub Beg from acting
independently but, rather, was useful to demonstrate both to his subjects
and other rulers that he was tied to a major outside power. It was also
a source of legitimisation of his rule that went beyond local Islamic
sources. Millward describes Yaqub Beg as a 'transitional figure'—
going from Central Asian strongman to practitioner of international
statecraft. He recognised the global power shifts occurring between
empires, understood how these were playing out in Central Asia, and
so sought to strengthen his position against Qing China.[43]

Likewise, Khalid regards the episode of the Kashgaria khanate as
significant because it demonstrates the 'collapsing of distances and
the incorporation of Central Asia into broader global politics'. It also
saw the Ottoman Empire becoming an important element in Central
Asian geopolitics and, while this was its only direct intervention
in Central Asia, it was to retain a certain 'allure in the minds of
Central Asian elites', which remained influential 'as colonial rule was
consolidated in the region'.[44]

## Qing Reconquest of Xinjiang

The Qing reconquest of Xinjiang in 1878 resonates with China's strategic geopolitical calculations today: consolidating its western territories, firming up its frontier borders, seeking security by asserting more influence over Central Asia, and expanding Han administration and values in Muslim lands. At the time, some Western commentators, who were unable or unwilling to recognise the vulnerability of China's western borders, saw it instead as:

> an example of backward continental thinking, an anachronistic echo of the Qing's Inner Asia strategic heritage at a time when more important matters demanded attention along China's coasts.[45]

The reconquest of Xinjiang was hotly contested in the Qing court. Maritime defence versus frontier defence had long been debated. Where best to allocate resources for security became an increasingly pressing problem, as the Qing dynasty's capacity was being depleted by domestic wars and insurrections, and incursions by foreigners. Now China faced coastal threats from Western powers and Japan, as well as security challenges along its Russian frontier.[46]

The argument against retaking Xinjiang was that it would be a costly venture to gain what was largely barren land populated by troublesome inhabitants. The opposing view pointed to Russian designs on the territory, arguing 'as Xinjiang goes, so goes Mongolia; as goes Mongolia, so goes Beijing'. In language reminiscent of the Cold War 'domino theory' rhetoric in the 1950s and 1960s, Russian occupation of the Yili Valley—some 3000 kilometres to the west—was said by the frontiersmen to be a 'dagger pointed at the heart of Beijing'.[47]

The most forceful proponent for recovering Xinjiang was General Zuo Zongtang, a scholar from Hunan province. He argued that the Eurasian frontiers were the most important for the empire's security and were where the Qing's military resources should be concentrated. He contended that in the northwest, there were no natural boundaries, so the frontier was permanently vulnerable to invasion. He claimed that

Beijing and the Northwest are connected to each other just like fingers are connected to the arm. When they are solidly united and connected, security can be guaranteed. However, if [our control over] Xinjiang is not solid, the various tribes of Mongolia would also become an unstable factor.[48]

But for General Zuo, the existential threat to the empire came not from local tribes and khans, but from the great imperial powers Britain and Russia:

When it comes to the management of the affairs of Xinjiang, the most important task is to prevent Russia's collaboration with Britain in violating our interest, rather than to suppress the Muslims.[49]

In time, the 'defending-the-frontier' faction prevailed over the 'coastal-defence' faction and Gerneral Zuo was awarded the campaign. He became the first Han to be put in charge of the region, previously the preserve of Manchu or Mongol warriors. The 1878 Qing reconquest of Xinjiang came to be viewed within China as a heroic triumph against the odds, rather than as an exercise of backward-looking revanchism. With so many defeats in the east, the fading Qing dynasty was able to demonstrate that it still had vitality and power. It was a tremendous morale boost for the court in Beijing. Since then, until more recent times, heavy stress on continental security has been a cornerstone of China's security policies and its grand strategy.

The Qing reconquest subsequently mutated into a major effort to sinicize Xinjiang from the east, while from the west, radically new political ideas of national identity were seeping in. Despite the reconquest and the creation of Xinjiang province in 1884, Xinjiang remained deeply embedded in the west. By this time, Russia had consolidated its control of Transoxiana and what today is Kazakhstan. Trade was predominately with Russia and British India, while China was too far away and uncompetitive to exert much influence. New ideas about government, statehood, nationalism and civil society were percolating in from the west, while in the east, China's imperial rulers held fast to old thinking and colonial rule over its western reaches. As Millward observes:

> Ideas moved along those same trade channels ... like peoples under colonial rule throughout the world, the Islamic and Turkic peoples of Central Eurasia were thinking in new ways about their situation.[50]

Jadidism—derived from Russia, and encouraging Muslims to modernise via education and self-improvement—was one expression of this. Throughout the late nineteenth century, modernist Muslim movements spread through Central Asia and became influential among Xinjiang's Muslims. Links to the Ottoman Empire were powerful conduits for educational experimentation and reform.[51]

With the Treaty of St Petersburg (1881), China recovered the territory of Yili from Russia, in return for an indemnity and trade concessions, and permission to open, initially, two consulates. The treaty was negotiated by Zeng Jize, who subsequently became the Qing's second appointment as ambassador to London.[52] This treaty replaced the earlier disastrous Treaty of Livadia (1879), in which China's concessions were so great that it nearly cost the lead negotiator his life; the treaty was never ratified. Dispute over the extent of Yili's western border and subsequent revisions to borders in the Treaty of St Petersburg, however, left China feeling as if it had been robbed of part of its territory: some 70,000 square kilometres. Today, China views it as another 'unequal treaty' imposed by a stronger imperial power.[53]

Establishing Xinjiang as a province within the Qing empire came as part of a broader administrative reorganisation, which included provincial status for Taiwan as well. Millward argues that:

> The implementation of provincehood in Xinjiang represented not annexation of a former protectorate by 'China', but rather a fundamental shift in the governing principles of the Qing empire as a whole ... The [internal] debates over the pragmatics

of provincehood thus hinted at deeper issues involving the
nature of the empire and the status of the Manchus, Mongols
and other Inner Asians in a realm dominated demographically by
Han Chinese.[54]

It was part of the ailing Qing empire's efforts to strengthen peripheral
security by sinicizing its frontier lands and administering them in the
same way as core China. The grand design did not work, however, and
the frontier lands were chronically short of funds. Corruption and
opium addiction were also commonplace. For Xinjiang, the burden
of centralised taxation greatly discouraged commerce with the rest of
China, especially because of the vast area's small population and long
distances. The Treaty of St Petersburg had also exempted Russian
traders from duties and levies, so Russian merchants prospered
greatly from Xinjiang trade. This trade integrated Xinjiang more
closely with Central Asia and Russia, rather than with China.[55]

During the period to World War I, the border of Xinjiang with
Russia saw large movements of people—including Muslim political
refugees, traders and migrant labour—into Russia. Brophy argues this
'Qing diaspora' resulted both from Qing policies, especially regarding
taxation and business, and individual choices about opportunity. In
Xinjiang, the Russian and Qing empires overlapped and meshed.
It was 'imperial subjecthood, rather than religion or ethnicity' that
distinguished foreigner from native. This made for great fluidity of
people between empires.[56]

Republican rule (1911–49) was a tumultuous period in Chinese
history. Xinjiang was largely a bystander to the events that, in 1911,
ended 367 years of Qing rule. Essentially, apart from some minor
non-Han involvement in anti-Qing activities, what occurred in
Xinjiang was a shift in military figures' political allegiances from the
Qing court to republican authorities. Nevertheless, across Xinjiang
sporadic violent uprisings against the Manchu rulers occurred and,
with the start of the twentieth century, the 'seeds of [a] Uyghur
nationalist movement had been planted'.[57]

Cosmopolitan industrialists and merchants who had travelled
frequently to the neighbouring Islamic lands to the west, and

beyond to Turkey and Europe, brought modernising concepts to the Tarim Basin cities and supported foreign teachers in espousing them. Through expanding Turkic media and schools, Uyghur nationalist ideas began to take shape in the 1920s. The Russian Revolution also had a big impact on Muslims in Xinjiang. They, like others in Russia's Central Asian borderlands at the time, looked on as the Bolsheviks' recasting of Russia unfolded, wondering where their interests were best served. Those with established links to Russia, especially merchants and traders, tended to align themselves with the Soviets.[58]

The ethnonym 'Uyghur' was a relatively modern creation, derived from the Soviets in the 1920s as they set about classifying and defining their own nationalities. The term spread to Xinjiang at that time and only became an official appellation during the KMT warlord government of Sheng Shicai.[59] Uyghur identity developed in a setting in which it was peripheral to the Soviets' efforts to classify their own ethnic nationalities in Central Asia, but nevertheless was influenced by what was happening in neighbouring Muslim lands. Uyghur identity was also localised, and varied depending on whether one was urban or rural, and on gender, educational attainment and even age.[60] It was far from being a concept related to homogeneous nationhood. Uyghur national identity was neither a result of 'state-sanctioned national construction', as in other Soviet Muslim republics, nor, as in the colonial world, the outcome of a national liberation struggle. Instead:

> [t]he Uyghur nation … emerged as a palimpsest of Islamic, Turkic, and Soviet notions of national history and identity and has remained a repository of these multiple discursive registers.[61]

## Soviet Buffer Territory

Xinjiang's first government in the republican period was under the autocratic rule of the brutal Yang Zengxin. Yang sought to isolate Xinjiang both from the rest of China and from neighbouring states from which he feared liberal, radical, modernising ideas were coming.

He sought the support of conservative elements in the Islamic clergy to shut the new schools. With the Bolshevik Revolution in 1917, Russia itself closed due to the chaos of its civil war and, as a result, Xinjiang's existing economic difficulties worsened. Despite Yang's ubiquitous secret police force, dissent spread throughout the province. By 1924, the Soviet Union had stabilised. Yang decided to negotiate a new treaty with it to replace the Treaty of St Petersburg. Many of the unfair elements, including Russian extraterritoriality and non-reciprocal duty-free movement of goods, were removed, while Moscow was granted permission to open additional consulates. For the first time, China was also allowed to open consulates on the other side of the Tian Shan mountains, including in Almaty and Tashkent. Xinjiang's trade with the Soviet Union surged. By 1928, it was ten times greater than its trade with the rest of China.[62]

With the assassination of Yang during a banquet in 1928, a period of political instability ensued, as successors vied for power, sought to implement administrative and land reforms, and played a multiplicity of factions off against each other to shore up their positions. This period cannot be reduced to Islam versus China, or modernisers against traditionalists, or a farrago of ethnic groups each against the other. Islam was a factor, but, with the collapse of authority, factionalism and opportunism were rife. Allegiances and alliances were constantly shifting and sides changing. Also a factor was interference from afar, both from the Nationalist government and the Soviet Union. Although the level has probably been exaggerated, both Britain and Japan also had some involvement in the rolling rebellions, through agents and proxies.[63]

By the 1930s, the Soviet Union was the most consequential influence over events in Xinjiang, even more so than distant Nanjing, which was now the capital of Nationalist China. In 1935, Ella Maillart provided accounts of conversations with local officials, as she travelled through Khotan, Yarkand and Kashgar, that turned frequently to Soviet influence in the Tarim Basin.[64] In the north of Xinjiang, where there was the largest number of Russians, new railways were reinforcing Russia's advantages of proximity. The Trans-Siberian Railway (1904) and the Turkestan–Siberia Railway

(1929–30) were close enough to Xinjiang for both to be of major economic and strategic significance. Xinjiang was being drawn closer to the Soviet imperial power.

In 1933, as political chaos and violence spread across Xinjiang, a short-lived East Turkestan Republic (ETR) was declared in Kashgar. While inherently Islamic and based on sharia law, it also embraced modernising trends in the areas of public education, libraries and industrialisation. However, as Moscow was attempting to consolidate its control over the Islamic regions west of the Tian Shan mountains, it did not relish the prospect of an independent Muslim state on its borders. When the weak Nationalist Chinese government of Xinjiang led by the warlord Sheng Shicai asked for Soviet assistance to quash the ETR, Stalin was only too happy to oblige. In the end, however, the Soviet Union played only a minor, indirect role in the crushing of the ETR. Local Tungan forces, aligned with the governing Nationalists, did most of the work.[65]

Following this, Sheng Shicai turned increasingly to Moscow for assistance. Millward and Tursun suggest that, in time, Xinjiang effectively became a satellite of the Soviet Union, 'much like Outer Mongolia'.[66] The Soviets were granted extensive mineral and oil concessions; Soviet advisers worked in local government in Urumqi, and were present in the military, intelligence and secret police. At the time, Moscow was also concerned about a possible Japanese advance on Xinjiang, after it had taken Manchuria from Russia and parts of Inner Mongolia from China. A Soviet regiment was stationed in Hami, in northeast Xinjiang near Gansu province, to defend the main eastern approach into Xinjiang.[67]

As isolated geographically as Xinjiang was from the main metropolitan centres of empire, distant events could and did disturb its domestic politics because of its geostrategic location. Stalin's non-aggression pact with Japan in 1941 protected the USSR's eastern flank for a time, while Moscow prepared for Hitler's invasion in the west. Stalin had neither the resources nor the need to keep propping up Sheng Shicai. For Sheng, the Nationalists were now a better option as a patron. He summarily expelled his Soviet advisers; stopped trade with the USSR; and executed Chinese Communist advisers who had been sent to him from Yan'an, where the CPC was holed up, and who were an important conduit to Moscow. One of these CPC advisers was Mao Zemin, brother of Mao Zedong. Sheng was welcomed by the Nationalists and made chairman of the KMT's Xinjiang branch. The US, which was now heavily financing the KMT, opened a consulate in Urumqi. [68]

In Xinjiang, the Nationalist government was a disaster. It set about sinicizing the administration; promoted mass migration from China; attempted to introduce sedentary farming on the grasslands; debased the currency; and, among much else, refused to recognise ethnic groupings, on the basis that they were ultimately meant to be all Chinese. The loss of trade with the USSR was devastating. Revolt was in the air. Rebellion broke out first in the wealthier areas of the north near Yili. It spread rapidly. Han Chinese were massacred en masse. The revolt's leader, an Islamic scholar, declared the formation of the Turkestan Islam government, which became the second ETR.

The Soviet Union had quickly infiltrated the ETR. Its founder soon 'disappeared' over the border into Russia, to be replaced by a Soviet-educated Uyghur who pursued secular socialist policies. Stalin had wanted to end the rebellion against the Nationalists after having signed the Sino-Soviet Treaty of Friendship and Alliance with Chiang Kai-shek in August 1945. This treaty formally recognised the agreements signed at the Yalta Conference in February 1945 between the great Allied powers. Among other territorial gains, the Soviet Union was granted railway concessions in Manchuria and the continuing 'independence' of Outer Mongolia was assured. The US had promised these to Stalin in order to bring the USSR into the war with Japan. With the Manchurian concessions, Mongolia's satellite status confirmed and a receding threat from Japan, Stalin decided not to push his luck in Xinjiang. Once again, Xinjiang's fate was shaped by great power politics. [69]

In late 1949, as the CPC extended its control across China, the retreating Nationalists held the southern part of Xinjiang, while the Soviet-influenced ETR was in the north. In October 1949, the People's Liberation Army (PLA) reached Xinjiang and met with little resistance. While the ETR held hopes for self-determination,

Stalin opposed this and instead welcomed the CPC's victory. A mysterious plane crash that wiped out the entire ETR senior leadership, as it flew from Almaty in Kazakhstan to Beijing for the inaugural meeting of the People's Political Consultative Conference, has variously been attributed to Mao, or to Stalin; or maybe the plane did in fact just crash.[70]

## PRC Embrace

Xinjiang was initially administered by the PLA's First Field Army. An early priority for it was to identify and train local Turkic cadres while avoiding those with ETR and Soviet sympathies. Another priority, as it was for the CPC across China, was land reform. This also enabled the PLA to recruit local-level officials to manage affairs at the grassroots. Collectivisation in Xinjiang, however, proceeded slowly, especially on the pastoral lands. The PLA seemed reluctant to force the pace, because of the existence of numerous ethnic groups with their own identities and customs.[71]

Forming government was particularly challenging because of the substantial size of the Islamic population. It was only in Xinjiang that the CPC faced a majority non-Chinese-speaking Islamic population, with 'a well-established clerical organisation that deeply penetrated society'.[72] Through to the mid-1950s, the CPC gradually stifled local clerical influence, by closing off tithes and religious taxes while coopting Islamic leaders into national-level religious, including Islamic, organisations.

As did the latter-Qing and the Nationalists, Beijing promoted mass Han migration into Xinjiang. A primary objective was to strengthen the security of the frontier. A key element of this was the state farm, which had ancient antecedents. The Han dynasty initiated military farms to support its armies in the far west. Under the Qing, state farms were known as *tuntian*. Their main purpose was to support the military administrative system of Xinjiang, as well as to provide frontier security. [73]

The modern PRC version was derived from the *tuntian*. After 1949, the first wave of new colonists in Xinjiang comprised over 100,000 demobilised soldiers, of whom some 80,000 were from the former Xinjiang KMT garrison. They were eventually organised into what became the Production and Construction Corps or *bingtuan*. *Bingtuan* were intended to be both production and militia brigades: 'one hand on the gun, one hand on the pickaxe'.[74]

*Bingtuan* were initially established mainly along Xinjiang's northern and western borders, to develop these hard-to-defend areas, increase population along the border regions, and provide security and social services. Later, they also became a means for populating southern parts of the Tarim Basin. In time, political and criminal prisoners, and volunteers encouraged by the government via incentives, began to fill out the *bingtuan* ranks, which also formed part of China's notorious *laogai* penal system.[75] *Bingtuan* were also involved in major campaigns to win against the wilderness, through land clearing, forest cutting, dam building, canal digging, and expanding the area of arable land. They were equipped with their own paramilitary security forces, and also provided welfare and medical services;[76] all of which have underpinned the CPC's recolonisation of Xinjiang.

In 2008, when I requested, as ambassador, the Xinjiang foreign affairs office to arrange a visit to the *bingtuan* headquarters in Urumqi, this was met with some puzzlement and resistance: a visit by a foreign diplomat would be most 'unusual'. But, in the spirit of growing openness at the time, my request was eventually granted.

This semi-secretive body was housed in a cavernous, seemingly sparsely occupied, tower block on the outskirts of Urumqi. It was clear from the awkward manner of my hosts that meeting foreign visitors was something of a novelty. When my meeting with the president of the *bingtuan* association concluded, I said I was now a little confused, and asked whether '*bingtuan* was a state within a state, or was Xinjiang a province within the *bingtuan*?' He wryly acknowledged the humour in the question and moved on without further comment. Beijing is ever vigilant regarding threats—real and perceived—to its control over the province, and so *bingtuan* remain an essential instrument for it to maintain peripheral security and internal stability in Xinjiang.

From the mid-1950s to the reform period under Deng Xiaoping, Xinjiang was again buffeted by geopolitical currents and storms from Beijing. Sino-Soviet relations went from warmly cautious in the early years to openly antagonistic by the late 1950s. The influence of the Soviet Union on local leaders, clerics, and scholars, and with their continuing sympathy towards the former ETR, was treated with greater hostility as time went on and Sino-Soviet relations cooled. From the mid-1950s, Xinjiang, like the rest of China, came under greater ideological pressure as Mao unleashed successive political campaigns: the Hundred Flowers campaign, the Anti-Rightest movement, the Great Leap Forward and the Cultural Revolution. These fell disproportionately heavily on Xinjiang because of the ethno-nationalism of its Islamic populations and attachments to the Soviet Union. These periods were also associated with 'aggressive assimilation' policies.[77]

Assimilation, forced collectivisation of agriculture, purges of Islamic officials sympathetic to the ETR and the Soviet Union, economic collapse with the Great Leap Forward, and Soviet propaganda highlighting these failures, combined to create the greatest security threat to Communist rule in Xinjiang since the founding of the People's Republic. Between April and May 1962, in what is known as the Yi-Ta Incident, some 60,000 to 100,000 refugees fled from northern Xinjiang to the Soviet Union. These included educated Uyghurs and Kazakhs, as well as many nomadic pastoralists taking large numbers of animals with them. PLA regular troops, supported by *bingtuan* units, were sent to seal the borders and stabilise the situation. One anti-CPC riot in Yili was repressed by the *bingtuan* 'Agricultural Fourth Division' firing into the crowd.[78]

The depopulation of areas in the northwest confronted Beijing with a new security threat along its borders. As was often the case, the *bingtuan* was called upon to secure these areas by moving in large numbers of people, and restoring industry and farming on the locations of the abandoned communes. In effect, it created a 'quarantine zone between Kazakhs in China and those in the richer Kazak SSR'.[79] The Yi-Ta Incident forced a temporary moderation of policies: stepping back from collectivisation, permitting a measure of private agriculture, and tolerance towards the 'unique characteristics' of Xinjiang's non-Han people. Official blaming of the Soviet Union for instigating the Yi-Ta Incident, however, led to purging of the CPC's non-Han cadres, who were generally assumed to be sympathetic towards Moscow. Security of the frontier was, again, a pressing concern for Beijing.

Xinjiang was not spared the violence and destruction of the Cultural Revolution (1966–76). When Mao Zedong declared war on his opponents in the Party by mobilising the masses against them, Xinjiang descended into chaos. Early in 1967, Premier Zhou Enlai ordered the military to take control and restore order, but it soon split into factions. The *bingtuan* militia were deeply engaged in the violence. On one occasion, in July 1967, 6000 *bingtuan* permanent troops together with 50,000 *bingtuan* workers attacked several targets in Urumqi taken over by Mao's Red Guards. On another occasion, the main railway line near Hami was seized by Red Guards and Xinjiang was cut off from the rest of the country for a time. With the heavy involvement of the *bingtuan* in the chaos causing disruption of agriculture, Xinjiang's economy was brought once more to the edge of ruin. Xinjiang switched from being a net grain exporter to the rest of China to being a net importer. The goal since Qing times of Xinjiang becoming self-sufficient was further out of reach.[80]

Red Guards arriving in Xinjiang in big numbers knew nothing of non-Han cultures. With the encouragement to see non-Han as equivalent to 'foreign invaders', terrible repression was loosed on their religious, community and family practices, with all festivals, public holidays and religious services banned. Jiang Qing—Mao's wife, usurper and red cultural tsar—was reported to have said, 'What is special about your tiny Xinjiang? I despise you.'[81] But even after the Red Guards were disbanded and the youth sent to work on *bingtuan* farms, attacks on Islam and non-Han culture continued, with the support of political leaders in Beijing and Urumqi. Across China, churches were desecrated, temples and icons smashed. In Xinjiang, pigs were often housed in mosques, among many other such atrocities.

In this period of ideological ferment and collective paranoia, non-Han Chinese were especially at risk of being targeted as traitors and counter-revolutionary class enemies. Non-Han political elites with ETR or Soviet backgrounds were accused of treason, and often tortured and summarily executed. Tensions on the Soviet–China border were elevated. Soviet troops were massing and exercising on the border; including, provocatively, a force called the 'Xinjiang Minority Refugee Army'. With almost continuous 'skirmishes, incursions, and some serious clashes' along the border, the PLA was fearful of a full Soviet invasion and made escape plans should one eventuate. With Soviet encouragement, some non-Han uprisings occurred. In addition, an East Turkestan People's Revolutionary Party operated for about two years, publishing newspapers. This group allegedly wanted an independent, secular, pro-Soviet ETR.[82]

## Xinjiang in the Central Asian Heartland

With the death of Mao in 1976 and the ascendency of Deng Xiaoping two years later, modern China's remarkable reform era began. All aspects of Chinese life, society and economy were transformed during this time, when pragmatism replaced ideology, moderation replaced radicalism, technical skill and knowledge replaced political correctness, and commerce replaced communism. These changes also swept through Xinjiang, and it too changed fundamentally. But four structural issues that had long shaped it remained: Xinjiang's distance from Beijing, despite a massive investment in transport infrastructure; its borderlands and proximity to Central Asian states; fraught relations between its sizable Islamic and Han populations; and its quest for some degree of cultural autonomy, if not outright independence.

Under Deng's policies of moderation, assimilationist policies were relaxed in favour of greater recognition of cultural and religious diversity. Local-level autonomy was encouraged with new laws to ensure minimum percentages of non-Han representation in local administrations. Restrictions on Islam were also relaxed: Mosques were repaired and reopened, new ones built; restrictions on travel to Muslim countries were eased. Recruiting of non-Han cadres was encouraged and publishing in non-Han languages was promoted. The economy began to recover rapidly under Deng's market-oriented policies and with the opening of borders with the neighbouring Soviet republics.

Following the collapse of the Soviet Union in 1991, independent Islamic states named after their majority ethnic groups—Tajikistan, Uzbekistan, Kyrgyzstan and Kazakhstan—emerged on Xinjiang's borders. When I first visited, early in 1989, Xinjiang was merely a buffer state, remote and isolated, against the Soviet enemy. The collapse of the Soviet Union presented Beijing with new opportunities in Central Asia. Xinjiang was to be tied more closely with the rest of China, to deepen integration; especially via mass Han migration, expanded transport infrastructure and investment from the rapidly growing provinces on China's eastern littoral. At the same time, Xinjiang was opened as a new international conduit to Central Asia. China's external trade was growing rapidly, and Xinjiang's trade with Central Asia, Russia, Turkey and the Middle East did so as well. But whereas for most of the nineteenth and twentieth centuries Xinjiang exported raw materials to import manufactured products, this was now reversed.

In 1992, the Urumqi Economic Relations and Trade Fair was launched by Premier Li Peng. It was intended to promote commerce between northwest China and Central Asia. In 2008, as Australia's ambassador, I attended as a guest of the Xinjiang party secretary. I had not heard of the fair, but when meeting with the party secretary, he insisted I join the opening celebrations the next day. Ministerial and senior government representatives from across Central Asia, the Caucus and Middle East were present. The guest of honour that year was Turkey's trade minister, and China's minister of commerce attended as well. It is not surprising that the fair's clunky title was changed, two years later, to the snappier China-Eurasia Expo. This also underlines the reach and ambition of China's Eurasian strategy at that early time, well before the BRI was launched in September 2013.

When I attended, a vast newly constructed convention centre housed thousands of stands representing companies from across Eurasia. It was here that I learned Xinjiang's *bingtuan* produced 80 per cent of the world's tomato paste. *Bingtuan* also produced the bulk of Xinjiang's cotton crop. The pressure from China's strategic planners to diversify sources of energy away from seaborne trade that is potentially vulnerable to trade embargoes is such that pipelines from Xinjiang to the east coast are built even when they may be uneconomic. In 2022, highlighting its continuing remoteness from core China, Xinjiang's foreign trade remained highly focused on its neighbours, with Kazakhstan, Kyrgyzstan, Russia, Tajikistan and Uzbekistan its five top trading partners. Of its ten top trading partners, only the US is not from the Eurasian or subcontinent regions.

During the reform era and continuing through into the Xi Jinping period, economic development in Xinjiang has been state led and financed. In this respect, it is a continuation of Qing dynasty policies. External security and internal stability prevail over commercial considerations. As with the Qing's state farms, *bingtuan* are the most important institution. Developed east coast provinces are required to relocate manufacturing to Xinjiang. Beijing has massively expanded investment in power and transport infrastructure. Xinjiang has also been a central focus of China's BRI. Four of its major east–west corridors run through Xinjiang: two cross from Urumqi to Kazakhstan; one from Kashgar to Kyrgyzstan; and a southern arm extends to Pakistan and on to the China–Pakistan Economic Corridor.[83]

On one visit I made to Kashgar in early 2015, officials readily conceded that they were struggling to understand what the BRI was all about. One thing all could agree on, however, was that Kashgar was to become a central focus, with transport routes from China, Central Asia and Pakistan (and hence the Middle East) converging there. The model was to be Shenzhen, notwithstanding the fact that Kashgar's hinterland was impoverished and remote compared with Shenzhen's. In January 2024, with China's effective recognition of the Taliban government of Afghanistan, new transport infrastructure, including a potential railway from Kashgar to Kabul, is being touted in the Chinese media; as well, significant investment in Afghanistan's resources sector is being spruiked. China has ambitious plans to one day run its standard-gauge rail lines across Afghanistan to Iran, and beyond to Turkey and Europe, providing an alternative to the current northern routes, which all run through Russia. Tensions in the Red Sea have increased the attractiveness of China's proposed overland rail routes to Europe.

## Fragile Frontier

Throughout the 1990s and 2000s, the incidence of 'separatist' attacks, seemingly random acts of terrorism and inter-communal conflict, waxed and waned. The 1990s saw ongoing ethnic tension and violence, with major demonstrations and even incidences of armed resistance. It was not unexpected that some in Xinjiang should seek to create an independent 'Uyghuristan'.[84] Initially, Beijing supported the US leadership of the Global War on Terror, leveraging international public opinion to support its view that any expressions of Uyghur dissent were acts of 'terrorism'. In 2002, Beijing achieved great success in this campaign by having the UN classify the Xinjiang-based ETIM as a terrorist organisation.[85]

In 2010–14, violence between Uyghurs and police escalated. The Chinese government attributed some hundreds of incidents that had occurred over the preceding decade to both ETIM and the Afghanistan-based TIP. Some foreign experts on terrorism, however, point out that both the government and the terrorist groups had their own reasons to exaggerate their claims.[86] Nonetheless, Beijing's assertion of an ever-present terrorist threat was certainly sustained by occasional high-profile attacks.[87] On 29 October 2013, for example, an SUV bearing the black Islamist flag with *Shahadah* printed on it was crashed into the south wall of the Forbidden City, almost beneath Mao's portrait, and caught fire. Five people were killed, including three in the vehicle, and another thirty-eight injured.[88] I was living in Beijing at the time, and remember how people were genuinely shocked that the extensive security cordon around Tiananmen Square could be breached, and that an incident of this type could occur in the heart of the capital city.

Violent actions, mainly against the police, continued to grow over the next three years. While they were labelled as 'terrorist' incidents by the government, some foreign commentators have stressed that they were spontaneous, random actions by individuals or small groups born out of 'frustration and rage' within the Uyghur population.[89] It is often argued by foreigners that Uyghur violence is a reaction to their being subject to 'structural racism' that results in 'discrimination and unfair and intrusive policing'. As such, harsh government assimilationist policies against Uyghur religious or cultural practices in effect become 'self-fulfilling prophecies'.[90]

While this is, no doubt, an important factor, radical Uyghurs within Xinjiang do have established links with Islamic militants abroad. The Uyghur diaspora across Central Asia and Turkey is an important source of support. In Kazakhstan, where a significant Kazakh population from China resides, a formal organisation, the Ata-Jurt, advocates on behalf of Xinjiang's Uyghurs. In Turkey, which has historically been an important destination for Uyghur exiles, public advocacy is muted due to their tenuous residency status, but nationalists and pan-Turkists are active on behalf of the Uyghurs. This occurs despite Ankara's close economic and political relations with Beijing. Uyghur advocate Sean Roberts also acknowledges that TIP, which he describes as 'mysterious', seems to be gaining more fighters. TIP has both Syrian and Afghanistan branches, which have developed along somewhat different lines: the former more aligned with internationalist jihadism and the latter more nationalist. In Afghanistan, Abdul Haq, who has been identified as TIP's emir, boasted in 2019 that it had relocated 'closer to the Chinese border than ever before', saying that:

> those seeking political solutions to what is happening to the
> Uyghurs through protests and advocacy are misguided. Instead …
> the only way to fight China's aggression towards Uyghurs is
> through armed struggle.[91]

The group has also adopted the flag of the first ETR, 'suggesting that it may be adopting a stronger nationalist orientation that is less associated with global jihadism'.[92]

In 2014, two years after becoming party general secretary and president, Xi Jinping ordered renewed 'strike hard' policies to be used in Xinjiang. This was to be a near-decade-long campaign by the state against Uyghur and Kazakh Muslim minorities, involving arbitrary and forced internment of perhaps a million non-Han citizens in 're-education' camps. From around 2017, many countries from the liberal West became increasingly concerned about human rights NGO reports of forced labour using mainly Uyghurs and other Xinjiang minorities. Such reports claimed that large numbers of them were being rounded up and incarcerated in re-education establishments, as part of a campaign of de-Islamisation by Beijing.

Following exposure in the West's media of the treatment of Uyghurs, Western public opinion turned sharply against China. Accusations of 'cultural genocide' were made by Western governments, led by the US, and raised in the UN. The US has been first to declare the situation 'genocide', the first to revoke its recognition of ETIM as a terrorist organisation, and the first to sanction Chinese officials in Xinjiang. China has responded with its own campaign of tailored information, sufficient to blunt the criticism in many countries. Reflecting China's global political reach, the Islamic world remained silent.

The use of the term 'cultural genocide'—which has a narrow definition within the UN—by Donald Trump's administration was deliberately provocative but nevertheless attracted support among Western allies. Roberts accuses both the US and China of having 'weaponised' the treatment of Xinjiang's Uyghurs as part of their heightened geopolitical competition.[93]

It is commonly claimed by observers, and vehemently denied by China, that, since 2017, 'likely over one million Uyghurs and representatives of related nations … were interned in "re-education" camps'. In early 2021, the BBC broadcast 'evidence' that Uyghurs were being dispersed as part of the state's coerced labour program, as a policy intended to reduce Ugyhur population density.[94] The reports captured global headlines, and resulted in democratic governments coming under pressure to take measures against China and for their own countries' companies to be subject to greater scrutiny under national anti-slavery laws. While much of the evidence is disputed, and while condemnation of the rounding-up of Islamic minorities was also cynically used by President Trump, and other Western states that had scores to settle with China (for example, Canada was vociferous in claiming genocide, at a time that two of its citizens were in Chinese prisons on dubious charges), no doubt reprehensible and large-scale abuses of human rights have occurred, and are likely to be continuing.

The campaign to 'strike hard' seemed to have moved into its forced-detention stage sometime around 2017. I was in Kashgar again in October 2017 and the city appeared to be in total lockdown. Moving around by car was difficult because, at intervals, paramilitary and the police had erected roadblocks, which needed to be passed at a snail's pace. The People's Square in front of Mao's gigantic statue, signalling the way to a glorious socialist future, had been turned into a parking lot for armoured personnel carriers. Heavily armed black-uniformed SWAT teams patrolled the streets in their golf buggies—two soldiers facing backwards in case of an attack from the rear. These were supplemented by sci-fi-style black mobile armoured boxes big enough to fit four troops inside, bristling with antennas and satellite dishes. These crept along some hundred metres from each other, with high-pitched sirens piercing the air twenty-four hours a day. This alone was torture. I asked my Uyghur driver if the noise drove him nuts. He replied he no longer heard it. With so much military around, with checkpoints, lights and noise, the city had a surreal atmosphere, as if it were the set of a movie about a military coup in some banana republic. It was so far removed from the ancient mudbrick Central Asian oasis on the Silk Road, of donkey carts, street vendors and craftsmen, as to be unrecognisable as the place I made so much effort to visit in 1989.

Over the years of visiting Xinjiang, I had befriended the Uyghur owner of a carpet shop located down a side street off the expansive square in front of the Id Kah Mosque in the centre of old Kashgar. His son had explained that, as part of the crackdown, he had been designated to join the neighbourhood watch team. With a red armband, reminiscent of those worn by Mao's Red Guards during the Cultural Revolution, he was to monitor 100 metres of the street outside his shop and report suspicious behaviour. As excessive, even silly, as it sounds, it was not necessarily without risk. Three years earlier, on the morning of my departure from Kashgar on another visit, with my daughter, the grand iman of Kashgar was knifed to death by three assailants outside the Id Kah Mosque after morning prayers, in what was seen as a factional religious attack. The iman was viewed as being too accommodating of Beijing and was, for a period, vice-president of the official Islamic Association of China.[95] Predictably, the attackers were immediately tagged as 'religious extremists'.

So, the long historical patterns still play out today and will continue to do so. The themes explored in this chapter will shape future developments in Xinjiang: the interplay of its remoteness from the metropolis, frontier security and insecurity; it being a perpetual drain on central government resources; cycles of relaxation and oppression; limited autonomy and assimilation; neighbours that are at times intrusive and unstable; and great power influence.

When seen from Beijing's perspective, the long-standing Russian, and then Soviet, threats to Xinjiang have now been replaced by the menace of radical Islam. As with the Russian and Soviet threats, radical Islam has sympathisers within the non-Han communities of Xinjiang. Xi Jinping's 'strike hard' tactics can only expand this group, providing fertile soil for the radicals to till. The imperative of peripheral security in these circumstances offers no prospect of a return to more relaxed policies and some greater degree of local autonomy. Han migration will only press more heavily on the region, exacerbating deep ethno-nationalist tensions. In all of this, Beijing's policies are likely to beget the very thing they are designed to avoid: challenges to its authority and a perpetual cycle of instability along a fragile frontier.

# CHAPTER 5

# 'RUSSIA ENDS NOWHERE'

Vladimir Putin, 2016[1]

The Trans-Mongolian train to Moscow left Beijing station early in the morning on a bitterly cold day in December 1989. Sometime later, in the middle of the night, the train was being lifted off its bogies. Across the dark carriages, powerful arc lights cast sharp-edged, white-lit shadows of swaddled workmen. Compressors hissed, steel ground against steel in the freezing early hours. This was the first of two bogie changes to fit the different rail gauges as the train passed from China to Mongolia, and then into the Soviet Union. Eventually, conductors ushered us out of the dank, steamy waiting room with its painfully hard wooden bench seats and back onto the train. After some time, we lurched and rattled off into the black night.

Morning came with the uninterrupted vastness of the Mongolian grasslands. In the middle distance, as in a movie scene, a camel train of some thirty beasts was starting its working day. Steam from straining nostrils created clusters of cloud above the camels' heads before drifting away.

The train arrived at Ulan Bator station in the late afternoon. In Soviet days, stops along the Trans-Mongolian Railway from Beijing to Moscow were usually no more than twenty-five minutes. I would jump down onto the platform—the stairs were always about a hundred centimetres too short—to stretch a bit, and smoke cigarettes without choking up the small private compartment that was my home for five days across the Soviet Union.

On this occasion, Ulan Bator was a longer stop. A horn bellowed as a locomotive trundled heavily past our stationary train, pulling what seemed like a never-ending line of wagons, each of which was loaded with a Soviet tank, the painted red stars on their turrets catching the fading afternoon light.

For forty minutes, I stood smoking, watching the clattering retreat of the much-feared Soviet empire. *So, this is how it ends*, I thought, *for one of the greatest armies on earth, and without a shot having been fired.* The Soviet Union had previously been defeated in Afghanistan and fled from it in February of that year, but over the centuries, empires have come and gone from Afghanistan, tasting defeat with a certain regularity. These freight trains loaded with tanks heading north, back into the Soviet Empire, seemed different in scale and significance— an imperial army in full retreat, heading towards a collapsing empire.

Watching the spectacle of the tanks juddering by on their rail carts recalled another event seven months earlier. In May 1989, Soviet president Mikhail Gorbachev went to Beijing, the first visit by a Soviet leader in the thirty years since Khrushchev's secret one in 1959. From the balcony of a friend's apartment at the Jiang Guo Men Wei Diplomatic Compound, I had watched as Gorbachev's long cavalcade of black Chinese-made Red Flag limousines swept south along the second ring road, from the expansive Soviet embassy compound. Turning right, into the Chang'an Avenue, the procession headed west towards Tiananmen Square, where Gorbachev was to meet with Deng Xiaoping in the Great Hall of the People.

He had come to Beijing to help thaw diplomatic relations with China. This was to be a gradual process, as the problems included unresolved border demarcation issues that took many years to settle. Mutual mistrust ran deep. China still feared the Soviet Union's military on its borders, while Moscow was acutely alert to Chinese encroachment into the resource-rich but sparsely populated Russian Far East.

Deng Xiaoping was also deeply concerned about what he regarded as Gorbachev's reckless approach to reforming the ailing

Soviet Union. Deng foresaw that under Gorbachev the Soviet Union
was abandoning its Marxist-Leninist governing dogmas. Gorbachev
had begun by changing and opening the political system with his
Glasnost and Perestroika policies, which allowed for contesting
government views. Deng would never countenance a relaxation of
control by the CPC—although he opened and partly liberalised the
economy, he never relinquished authoritarian control.

In May 1989, as was common practice—and still is today, as a mark
of respect for heads of state when in China—the visitor's national
flag was displayed alongside the Chinese flag on the main roads, in
Tiananmen Square, and at the Gate of Heavenly Peace at the northern
end of the Square. The streets were bedecked with bright red Soviet
flags fluttering alongside the Chinese flag of the same colour.

On the day of Gorbachev's historic visit, another spectacle was
taking place in Tiananmen Square, as it had every day for the past
month. It was one the Chinese leadership would not have wanted
Gorbachev to see. Students from China's universities had been occupying the Square, protesting government corruption, and the lack of
transparency and accountability. At that early stage, it was less about
the CPC's rule as such and more about achieving a fairer society. The
number of protesters in the Square at the time of Gorbachev's visit
would later swell, ending in the bloody denouement on 3–4 June.

The early years of Deng Xiaoping's reforms and open-door policies
had seen greater personal freedoms: the Party was withdrawing from
managing the details of ordinary people's lives. Inflation was high,
which people had not experienced since the founding of the People's
Republic, but daily life was materially improving. Naively, the young
had high expectations that opportunities would progressively expand,
and that the state could be held accountable by ordinary citizens.
Although popularly dubbed a 'democracy movement' by breathless
Western journalists and politicians, demands for 'democracy' came
quite late to the Square.

At that time, Gorbachev too had more than enough dissent of
his own to deal with. During 1989, popular demonstrations had
spread throughout the Soviet Union's eastern satellite states. By May,
discontent and protests were breaking out in Eastern Europe, from

Poland to Hungary and the Baltic republics; six months later, the unthinkable happened—the Berlin Wall fell. The Soviet Union collapsed just two years later. None of this was foreseen, as officials of the two great Communist nations took in the scene from the upper floors of the Great Hall of the People. Among the makeshift camps and agitprop gatherings of students strewn across that enormous area over which the leaders gazed, protest leaders brandished a new symbol of power in that year of turmoil: the megaphone.

After Gorbachev had left Beijing, martial law was declared. The protests in the Square grew and the students were soon joined by all segments of society. I would watch from my balcony at the Qijiayuan Diplomatic Compound as waves of workers marched by, shouting slogans through megaphones. They carried enormous banners, some stretching across six lanes of Chang'an Avenue, identifying themselves as hospital workers; primary and secondary school teachers, bus and train drivers, and, remarkably, on at least one occasion, as being from the Party's own newspaper, the *People's Daily*.

The protesters now controlled central Beijing. While uniformed police still stood on their round, circus-tent-like, yellow- and red-striped sentry blocks, waving their arms while attempting to direct traffic, the students standing on the road had usurped their role. Traffic flowed smoothly, and people were smiling and friendly to each other. Parodying Communist Party propaganda, some students wore slogans on their sleeves or headbands saying, 'serve the people'. By this stage, the students exercised such command over the city that workmen were unable to remove the Soviet flags following Gorbachev's departure. They hung bedraggled until the military took back the city.

During this period, to present a veneer of control and normalcy, the Chinese government accepted visits from foreign delegations. In February of that year, Australian prime minister Bob Hawke surprised just about everyone in the East Asian region, and in Washington, when he proposed in a speech during a visit to Seoul that a new regional grouping—controversially, at first, minus the US—should be formed. It was intended to promote greater economic integration in the region by liberalising trade and investment.[2]

To sell the concept and attract support for a proposed ministerial meeting in late 1989, he assigned Dick Woolcott, veteran diplomat and secretary of the Australian Department of Foreign Affairs and Trade, to travel the region as his special envoy. China was always going to be difficult because of the questions surrounding Taiwan and Hong Kong. Its reforms and open-door approach were still at an early stage; China had not then joined the World Trade Organization (WTO) and wouldn't for the next twelve years; and Deng's market-driven policies were still under attack by the political elite—most notably, by Deng's archenemy and Long March comrade, Chen Yun.

Formally, the secretary of the Department of Foreign Affairs and Trade is equivalent in rank to the Chinese foreign minister. The Chinese are, however, always keen to elevate their side, so it is usual practice for the Chinese foreign minister to meet with the Australian foreign minister and allow the departmental secretary a short courtesy call. On this occasion, however, the Australian embassy was surprised to be told that Woolcott would be meeting with Premier Li Peng, an elevation of two levels. It was most unusual. But then, they were unusual days.

Li Peng was both a princeling from the Party's ruling elite and a traditional hardline communist, who had studied engineering in Moscow. He played a key role in having the more liberal party secretary, Zhao Ziyang, arrested after martial law had been declared in Beijing, and prior to the military attack on Tiananmen Square. This earned him from the Western media the sobriquet the 'Butcher of Beijing'.

At the time, I was economic counsellor at the Australian embassy, and so also had the opportunity to attend the meeting. It was to be in Zhongnanhai, the leadership compound on the western side of the Square, next to the Forbidden City: the seat of imperial authority and power for some six centuries. The route from the Australian embassy would normally be to go south along the second ring road, onto Chang'an Avenue and then directly to Zhongnanhai. In view of the disruption in the Square and along the main arterial roads leading to it, we took a circuitous route through tiny *hutong*s, the alleys that

were more common in those days, before most were swept away in
a rush of frenzied development in the 2000s.

The meeting was occurring after martial law had been declared
on 20 May, which sparked more protests, drawing ever-bigger crowds
to the Square. The political atmosphere was now incendiary. As such,
the feeling in the meeting room was tense as we sat down. Li Peng,
whom I had met earlier, when he was minister for transport, was
typically stiff, graceless, abrupt and humourless. A senior Chinese
foreign ministry interpreter once indicated to me where her political
loyalties lay, by saying that when she interpreted for Party Secretary
Zhao Ziyang, the words came naturally and flowed. When she did it
for the then President, Yang Shangkun, she was less fluid and more
halting. But she found interpreting for Li Peng hardest of all. She
implied that she had no empathy with what he was saying.

While it was, in any case, generally characteristic of the man, Li
Peng was understandably short with his guests at this time. He was,
as we later learned, in the middle of a full-throttle power struggle
with Zhao Ziyang. Li Peng had little interest in discussing the
proposed Asia-Pacific Economic Cooperation (APEC) group with
the Australian special envoy. Rather, all he wanted was to try to have
Dick Woolcott say something critical about the demonstrations,
which would presumably be presented to the media as commentary
from 'China's foreign friends'.

Wily Woolcott would not be trapped. No matter how many times
Li Peng tried to draw him into a comment about the inconvenience
of the circuitous route he had taken, or the mess the city was in with
the bedraggled Soviet flags along the main roads, Dick—unflappably,
and to Li Peng's obvious irritation—said how much he had enjoyed
looking at the narrow lanes and *hutong* houses up close, and how
interesting the back streets were, as he attempted again and again to
steer the conversation back to APEC. It felt like a fencing contest
between an old pro and a clumsy student.

Later, on the train in Ulan Bator, I was looking forward to
spending a few days in Moscow with a colleague from the Australian
embassy. I had been given extended leave because of a mild case of
post-traumatic stress syndrome caused by what had been happening

that year in Beijing. I had ahead eight weeks of travelling mainly across Russia, the Eastern Bloc and Western Europe to Rotterdam. The awful events of June, and subsequent bleak repression, were mentally and physically being left behind. In Moscow and Budapest, my excursion would be more like a work trip, with a busy schedule of visits to academics, think tanks and media people to discuss Gorbachev's reforms and, of course, China. After Tiananmen Square, I wanted to throw myself into the new open, liberal environment of Moscow.

Little did I know that my trip would be a farewell tour of a world that no longer exists. All the distortions, inefficiencies, inequities, injustices and repression of the old communist system were about to be swept away. Gone would be dining like a king if you had $US20 for a four-hour meal in the famous Café Prague in Moscow; or, if you had $US5 for a ticket, a private box at the gorgeous National Ballet in Budapest, with its scarlet velvet-lined walls looking like the inside of a box for precious jewels. Just two years later, Mikhail Gorbachev signed the Soviet Union out of existence. He did so with a look of sad resignation captured in HS Liu's magnificent Pulitzer Prize–winning photograph, shot in slow motion as the flicking pages of the document in Gorbachev's hand blurred.

As one empire was disintegrating, Beijing was watching intently, determined to defend the CPC's rule and preserve China's territorial integrity. For the rulers in Beijing, having two years earlier supressed the first flickering of organised opposition since taking power in 1949, Gorbachev was a wrecker and a villain. They were determined his actions would never be repeated in China. For the ensuing decades, one of the events of contemporary history most studied by Chinese political elites was the collapse of the Soviet Union.

## Russia and China's Divergent Approaches to Security

The weight of historical experience hangs heavily on strategic thinking in both Russia and China, as it does for all great powers. Russia views its security as coming from colonising neighbouring territory to act as buffer states. In its experience, restraints on power spelled catastrophe. Russia's failure to dominate its surroundings, according to this view, had exposed it to the Mongol invasions. Henry Kissinger argued that where the Peace of Westphalia saw international order as 'an intricate balancing mechanism', the Russian view 'cast it as a perpetual contest of will, with Russia extending its domain at each phase to the absolute limit of its material resources'.[3] In the mid-seventeenth century, Tsar Alexei's foreign minister, Afanasy Nashchokin, observed that 'expanding the state in every direction ... is the business of the Department of Foreign Affairs'.[4]

Although Russia's contemporary invasion of Ukraine stems from a complex mix of reasons both internal and external to Russia, it ultimately rests on this fundamental understanding of how Russia achieves security. For centuries, this 'national impulse' drove Russian geographical expansion, unhindered by major natural boundaries, across the Caucasus, Balkans, Eastern Europe, Scandinavia, the Baltic Sea, and Central Asia to the Pacific Ocean, coming to rest at the Chinese and Japanese frontiers. Its expansion averaged 100,000 square kilometres per annum from 1552 to 1917.[5]

After the 1917 Bolshevik Revolution, the communists fought on for nearly six years in a civil war to retake all the tsar's lands for the Soviet Union. The Bolsheviks had to capture territory from White Russian counter-revolutionaries, supported for a period by foreign interventions from the West, and to strike down local insurrections in Muslim lands where efforts were made to re-establish ancient khanates.[6] The swashbuckling, murderous Enver Pasha, Ottoman military leader during World War I and an architect of the Armenian genocide, who had been exiled to Central Asia, attempted to seize on the chaos of the Bolshevik Revolution, leading a jihad to establish a Central Asian caliphate.[7] The Bolsheviks, in time, prevailed, fighting all the way to the Pacific Ocean. The USSR resumed control of all imperial Russian territories, and added Mongolia as a puppet client state until its formal independence in 1990.

China derives its security from 'pacifying' neighbouring states as tributaries. Where Russia's statecraft rests primarily on territorial occupation, and hence violence, China's requires neighbours to recognise its authority. Its statecraft is based on diplomacy, reinforced by cultural, political and, most prevalently, economic influences.

According to Kissinger, both Russia's and China's approaches to security are at odds with the Westphalian system of 'balance of power'.[8]

While the Chinese emperor, like the tsar, was an autocratic ruler of a vast territory, in the Chinese view 'the emperor ruled through the serenity of his conduct and was conceived of as the embodiment of the superiority of Chinese civilisation, inspiring other people to "come and be transformed"'.[9] The Chinese imperial court in successive empires based its foreign relations on the tribute system. According to this belief, there was a hierarchy with the Chinese emperor as the head of the civilised world that was China, and all outside of China being barbarians. The emperor's role was to maintain order through a carefully constructed and time-endowed system of rituals. People outside the Chinese world were expected to participate in the rituals, through visiting the imperial court and paying tribute to it, for which they were richly rewarded. Challenges to this system from beyond the frontiers, which often occurred during dynastic transitions, were seen as signs that the emperor's mandate from heaven had been lost. Failure to comply with the tribute system therefore could not be tolerated.

Again, the concept of world order was not derived from a balance of power between competing states but from a universal hierarchy of authority, with the Chinese emperor at the top. So, for China, diplomacy was not about bargaining between states, but a 'carefully contrived ceremonial ritual', which gave a barbarian state the opportunity to affirm its assigned position in the hierarchy. The tribute system applied to foreign states was to 'foster deference, not extract economic benefit or to dominate foreign societies militarily'. Kissinger argued that China's Great Wall, while demonstrating vast power, was a statement of China's enduring sense of vulnerability to the lands beyond its frontiers: '[f]or centuries, China sought to beguile and entice its adversaries more often than it attempted to defeat them by force of arms.'[10]

Both the conquering Mongols in the thirteenth century and the Manchus in the seventeenth century eventually became assimilated into Han China in order to administer it, adopting its language and customs. This occurred to such an extent that, over time, the conquerors' territories came to be regarded as part of China. Rather than exporting its political system, China expanded its territory 'not by conquest but by osmosis'.[11] Kissinger was overstating the point here, as the Manchu in fact conquered large areas of western China and parts of Central Asia by violent military campaigns. While the expansion of the Manchu empire involved the interplay of many forces—ecological, political and economic—securing its frontiers from 'barbarians' was of the utmost importance.[12] The existential fear of distant lands across Eurasia was ever present. It was only by 1750, after more than a century of central Asian colonial expansion, that Emperor Qianlong felt able to declare that the empire was 'secure against invaders and broadly self-sufficient in terms of agricultural supplies'.[13]

With these two great Eurasian powers having fundamentally different understandings of how to ensure their security, tensions and conflict between them were baked into their respective DNA. China seeks frontier security and pliant border states; Russia occupies territories as buffer states. Whatever the professions of affinities and friendship, and desire for accommodation against a common enemy, the structure of their respective security needs is incompatible with stable, enduring alliances between them. As soon as their relative strengths turned decisively in Russia's favour in the middle decades of the nineteenth century, following the Opium Wars, Russia moved successfully to occupy vast swathes of Chinese territory in the Far East and Manchuria, and, in the twentieth century, detach Outer Mongolia from China as an 'independent' client state.

China's world view did not recognise fixed frontiers or borders. The areas populated by frontier peoples would expand or contract depending on their changing fortunes, and as dynasties waxed and waned. Control over the frontiers was maintained by the traditional policy for barbarian management: 'using one barbarian to control another'. The converse of this was to apply diplomacy to prevent barbarians uniting against China. As Sarah C Paine, US historian of Eurasian conflict, argues, the Manchus' traditional approach prevented them from understanding the nature of the Russian threat. They saw

Russia as just another barbarian tribe to be managed in the context of fluid control over peripheral territory as buffer zones. They did not understand that Russia was a European power that thought and acted in terms of fixed boundaries that would not accommodate the old system of fluid buffer zones.

Until early in the twentieth century, the Qing court distinguished between 'overseas barbarians' (the UK, US and France) and 'overland barbarians' (Russia). It thought it could deal with Russia differently: it had long experience in managing overland barbarians, but at the same time greatly underestimated Russia's power. Accordingly, it dealt with Russia bilaterally and did not seek to engage with overseas barbarians to balance it. Moreover, to enlist the assistance of barbarians would cause the emperor to lose face, as it would be an admission of weakness. Again, according to Paine:

> This would have undermined the Chinese myth of absolute superiority, which for centuries had been the official ideology and a basis for the imperial system. So in an increasingly strained effort to 'keep face', the Qing court long resisted playing the balance-of-power politics practiced in the West.[14]

This suited Russia nicely, and for China came at a very high price.

**Pre-1949 Eurasian Triptych: Manchuria, Mongolia, Xinjiang**
For centuries, its Eurasian frontiers appeared to Beijing as a three-panel painting of their external security threats and challenges. This triptych—Manchuria, Mongolia, Xinjiang—each presented different pictures, depending on the time and place, but were united as a single world view of China's geopolitical vulnerabilities. As British historian of Sino-Russian relations Philip Snow has argued:

> we need to think of the Russo-Chinese borderlands as an immense triptych on which an incessant struggle for influence between two imperial powers would be displayed—Xinjiang with its deserts, Mongolia with its grasslands and Manchuria with its forests and rivers.[15]

And for the Qing rulers, these panels were closely interconnected. The loss of northeast Xinjiang would threaten control of Mongolia, which would lead to the loss of the Manchurian homelands.

### Manchuria

Relations between the Manchu and Russian empires were remarkably stable for much of the Qing rule. The Treaty of Nerchinsk (1689) was the first time China had signed a treaty with a Western power. Two Jesuit priests acted as translators, with the treaty originally in Latin and not translated into Chinese for another two years. Significantly, it was to settle relations between the two great imperial projects: the Russian Empire was pushing eastward and the Qing northward into the ancient ancestorial Jurchen homelands of what was to become Outer Manchuria.

In the east, Russia ceded the area north of the Amur River, up to the Stanovoy mountain range and all land up to the Sea of Japan. To the west, the new border was the Argun River and Lake Baikal. At the time, this represented considerable territorial gain for the Qing. Russian nationalists have long regarded this as an 'unequal treaty' because of the Qing's superior military power employed relatively close to home.[16] So, while seemingly it was a successful outcome for the Qing in having achieved control of the entire Amur basin, it contained the seeds of future instability, as the Amur valley would enter Russian nationalist consciousness 'as an idyllic lost realm they must one day recover'.[17]

As with any treaty between states, each side could interpret it to their respective advantage. For Moscow, it provided frontier security in an area where, because of its distance and sparse population, it was hard to project power. For Beijing, it settled the frontier with Manchuria, allowing the Qing to expand westward in what was to become Xinjiang, and to consolidate it within the empire. But first, the Qing had to deal with the Dzungar peoples of western Mongolia and northern Xinjiang, who, in alliances with Kazakhs, had long threatened the Qing's western frontier.[18]

The Qing also feared Dzungar forces might combine with Russian Cossacks against them, and with good reason. Indeed, shortly after the Treaty of Nerchinsk was signed, the Dzungar chief, Galdan, urged the Russians to join him against the Qing, arguing that Mongolia did not belong to them. Russia rejected Galdan's repeated requests. It might have been that both the Russians and the Manchus preferred to deal with each other as sedentary powers, rather than with marauding nomads of the steppe, with whom they each had had unfortunate experiences.[19] With the Dzungar having gained no support from Russia, Emperor Qianlong was determined to settle the Dzungar question once and for all, and embarked on their genocide. As Odd Arne Westad observes, the settlement of relations between Russia and China:

> turned out to be a remarkably successful grand bargain from the
> perspective of both empires, though the [Dzungar], slaughtered
> to almost the last man, woman, and child by the 1750s, would
> have disagreed.[20]

The threat to the northwest frontier from the nomadic Dzungar was no more.

Although the settlement achieved with the Treaty of Nerchinsk stabilised cross-border relations in the Far East for 189 years, the Qing and Tsarist empires 'were contemporaneous, competing imperial projects, that achieved rapid expansion in the modern era'. In time, their respective interests would inevitably collide.[21]

Meanwhile, trade flourished, especially after the 1727 signing of the Treaty of Kiakhta, which affirmed the terms of the earlier Treaty of Nerchinsk and extended commercial arrangements between the empires. Throughout the eighteenth and nineteenth centuries, commerce was considerable, accounting for some 10 per cent of total Russian trade. As in modern times, Russia exported mainly natural products (particularly fur from sables, tigers and wolves), while China exported mainly manufactured products (silk, porcelain, cotton and furniture), and the balance was heavily in China's favour. Through mutual benefit in trade and artful diplomacy, relations between these two great neighbouring imperial powers remained settled until the nineteenth century.[22]

Russia's opportunity to recover territory lost with the Treaty of Nerchinsk and continue its eastern expansion came in the late 1850s, when the Qing empire was wracked internally by the Taiping Rebellion and threatened externally by interventions from other European powers. The Taiping Rebellion was perhaps the most significant event in nineteenth century China. Lasting fourteen years, from 1850 to 1864, fighting raged across central and southern China, with some 20 million dead at its end. Once understood mainly as an eschatological religious movement led by a messianic believer in Jesus Christ, it is seen in more recent interpretations as the first major popular uprising by ethnically Han Chinese against their foreign Manchu rulers. Soon after the Second Opium War (1856–60) concluded, Britain joined with the Manchus to supress the rebellion. The US Civil War had interrupted cotton supplies to Lancashire mills, from which 75 per cent of Britain's cotton had come before the Civil War. In response to skyrocketing prices, Britain turned to China and the lands controlled by the Taiping to fill the gap in supply.[23]

The British and French seized on the weakness of the Qing at this time to insert themselves further into China. Moving north from treaty ports in the south, they increasingly threatened ports further along China's coast. At this, the Manchu court panicked and opened negotiations with the British. During and after the Second Opium War came the signing of the Treaty of Tianjin (1858), permitting, among the many concessions made by the Manchu court, embassies to be established in Beijing, unrestricted travel across China for foreigners, and the opening of Yangtze River ports to foreigners. Today, in Wuhan, nearly a thousand kilometres inland from Shanghai, the nineteenth century European-style buildings that housed British banks, insurance companies and commodity exchanges are reminders of the extent of European penetration into the heartland of China at the time.

Also in 1858, the Treaty of Aigun, and then the Convention of Peking (1860), saw the Qing make major territorial concessions north of the Amur River and east of the Ussuri River. Russia took advantage of the Qing's weakness to press for these, as it was expanding into outer Manchuria. At the height of the Taiping crisis, and with China at war with Britain and France, Moscow presented its demands to the Manchu court.[24] For the Qing, this was as alarming as British and French encroachments: the threat to its frontiers was again coming from inland, across Central Asia. So, when Russia supported Muslim separatist regimes in Xinjiang in the 1860s, the Manchus struck back aggressively.[25] It was an assertion of strength against inland barbarians—essential, in the minds of the Qing, to retain regime stability, even while showing weakness against the overseas barbarians.

Despite the harshness of its winters, Manchuria had long been set aside by the Qing as a traditional and pristine preserve for Manchu rulers to hunt among its forests and lakes. An essential feature of the Qing imperial court, especially during the long reign of Emperor Qianlong (1736–95), was the maintaince of Manchu traditions of horsemanship and hunting drawn from the tribal grasslands. Moscow was increasingly encouraging Russian immigration along the rivers of the Manchus' homelands that were largely empty of settlement.

As a result of the Qing's weakness, and defeats by the British and French in the Second Opium War, in which Russia was not a combatant, St Petersburg was able to force upon the Qing court the two treaties that handed it control of Manchuria. With these the Qing ceded almost 1 million square kilometres to Russia and lost its access to the Sea of Japan. Together, the treaties are known as the Amur Annexation—seen as a major humiliation for China at the hands of foreigners. The capital of this region became Vladivostok, meaning— in case anyone had missed the Russians' intentions—'Conqueror of the East'.[26] Ninety years later, the newly installed revolutionary leader of China, Mao Zedong, was railing against the Amur Annexation and using the grievances over it to fuel nationalistic resentment, in support of his new government. Although today the Chinese government does not speak of these as 'unequal treaties'—as it does of those made with the West, such as when the Qing ceded Hong Kong and Kowloon to Britain—an older generation sees them as a reminder of when the Soviet Union was an enemy.

Having secured Outer Manchuria with the Amur Annexation, Russia soon began pushing south into Qing Manchuria. From the

1860s, Beijing encouraged internal migration to Manchuria, as a bulwark against pressure from Russia. Immigrants came mainly from Shandong on the Bohai Gulf, where the population was heavily taxing resources. Following Russia's example, Japan also began eyeing these sparsely populated and fertile spaces. Manchuria would soon become contested territory between Russia and Japan, with the ailing Qing dynasty and, later, Nationalist governments onlookers until 1949.

In 1904, the first major military contest between an Asian and European power since the Mongol invasions occurred at Port Arthur (Lvshun), near today's port city of Dalian, when Russia and Japan fought each other in a massively destructive battle over nearly two years, resulting in the first defeat of a European power by an Asian power. The Battle of Port Arthur can also be seen as a precursor of World War I, in which armies deployed the firepower from their new heavy industries but still used static tactics such as trench warfare.[27]

In 1898, Moscow had forced the Qing to agree to lease Port Arthur for twenty-five years. By then, Russia was already occupying large areas of Manchuria and wanted to extend the Trans-Siberian Railway south, through today's Liaoning province. Port Arthur became the terminus of the line and gave Russia its first all-year-round warm water port. Its magnificent protected harbour became the base for Russia's august Far East Fleet, the pride and joy of Tsar Nicholas II. Japan, alarmed by Russia's push down the Liaoning Peninsula—fearing it was heading towards Korea, its self-proclaimed sphere of influence—launched a surprise attack on the Russian fleet in Port Arthur on 8 February 1904. Overnight, the Japanese navy had blocked the narrow entrance to the harbour, and as dawn broke, began sinking Russian ships with a naval barrage. By April, fighting had shifted to the high ground overlooking the harbour. Using heavy artillery at close range, Japanese troops attacked the Russian forces controlling these strategic positions. With Japan's eventual victory at Port Arthur, it fought the Russians back up the Liaoning Peninsula and quickly gained control of all Chinese Manchuria. The Chinese were bystanders as this titanic global struggle was fought on their territory; still, some 20,000 Chinese died, in addition to the 120,000–150,000 foreign soldiers who perished.[28]

The cost of the war compounded looming social and economic crises in Russia that triggered events on the far side of Eurasia, notably the 1905 Russian Revolution. With both sides exhausted from the war, they agreed to mediation by the US. The Treaty of Portsmouth (1905), named after the New Hampshire naval dockyard where negotiations were held, marked the US's entry into global affairs and established it as a Pacific power. The treaty did not provide for war reparations from Japan, which became an ongoing source of criticism by Russian nationalists. Moreover, it handed Port Arthur to the Japanese, and required Russia to recognise that Korea was part of Japan's sphere of influence and to leave Manchuria to the Japanese. Russia kept the Far East, and half of Sakhalin Island.[29]

It is doubtful that European powers a world away understood the global implications of the Battle of Port Arthur, which marked the beginning of a new world order. By 1919, the great Eurasian empires had been swept away—first the Qing, in 1911; then the Russian Empire, in 1917. Japan emerged as the dominant imperial power in East Asia and threatened all of China. The Pacific, for the first time, became a major theatre for global competition, and the US, also for the first time, became a major world actor.[30] Russia and China, which for nearly 300 years had been the dominant powers in Eurasia, were breaking apart due to domestic upheavals and foreign intervention.

By 1931, the military had come to dominate Japanese domestic politics. Modernisation, the spreading of Asian Values—'Asia for the Asians'—and Japan's need to control more of the Asian continent's resources led first to the occupation of what is today Liaoning province and then, beyond that, the rest of Chinese Manchuria. Manchukuo, or Manzhouguo—with Shenyang as its capital, and the last Qing emperor, young and hapless Puyi, its puppet ruler—saw dramatic economic development under the Japanese, with substantial investments in heavy industries, transport, urban infrastructure, education and public health.[31] In the major urban areas of Dalian, Shenyang and Changchun, the Japanese presence during this period strikingly featured in their urban architecture, town planning and traffic management systems until well into the 2000s.

The prevalent Japanese imperial architecture was heavily influenced by the West, echoing the Bauhaus approach in its modernist, minimalist and brutalist character. An example of Japanese architecture in a more decorative but still European style is the Lvshun Museum at Port Arthur. Built by the Japanese in 1915 as a products exhibition hall, it houses a fine collection of treasures from Dunhuang's Thousand Buddha Caves, and elsewhere from the oases of Xinjiang, collected by the Japanese explorer Count Otani. Otani was a contemporary of the famous European explorers on the Silk Road in Gansu and Xinjiang, such as Sven Hedin and Aurel Stein, but was believed by Russian and British explorers to be using his collecting as a cover for spying operations on behalf of the Japanese government. It would seem that collecting and spying are incompatible only when done by a 'secretive' Oriental. It is well known now that Aurel Stein, for one, was a regular visitor to the British consulate in Kashgar, debriefing Her Majesty's consul general, George Macartney, on the lands that he traversed in Xinjiang.[32]

Otani's collection was abandoned in Lvshun when Japan collapsed in 1945 and the Japanese fled Manchukuo for home. Another relic from that period that has survived, and is used flagrantly by the Chinese government in its anti-Japanese propaganda, is a former Japanese concentration camp outside Harbin. Notoriously, biological experiments were conducted on live Chinese prisoners; it was the subject of war crime trials in the post–World War II period. Unit 731, at a town called Anda, is estimated to have involved some 3000 live victims. The site today is a monument for remembrance, but also a tool of propaganda, where visitors can view the tiny, unheated cells and see a range of grisly equipment. Recently, Chinese archaeologists have found evidence of more crimes committed at the site.[33]

After Japan's abrupt collapse, Stalin moved quickly to occupy all of Manchuria. The three-power (US, UK, USSR) Yalta Conference of February 1945 made extensive concessions to Stalin over Manchuria, in return for the Soviet Union entering the war against Japan. These included:

The commercial port of Dairen [Dalian] shall be internationalized, the pre-eminent interests of the Soviet Union in this port being safeguarded: the Chinese-Eastern Railroad and the South Manchurian Railroad, which provide an outlet to Dairen, shall be jointly operated by the establishment of a joint Soviet-Chinese company, it being understood that the pre-eminent interests of the Soviet Union shall be safeguarded and that China shall retain sovereignty in Manchuria ... [with the] concurrence of Generalissimo Chiang Kai-shek. [The US] President will take measures in order to maintain this concurrence on advice from Marshal Stalin.[34]

In other words, Stalin had recovered all of the Soviet Union's interests in Manchukuo and effectively extended its control over all of Manchuria. The Soviet Red Army occupied Manchuria and the northern part of Korea, with more than 700,000 troops. In 1945, the Sino-Soviet Treaty of Friendship and Alliance was agreed between Stalin and Chiang Kai-shek to implement the 1945 Yalta Conference understandings, which would require the withdrawal of Soviet troops from Chinese Manchuria. The Nationalist forces were at this time on the ascendency across China, as Chiang strove to put the fractured country back together as a coherent political entity. Mao and the communists were being sidelined by the international situation, with the US continuing its long-standing support for the KMT, and Stalin cooperating, at least for a time, with Chiang. Mao blamed the US for the turn of events against him, but he 'also viewed Stalin's role with scepticism and doubt'.[35]

Under pressure from the US and Britain to honour the terms of Yalta, in the spring of 1946 Stalin ordered a full troop withdrawal from Manchuria, while arming CPC forces on the way out. Hoping that the Soviets would continue to train and support his troops, Mao ordered those troops to fight for and hold 'every inch of land' against the far superior US-backed-and-funded KMT army. Thus, in Manchuria began China's civil war that lasted until 1950 and 'defined China's foreign relations for more than a decade'.[36]

## Mongolia

In 1206, a group of tribal chiefs gathered under the command of Chinggis Khan in what is now central Mongolia and pledged their allegiance to a campaign of trans-Eurasian conquest. By 1215, northern China had succumbed, and soon after, Afghanistan and Iran were conquered. The Mongols then swept westward, defeating Russian tribes, but Chinggis Khan died before crossing the Volga River. It was one of his grandsons, Baru, who pushed on past the Ural Mountains to attack Eastern and Central Europe between 1236 and 1241. With an army of some 100,000 men, he first captured Kiev, and then the whole of Muscovy fell, in what was a 'brutal and terrifying' campaign. Mongol domination of the region lasted for the next 250 years. The 'Golden Horde', as the Mongol or Tartar overlordship became known, could be harsh but was perhaps no more barbaric than the times themselves. Systems of governance, including regular and systematic taxation, as well as military organisation, were also put in place. Following the collapse of the Mongol empire, these innovations allowed Muscovy to begin its outward expansion and itself become an empire.[37]

But this was a process that took over two centuries, during which the Grand Princes of Muscovy gradually built and extended their political and military power, while chafing at paying tribute to Mongol overlords. After repeated failures to shake off the control of the Mongols, the military revolution in Europe in the sixteenth century, especially the use of new and more powerful artillery, shifted the balance of power between Moscow's Grand Princes and the Tartar khans. Russia's expansion across Eurasia's forests and steppes began under Ivan IV, 'The Terrible' (1547–73), who adopted the most modern European artillery and hand-fired weapons of the time. Ivan was the first Russian ruler to take the title of tsar (the Russian version of Caesar). Under him and his successors occurred the 'most successful of European expansions overland'.[38]

Philip Snow argues that Mongol rule psychologically scarred Russia's geopolitical mind: 'The rule of the Mongol Golden Horde ... [left a legacy of] ... a deep horror of invasion from the east.'[39] By the seventeenth century, Mongolia was no longer a united empire but was divided between the Dzungars and the Khalkhas. Central Eurasia now had a power vacuum that a determined, unified Russia under a wilful tsar would fill. The Russian Empire set out to colonise lands to the east, acquiring vast territories and resources, and, in so doing, strengthen its security against potential invaders from Asia. Kenneth Harl, British historian of pre-modern Eurasia, notes that 'Russia's rulers never forgot nor forgave the Mongols, who alone hold the honour of conquering Russia.'[40]

In this eastward expansion, Russia pushed more and more on areas that the Qing customarily regarded as its frontiers. In the seventeenth century, these two expanding Eurasian empires came into conflict periodically, until their frontiers were settled by the Treaty of Nerchinsk. Fearing a rising Mongol threat on China's northwest, Emperor Kangxi was keen to settle relations with Russia. By the 1680s, the Dzungar were seeking to unite the Mongols under the banner of Tibetan Buddhism, with the potential to create a new empire in Central Asia, and so were challenging the other imperial rising power, Qing China. The Treaty of Nerchinsk 'regularised trade relations, demarcated their eastern border, and set rules governing the unsettled peoples in frontier territories'. This accommodation with Russia cleared the way for Emperor Qianlong's genocidal campaign against the Dzungar people.[41] The treaty, plus the near obliteration of the Dzungar, fixed Qing control of Mongolia until the twentieth century.

From the seventeenth century until the fall of the Qing dynasty in 1911, Mongolia was part of the Manchu empire. Accordingly, China has long regarded Outer Mongolia as part of its 'lost' territories; Taiwanese official maps still show it as being part of China. With the collapse of the Qing, peripheral regions along the frontiers of China seized their chance to separate. Foreigners participated in the project as per their interests: Russia insisted on full autonomy for Outer Mongolia; Britain for Tibet; and Japan for parts of the northeast.

Only Russia succeeded fully in its demands, because of its proximity, and the determination of Mongolian separatist leaders, supported by St Petersburg, who declared their independence in 1911. Westad regards the nationalists' desire for independence from the hated Qing as more decisive than Russia's preponderance of military power.[42] In November 1912, St Petersburg concluded with the princes of Outer Mongolia the Russo-Mongolian agreement, which included a Russian commitment to train a Mongolian army; and a Russo-Mongolia Commercial Treaty, extending to Russia rights over mining, fishing, forestry and trading.[43]

Following its defeat in the Russo-Japanese War of 1904–05, and its eviction from much of Manchuria, St Petersburg turned its attention to Mongolia as a buffer state against the Japanese. In time, Japan and Russia began to draw closer in their resolve to resist third-party interventions in China, as both were pressing on Mongolia and Manchuria. From 1907 to 1916, in a sequence of four secret treaties, respective spheres of influence were reaffirmed: Japan reassured Russia that it had no interest in expanding its influence over Mongolia, giving Russia a 'free hand' there.[44]

For St Petersburg, Mongolia was seen as a strategic vulnerability, as the frontier comprised long stretches of territory bordering Siberia. Japan could cut the all-important Trans-Siberian Railway were it to gain a position in Mongolia, which was thus viewed by St Petersburg as essential to its Siberian and Far Eastern security.[45] In 1911, after the founding of the first Chinese republic, Russia made full independence for the breakaway province of Outer Mongolia a precondition for recognition of the new Republican government. Hoping for Russian support and economic assistance, in an act that would be repeated when the Communists came to power nearly half a century later, the Republican government accepted this condition. With this, St Peterburg achieved its objective of securing a pliant buffer state.[46] Chinese nationalists at the time saw this as further evidence of China's weakness, even though Outer Mongolia would, for a period, remain under Chinese suzerainty. The tsar's detachment of it from China was 'bitterly resented, and outbreaks of Russophobia were reported from Chinese communities all over the border lands'.[47] Independence for Outer Mongolia—although, in practice, it was hugely under Russian influence—was a major concession forced by a much more powerful Russia on China's leaders: at first Republican, then Nationalist, and finally Communist.

Mongolia was the first Asian state and the second in the world to adopt communism. The Mongolian People's Republic was proclaimed in 1924, after the death of ruler Bogd Khan. Soviet troops fought the White (anti-communist) Russian Baron Ungern at the request of the Mongolian People's Party (MPP) and eventually occupied the entire country before returning government to the MPP. In 1939, the Soviet Union successfully defended Mongolia against a major Japanese incursion at a battle on the Manchukuo–Mongolia border. The Soviet forces were led by the soon-to-be-famous General Zhukov.[48] Mongolia continued as a Soviet satellite state from then until 1990, when it gained independence. The Soviet Union maintained huge armies along the 3500 kilometres of border between Mongolia and China.

Mongolia is a vast country, about half the area of India, with just 3.5 million people in 2023. For the best part of seventy years, it was a de facto republic of the Soviet Union. Its ethnically homogeneous population has been generally well disposed towards Russia. The Qing rule was particularly repressive, and hateful attitudes to the Chinese have been passed on through the generations. Mongolia also fears China's intentions, believing that the Chinese have not given up on recovering their lost territories. At the same time, China has become the largest trading partner and investor there, so Mongolian diplomacy seeks to balance these interests with its fraught mutual history and great power rivalries.

### *Xinjiang*

In the later decades of the nineteenth century, Russia and Britain vied with each other for influence in Xinjiang. Russia did this mainly from the north, from Yili; and Britain from the North-West Frontier of India. At times, the influence exercised by their various embassies in Xinjiang was greater than that of the Qing rulers. In the early years of the twentieth century, as we have seen, British interest and influence waned, while the Russian Empire pressed further on Xinjiang and the other Qing frontier lands.[49]

By 1949, Soviet influence in Xinjiang was pervasive. During the period of Nationalist government, Nanjing exercised little authority over Xinjiang; competing warlords fought for control. Opportunistically, Stalin sought to influence events in the USSR's favour, by extending economic and military aid to support rival factions as determined by Soviet interests. During the 1930s, Stalin had two principal strategic concerns in Xinjiang beyond access to its resources, especially crude oil. One was his fear of Japan's intentions following its occupation of Manchuria. The other was the need to prevent an independent Uyghur state forming in southern Xinjiang, next door to his recently acquired Islamic republics.[50]

With Soviet backing, as we saw in Chapter 4, Nanjing's military governor, Sheng Shicai, was eventually able to extend control over the entire province.[51] He became beholden to Soviet economic and military aid, and the Soviets gained access to valuable resource concessions. As was to occur later through all of China, Soviet technicians, experts and military personal came to Xinjiang in large numbers, including to help Sheng establish internal security services modelled on the NKVD, Stalin's secret police. Xinjiang had turned 'red', complained the Nationalists and Japanese alike.[52]

Sheng then unleashed his own local version of 'red terror', at the same time that Central Asian republics were being purged by Stalin. On a trip to Moscow, Sheng was honoured by Stalin and Vyacheslav Molotov, the Soviet foreign minister, who enrolled him in the Communist Party of the Soviet Union (CPSU). Some 50,000 to 100,000 souls fell victim to Sheng's purges. By 1942, Xinjiang was almost in Stalin's hands when the US entered the war against Japan. Substantial US aid was beginning to flow to the Nationalist government, giving it the possibility of reasserting control over Xinjiang. By October 1943, the Nationalist government, now located in Chongqing, had taken control of Xinjiang from the Soviet Union and strengthened its western borders.[53]

The Soviets withdrew all military personal and technical advisers, and capped the Dushanzi oil fields, taking their equipment home. In one last twist, when the Soviet Union prevailed over Nazi Germany at Stalingrad and the tide of the war turned decisively against Germany, Sheng Shicai tried to swap sides again, back to Moscow, but to no avail. Stalin was by now so fed up with Sheng that he informed Chiang Kai-shek of his shenanigans. Sheng was hastily removed and sent to the east, lucky not to have lost his life.[54]

Moscow then shifted its support to the province's Turkic Uyghur and Kazakh groups, with whom it had maintained influence for decades. Discontent with the Han rulers was widespread and deep. After Sheng's departure, local insurrections and rioting were supported by Moscow, leading to the mounting of a major insurgency based around the northern region of Xinjiang around Yili. In November, a fully-fledged border war broke out, backed by the Soviets, leading to the establishment of a new ETR in northern Xinjiang. The ETR proclaimed friendship towards the Soviet Union and opposition to Chinese misrule. Stalin returned the favour, with military and economic aid, and a bevy of military and civilian advisers. In January 1945, the Yili National Army was formed, led by a Soviet Kyrgyz general. It quickly grew to some 45,000 troops, in addition to 3000 Soviet Kazakh and Kyrgyz recruits from across the border. Stalin was now in control of the northern part of Xinjiang; oil and other resource extraction resumed. By August 1945, the Yili National Army was advancing on Urumqi.[55]

At that point, during negotiations with Chiang over the Sino-Soviet Treaty of Friendship and Alliance, Stalin acknowledged that Xinjiang was Chinese sovereign territory and agreed to stop supporting the ETR. Stalin's objective was gaining Chiang's agreement to return in full the tsarist lands in Manchuria and relinquish claims to Outer Mongolia. In return for Chiang's concessions, Stalin made good on his promise to stop supporting the ETR. The advance of the ETR's troops was halted, and a peace agreement negotiated, overseen by the Soviets, which established a Xinjiang provincial government under the KMT. The northern areas controlled by the Soviet-backed ETR were to remain autonomous entities within Xinjiang, but the nomenclature of the 'East Turkestan Republic' was banned.[56]

After this, until the CPC's victory, Moscow maintained cordial relations with the KMT, as it sought commercial advantage and access to the region's resources. But Moscow had not entirely given up on Xinjiang. At one point, the Soviet consul general, displaying the usual high-handedness of Russian and Soviet officials towards

Chinese territorial sensitivities, went so far as to offer to halt the CPC's western advances if the KMT would declare Xinjiang to be independent in the same way as Outer Mongolia.[57]

As a result of these 'reciprocal' concessions, after 1949 and with the CPC's accession to power, Xinjiang for a time became a less acute national security concern for China than it had been since the mid-nineteenth century and the caliphate of Yaqub Beg. The Sino-Soviet accommodation lowered Beijing's perceived risks along China's western frontier with the Soviet Union. And yet, as in most periods of détente between China and Russia, mutual suspicion continued to churn beneath the surface. Sections of the border had still not been officially settled and Mao came to hold deep grudges against Stalin and the USSR, over what he felt were excessive territorial compromises he was forced to make to secure Soviet military aid.[58]

# CHAPTER 6

# THE OTHER COLD WAR

*'About a hundred years ago the area east of Baikal became Russian territory … and other points have become territories of the Soviet Union. We have not yet presented the bill for this list.'*
Chairman Mao Zedong[1]

While travelling in Tajikistan along the Afghan border near the Wakhan Corridor, which once was the buffer zone between British India and Imperial Russia, two massive rusting domes can be viewed in the distance under the shadow of Lenin Peak, relics of the 'Other Cold War'. These were part of the Soviet Union's forward nuclear arsenal aimed at China. This was from the time when the Soviet Union and China were engaged in sporadic military actions along China's western frontier. Nuclear war between these two communist empires threatened in 1969, when Chinese troops attacked at Zhenbao/Damansky Island, in the Ussuri River, in Manchuria. Unlike the 'Cold War' between the Soviet Union and the West, which attracts the most attention, that between China and the Soviet Union became hot at times, and the situation was far more unstable, and more pregnant with potential risks of nuclear armed conflict.

In the years following the clashes on the Ussuri River, renowned Chinese modern artist Shen Jiawei was in the PLA, painting propaganda works. One of them was a monumental piece depicting Chinese sentries in the depths of winter, keeping watch over a frozen Amur River. *Standing Guard for our Great Motherland* was so prized by Madame Mao, Jiang Qing, that she described it as the greatest work of art in modern China. It was the major item at the National Art Museum's annual exhibition in 1975, and a propaganda song of the same name was created.[2] The Soviet threat engendered great nationalist fervour at the time.

### 'Fraternal' Revolutionary Comrades

After proclaiming the People's Republic of China on 1 October 1949, such was the importance of the Soviet Union to the new Communist government in Beijing that Mao's inaugural international trip was to Moscow, in December 1949. It was the first time he had left China. Mao and his delegation travelled on the Trans-Siberian Railway across the wintery vastness of Siberia. He expected to be received as a fellow victorious revolutionary and as an equal but, instead, Stalin kept him and his delegation loafing around Moscow for nearly two months. Mao's frustration and anger at this were to scar permanently his attitudes towards Stalin and the Soviet Union. It can hardly be imagined how it must have felt for Mao and his party of senior officials—having just achieved power after civil war, following years of Japanese occupation and conflict, with so much urgent business to attend to in building a new state—to be kept in suspended animation in a Moscow winter, toyed with by Stalin.

During that time, Mao was regularly interviewed by Stalin's senior aides, his living quarters bugged by the NKVD, and his fealty tested. Mao presented the ever-cautious, suspicious, even paranoid, Stalin with a dilemma. There was at once an opportunity for Moscow to establish permanently its dominance over neighbouring China, which had waxed and waned over centuries; and, as relations with the US worsened, a heightened threat of direct confrontation with an enemy that Stalin knew his country was not yet ready to meet. He was also suspicious of Mao's real intentions towards the US. On one occasion, in January 1950, US allegations that the USSR was intent on gobbling up northern China so incensed Stalin that he demanded Mao issue a formal rebuttal through China's foreign ministry. When the statement was eventually issued, it was done at a lower level via Xinhua news agency, not the ministry, implying that China was ambivalent, at least, about the US's charge. This earned

Mao a severe reprimand from Stalin; the foreign minister, Molotov; and the NKVD chief, Lavrentiy Beria.[3]

It was only on 14 February 1950 that Mao received what he had come for and so desperately wanted. The two countries signed the Treaty of Friendship, Alliance and Mutual Assistance, known as the Valentine's Day Treaty. With this, Moscow pledged to defend China from attacks by the US and its allies, notably Japan. The Soviet Union would also provide military and civilian assistance in the form of economic and technical aid to support the task of national reconstruction. In return, Mao agreed to Moscow's demands to establish joint stock companies to cover everything from food processing and textiles to aviation. Stalin's main objective with the Valentine's Day Treaty, however, was to force Mao to accept Chiang Kai-shek's territorial concessions and reinforce China's junior-party status in the relationship. Mao had to accept the independence of Outer Mongolia and, in addition—reflecting Moscow's long-standing interests in Xinjiang and Manchuria—China would have to prevent any other country from operating in, or having a presence in, these two Chinese provinces.[4] With the treaty in his pocket, Mao could return home and attend to the construction of New China, in the knowledge that the Soviet Union would support the enterprise financially and guarantee its security.

The treaty, however, marked a humiliating backdown for Mao. The concessions on Outer Mongolia, Xinjiang and Manchuria were tucked away in secret annexes, and he ordered that they not be mentioned publicly. Xinjiang and Manchuria would continue as Soviet spheres of influence. Mao described these as the 'two bitter pills' he had been forced to swallow. Stalin also sought, and obtained, the right of extraterritoriality for the treatment of USSR nationals who broke Chinese law. This was particularly demeaning for Mao, as it undermined sovereignty in the way that earlier Qing and Nationalist treaties with foreign colonial powers, including Russia, had done. Stalin is reported to have told his inner circle, 'Comrades, the battle of China isn't over yet. It is only just beginning.'[5]

The Korean War was another source of heightened tension between Mao and Stalin, despite outward impressions of being comrades in arms. At Stalin's urging, Mao overruled his politburo's deep reservations about committing troops to the conflict, in the absence of direct combat involvement by the Soviet Union. On 19 October 1950, Chinese troops crossed the Yalu River, and drove the US and UN forces out of Pyongyang, and back down the peninsula. Stalin provided fighter jets, tanks and equipment, and big numbers of advisers, to sustain the Chinese frontline effort. But Chinese commanders in the field often had cause to complain about the quality of the matériel and to note that superior Soviet fighter jets were being held in reserve by Stalin. Mao and his officials were outraged when they learned that Moscow expected China to pay for the equipment, despite China having committed 3 million troops to the cause, with the loss of some 400,000 lives. Humiliatingly for China, funds were recovered by Moscow from the loans extended under the recently signed Valentine's Day Treaty.[6] Stalin's urging Mao to enter the war may also have cost the CPC its only chance to have taken Taiwan militarily. Mao had been amassing troops for a large-scale invasion, which he reluctantly diverted from Fujian to North Korea. It was a Hobson's choice for Mao: not to enter the Korean War would almost certainly have meant that China had a US military presence on its Manchurian border—a presence that has been an abiding fear of the PRC's strategic planners.

While Stalin had ideological reservations about Mao and the CPC, his successor, Nikita Khrushchev, initially had none. In 1953, with Stalin's death, Soviet aid to China ramped up massively. It extended to every sphere of Chinese life, both urban and rural, including advanced industrialisation, technology transfer, education and training, public administration, urban planning and major infrastructure projects. It is little remembered that the first bridge across the mighty Yangtze River, in all of China's 3000 years of continuous recorded history, was built at Wuhan, in 1953, by the Soviet Union. In China's First Five-year Plan, one third of the projects were to be built and paid for by either Moscow or fraternal East European communist states. By 1955, some 60 per cent of Chinese trade was with the Soviet Union.[7]

The Soviet Union played a massive role, in all respects, in the creation of Communist China: from political and heavy industrial organisation, to arts and culture. Relics of those times can still be seen, embodied in the organisational structure of the CPC and the old-fashioned, anachronistic names of its institutions; and China's love of classical ballet and orchestras, in the Russian tradition. Significantly, the PLA was progressively reorganised along the lines of the Red Army. Nothing reveals this more than the ceremonial uniforms and goosestepping parades for visits of heads of state or at the decennial National Day military parades. At such a military parade, if one were to photoshop out Tiananmen Square and replace it with Red Square, it would all look much the same.

Khrushchev, in part, saw his support for China as an important point of difference from his predecessor. For him, China was a large communist neighbouring state that wished to mimic the Soviet Union. In 1954, Khrushchev's first overseas visit as party general secretary was to Beijing. This flattered Mao enormously. Finally, he felt as if he was being treated by Moscow in the manner he deserved: as a peer. But no sooner had the romance begun, than it began to sour.

Initially, the Soviet leadership accommodated Mao's demands, other than the return of Outer Mongolia, and expanded economic and technical assistance. While not conceding the gifting of nuclear weapons, a collaborative nuclear research institute was established near Moscow, to work on the peaceful use of nuclear energy.[8]

However, Mao's ambitions were great and began to alarm the Kremlin. He intended to position China as the joint leader of the communist world and his demands on Moscow were heavy. Beijing was also flirting with a foreign policy that was more independent from Moscow, including having secret talks in Warsaw with the US. Increasingly, Mao was being seen as reckless, especially over Taiwan and the attendant risks of provoking nuclear war with the US. In September 1955, Khrushchev told visiting West German chancellor Konrad Adenauer that 'the Soviet Union faced two enemies, the United States and China; but the greater of these was China'.[9]

## Sino-Soviet Split
The post-1949 period in Sino-Soviet relations has had five distinct phases: naivety, mistrust, and disappointment on China's side; comity;

mutual hostility; gradual normalisation; and today's 'friendship without limits'. The previous period of Sino-Soviet comity lasted barely eight years (1953–61)—far shorter than the twenty-eight years of hostility (1961–89) that brought these great Asian communist powers to the brink of nuclear war. The current phase of warmer relations began in the 2010s, and is based on a mutual interest in resisting the US and reshaping the liberal international order; not on ideology. This phase is now into its second decade.

As mutual suspicions, disappointments over unfulfilled expectations of each other, and geopolitical divergences between Moscow and Beijing became entrenched, ideological differences were elevated. It is in this context that Khrushchev's speech denouncing Stalin, in February 1956 at the CPSU's Twentieth Congress, became the key turning point in the bilateral relationship. He attacked Stalin for his crimes against innocent citizens and for the extreme cult of personality that surrounded him. For Mao, on the one hand, the speech provided the chance to question Soviet orthodoxy in the communist world, and opened a space for him to position himself as an equal leader of it—a brotherly relationship, rather than one of 'father and son'. On the other hand, the criticisms of Stalin, especially those regarding the cult of personality he engendered, could be directed at Mao himself, by his own party.[10]

Mao was determined to use the opening provided by Khrushchev's denunciation of Stalin to position the CPC as the champion of hard-line communist orthodoxy and as an alternative to the CPSU. Snow observes that:

> From this point we begin to detect a change in the whole dynamics of Russia–Chinese interactions. Ever since the 1850s, under both tsarist and Soviet regimes, it had been Russians who took the initiative, pushed the limits, set the agenda, with the Chinese largely confined to reacting ... From now on it is the Chinese who are making the running, with the Russians increasingly passive and on the defensive.[11]

The Sino-Soviet split occurred in 1961 but only became public in the West in 1963. It was the culmination of slights small and big, ideological differences, misunderstandings, long-standing grievances and geopolitical shifts. Moscow suspected China's ambitions in its traditional spheres of influence, including Eastern Europe and, especially, the Soviet Far East. Beijing had come to see the USSR as a hegemonic power determined to manipulate and dominate China, while denying its claims to leadership of world revolution and the legitimacy that Mao sought from that status.

The 'split' was more a slow melting of relations from 1956 onwards. Internationally, Beijing increasingly asserted its independence from Moscow in the communist movement and promoted conflict with the West, rather than advocating the coexistence of two distinct orders that Khrushchev favoured. Domestically, policies promoting 'self-reliance' were coming to dominate Chinese domestic politics, reaching full force with the Great Leap Forward. Launched in 1958, it aimed to supercharge industrialisation and reach a higher level of communism, through the mass collectivisation of agriculture, based on the people's communes. In doing so, Mao was rejecting the advice of the numerous Soviet advisers by now embedded within various ministries and departments who urged gradual transformation. Mao saw this as Moscow's attempt to keep China in a subservient role forever. He believed a new self-reliant China would have no need of Soviet support and technical advisers, and would even end up outstripping the Soviet Union, reaching a higher level of communism much sooner. Mao dismissed the Soviet Union's progress towards communism, saying, 'One hears footsteps without seeing anyone coming down the stairs.'[12]

Bizarrely, in view of the tensions building in the relationship, in July 1958 Khrushchev proposed that a joint fleet be built as part of an East Asian defence mechanism—under Russian command but crewed by Chinese sailors. This was a supreme misreading of Mao. Khrushchev's tin ear earned him a sustained diatribe via his Beijing ambassador, in which Mao returned to all the grievances resulting from Russia's long-standing mistrust of China. These ranged from Russia's lack of support for the CPC during the civil war, to the 'bitter pills' of Xinjiang and Mongolia he had been 'forced to swallow' with the Valentine's Day Treaty, and Moscow's attempts to control and manipulate the CPC, to keep it in a subservient relationship.[13]

During this time, Beijing also made advances in the borderlands. As the Qing had done in the nineteenth century, more Han Chinese immigration to the grasslands of Inner Mongolia was encouraged, to shore up these sparsely populated areas against encroachment from the Soviet-backed Mongolian People's Republic. Meanwhile, trade was expanded to the point where China was close to replacing the Soviet Union as Mongolia's biggest trading partner. Soviet influence was purged from Xinjiang, in several campaigns. To derail Moscow's efforts at coexistence with the US, Mao provoked a crisis in the Taiwan Straits, warning Moscow that China would prevail as leader of the developing world after a nuclear war. China then ramped up its diplomacy in Africa, in competition with the Soviet Union.

By mid-1959, Khrushchev was fed up with Mao's impudence, as the Kremlin's efforts to placate him were reciprocated by higher levels of effrontery. In July, in a speech in Poland, Khrushchev began openly to criticise the Great Leap Forward, both in terms of efficiency and, more tellingly, on ideological grounds—arguing that the people's communes, so central to the Great Leap's narrative of leading the communist world, revealed a poor understanding of communism.[14]

## Crisis in the Himalaya

By the end of the 1950s, the Nehru government in India was drifting away from a socialist stance on economic and social policies domestically, and, at least in the Chinese view, leaning internationally towards the US. With echoes of today, China accused India of making itself 'the pawn of the international anti-China campaign'. According to Beijing, this was the root cause of the intensification of Sino-Indian boundary disputes.[15] Initially, Beijing reacted more in sorrow than in anger to what it alleged were Indian provocations along the border. As with China's other frontiers, notably Xinjiang and Manchuria, disputes often became embroiled in wider geopolitical moves. With India, it was the intensifying Sino-Soviet split. When clashes occurred between China and India in disputed border areas, the Kremlin would remain neutral, despite its obligations under the Valentine's Day Treaty to come to China's assistance. Beijing accused Moscow of 'feigning neutrality' while in fact siding with India and its tilt towards the US. China's disputes with India and Russia amplified and fed into each other.

In August 1959, five months after the Dalai Lama fled Tibet, a violent clash occurred between Chinese and Indian troops at a village called Longju on the frontier of Arunachal Pradesh. This is known as the 'Longju Incident'. In a pattern familiar today, China claimed that it repelled an attack by Indian troops; India said it was the victim of unprovoked aggression by Chinese troops. The Longju Incident occurred virtually on the eve of Khrushchev's departure for the US. This was to be the first visit by a Soviet leader, in which he hoped to ease Cold War tensions and reduce the threat of war by promoting 'co-existence'. Unexpectedly, the Longju Incident, in the context of the Cold War, had loud geopolitical resonance and nearly derailed Khrushchev's visit.[16]

In language eerily like that used sixty years later, when China and India clashed in 2020 on the Line of Actual Control near Lake Pangu, China was roundly denounced in the West by those opposed to coexistence as a 'bellicose and bullying power'. The Longju Incident was used to argue that this 'unprovoked' attack on India 'had bared the true face of international Communism—unreliable and predatory'. As Neville Maxwell, in his at times controversial study of the causes of the subsequent 1962 Sino-Indian border war, said of the Longju Incident:

> [This] small spark in the Himalayas was treated as if it were a flare, irradiating the risks of attempting coexistence with Communist powers, and thus putting Khrushchev's protestations about the peaceful settlement of disputes [between blocs] in what, to the Russians, was a false light.[17]

To Beijing's unholy fury, Moscow's position on the incident publicly remained neutral while it privately moved to support India against

China. Worse still, other fraternal communist countries in Eastern Europe fell into line with Moscow, to imply that China was the aggressor and recklessly stirring up trouble. The reaction to the incident highlighted the extent by then of the rift in the communist world, with Moscow arguing that it was essential for the development of world communism to avoid war with the capitalist countries. Beijing's view was stridently opposite: war with the capitalist world was inevitable and a necessary step for world communism to prevail. On his way home from Washington, Khrushchev stopped in Beijing. He was left in no uncertainty about Chinese anger over Soviet 'neutrality' regarding the Longju Incident.[18] Moscow then doubled down on the border dispute, and by late in 1960 had begun to provide India with military support. With this, together with US assistance, India was quickly acquiring the means to support its forward policy along the remote Himalaya frontier against China.

Fissures in the Sino-Soviet relationship burst into the open at the Romanian party congress in Bucharest in June 1960. Khrushchev openly attacked the 'left revisionists in Peking', accusing them of setting back the international communist cause. By ignoring Moscow's direction and stirring up trouble with India, Beijing had pushed Nehru towards the US, just when the Soviet Union was having some success in encouraging India to turn away from capitalism to communism. Moscow was also acutely aware of the parallels between India and China's border disputes and its own with China. It rejected China's version of events, and instead stressed the importance and inviolability of existing treaties and boundaries. Beijing responded with accusations of revisionism and counter-revolutionary behaviour.

### Sino-Soviet Relations Freeze Over

In July 1960, following Beijing's attacks on Moscow at the Romanian party congress, Khrushchev recalled most of the 1400 Soviet advisers working in China, together with their families, and cancelled hundreds of contracts. Many Soviet advisers were dismayed by this sudden recall, which they saw as having been provoked by Mao. Domestic and foreign policy trends again reinforced each other, culminating in a complete rupture in relations by 1963. That year, China successfully tested its first atomic weapon, which, to Moscow's consternation, was achieved without Soviet assistance.[19]

For Beijing, the dispute with Moscow had now gone beyond past grievances and ideology to come from a feeling of deep betrayal. Suggestions of some reproachment with the Soviet Union, for both sentimental and hard-headed economic reasons, fused to become opposition to Mao, which he struck down as 'revisionism' and 'right wing opportunism'. In 1963, for the first time, the CPC's official mouthpiece, the *People's Daily*, began to editorialise on the 'unequal' nineteenth century treaties between Russia and Qing China. Later in the year, the Chinese foreign ministry formally raised the 'unequal treaties' as a subject to be addressed by both sides.[20]

Surprisingly, in this time of deep rancour, Moscow responded that it was prepared to negotiate over border demarcations in Manchuria. During 1964, these proceeded steadily and reached an agreement that would have returned territory to China had it not been for Mao's wilful intervention. The Soviet delegation returned home empty handed.[21] Insult continued to pile on insult, and repeated efforts by Moscow for some sort of reconciliation were rebuffed.

Even after Khrushchev's fall in 1964—in part, due to the Soviet Politburo's misgivings over his handling of China—Mao would not yield, and matters went from bad to worse. He then started to close China to the rest of the world, in preparation for launching the Cultural Revolution in the spring of 1966. He also warned the nation to prepare for war and not to be afraid of it, including war with the Soviet Union, saying that:

> We cannot only pay attention to the East [US] and not the North, only pay attention to imperialism and not revisionism, we must prepare for war on both sides …

Later, he said:

> About a hundred years ago the area east of Baikal became Russian territory, and since then Vladivostok, Khabarovsk, Kamchatka,

and other points have become territories of the Soviet Union. We have not yet presented the bill for this list.[22]

From the late 1950s, in the context of deteriorating relations between Beijing and Moscow, the northwestern border became volatile again. In April–May 1962, 62,000 'Soviet' citizens and their Chinese families fled across the border into Soviet Kazakhstan to escape famine caused by Mao's Great Leap Forward. Attempts to stop this exodus provoked demonstrations at various places along the border, culminating in April 1962 with the Yining Incident, where the PLA attacked Kazakh demonstrators. This in turn sparked further demonstrations, leading Beijing to garrison sections of the border, and close the Soviet consulates at Urumqi and Yining.[23]

When instability broke out in Xinjiang, Moscow, for its part, adopted its default position: supporting the Turkic minorities against the Han Chinese and encouraging refugees to cross the border. Propaganda reminded the Turkic population of the Soviet Union's support for the ETR of 1944–49. Before they were shuttered, Soviet consulates in Yining and Urumqi were handing out passports to anyone wishing to leave Xinjiang, and border guards on the Soviet side facilitated crossings. China listed 1674 border incidents it claimed were provoked by the Soviet Union between 1960 and 1964. For its part, China was stirring up trouble on both the Xinjiang and Manchurian borders. In 1962, the Soviet side reported 5000 Chinese transgressions of Soviet territory for the year.[24]

Directly challenging China's territorial integrity, Moscow focused an increasingly vociferous campaign on encouraging separatist groups, with the aim of delegitimising China's sovereignty over Xinjiang. Using the chaos of the Cultural Revolution and persecution of Uyghurs, and attacks on those of the Islamic faith by Mao's Red Guards, Moscow increased Uyghur broadcasts on Radio Tashkent in Uzbekistan, urging Uyghurs to revolt against Chinese rule and offering shelter within the Soviet Union. Propaganda against each side escalated, with Moscow—in terms resembling the criticism of Beijing's policies towards the Uyghurs in the second decade of the twenty-first century—accusing China of 'building concentration camps in Xinjiang, persecuting Soviet citizens, and suppressing national minorities by force'.[25] Moscow was also involved in organising Kazakhstan-based ethnic guerrilla groups to attack Xinjiang's frontier posts along the northwestern border.[26]

## A Time of Madness

During the Cultural Revolution, the Soviet Union was portrayed in relentless propaganda campaigns as China's greatest enemy: Soviet 'revisionism' threatened from abroad and 'revisionist' traitors threatened from within. All high-level contact was frozen. Past associations by senior CPC figures with the Soviet Union—which were numerous and reached deep into the Party—became the justification to bring them down, on the grounds of 'conspiring with a foreign power' against Mao.[27]

Following the Soviet invasion of Czechoslovakia in the summer of 1968, and the adoption of the Brezhnev Doctrine justifying military intervention in socialist countries, the Red Army again began to make incursions into Xinjiang. China claimed over 400 Soviet incursions occurred over the spring/summer of 1969, involving tanks and armoured cars. On 13 August, the PLA engaged the Red Army, resulting in casualties on both sides. Beijing was now convinced an all-out military invasion of Xinjiang, which would include an air attack on China's Lop Nor nuclear facilities in the Gobi Desert, was likely.[28] On 23 August, Premier Zhou Enlai established a Leading Group on Air Defence, to prepare for a sudden nuclear attack. All provinces and regions bordering the Soviet Union and Outer Mongolia were put into a state of war alertness. Mass mobilisation campaigns to prepare for war were launched by the propaganda departments.[29]

In Manchuria, border incidents escalated from 1968. In February 1969, an elite detachment of PLA troops lethally attacked Soviet border guards on the Zhenbao/Damansky Island in the Ussuri River, a part of the Manchurian frontier claimed by both sides. Deaths numbered some thirty soldiers and officers on the Soviet side, and fifty to 100 on the Chinese side. Moscow's retaliation was as swift as it was substantial, with a full Red Army assault launched in March. Chinese losses were put at around 800 to the USSR's thirty. It seemed to Beijing that its worst fears were about to be realised. The PLA was put on full alert.[30] Mao ordered Zhou Enlai to disperse the top leadership, saying that if he did not, 'Many will die in the attack by one atomic bomb'. Under Zhou's plan, Mao would move to Wuhan, and marshal Lin Biao to Suzhou. Only Zhou and chief of staff Huang Yongsheng were to remain in Beijing.[31]

A few months later, China was at it again, but this time on the northwest frontier, where soldiers made border incursions under the guise of being local herdsmen. Soviet forces responded with a preponderance of armoured vehicles and aircraft. Reports of casualties are vague but the numbers were high enough for the Chinese government to issue orders to prepare national defences, including digging tunnels and storing grain. There were large-scale civilian evacuations from the borderlands.[32]

Moscow had indeed planned for a pre-emptive strike on China's nuclear facilities at Lop Nor in Xinjiang. When Kissinger was asked by the Soviet ambassador to the US whether the US would remain neutral if the USSR attacked China's nuclear facilities, he replied that it would not and was prepared to strike Soviet cities. Bravado it may have been, but it led Moscow to step back from the abyss. By the end of 1969, still fearing war with the Soviet Union, Mao accepted advice from a group of old revolutionary marshals, who he had convened to report their 'mature ideas' on the 'international situation'. They reported that the US imperialists could not easily launch an attack against China, and warned Mao that 'the Soviet revisionists see us as the main enemy, so they are a more serious security threat'.[33] Although not explicitly advising how China's international policies should be changed, their conclusion was crystal clear: open dialogue with the US.[34]

Tensions with Moscow also eased somewhat, as Mao sought to lower the temperature. Premier Alexei Kosygin was permitted to visit Beijing after attending the funeral of Vietnam's revolutionary leader and president, Ho Chi Minh, in September 1969. In the meeting between Zhou and Kosygin at Beijing airport during his stopover, each indicated that they wished to improve relations and avoid war.

Zhou advanced three proposals for taking the relationship forward, but Moscow subsequently merely noted these.[35]

Nevertheless, following the visit, Beijing and Moscow eventually consented to commence discussions to settle the border demarcation in Manchuria and Mongolia. Both sides agreed to respect existing border lines and to withdraw troops. Significantly, Beijing conceded that it would not demand the return of territory Imperial Russia had annexed by means of 'unequal treaties'. Their respective ambassadors would also return to their posts in Beijing and Moscow. But little came of this, as Mao was still reluctant to compromise.[36]

With an understanding between Beijing and Moscow to de-escalate military tensions, Xinjiang was a second-order concern after the boundary issues in Mongolia and Manchuria. Nevertheless, it was still of sufficient concern for Premier Zhou Enlai, in February 1972, when meeting President Nixon, to warn of Moscow's aggressive intentions towards Xinjiang, saying that it:

> will try to create a Republic of Turkestan ... [but it] will not be so easy for them to enter [Xinjiang], and even if they come in it will be hard for them to get out. No matter what, we will make no provocations.[37]

Over the next decade, Sino-Soviet relations settled into a pattern of uneasy stability. Occasional border flare-ups occurred along the Xinjiang frontier, but these were relatively minor. As bilateral relations with the US deepened, Beijing grew much less fearful of the Soviet Union. Meanwhile, Moscow, ever mistrustful of China, continued its relentless accumulation of miliary forces in Mongolia and the Russian Far East. A quarter of the Soviet Union's total military strength was directed towards China in those years.[38]

### Ice Begins to Break
By the late 1960s, Eurasian geopolitics was once more shaping global events. Ideologically blinkered US policy makers took the best part of a decade to understand and accept that the Sino-Soviet split was real. The idea of working with China against the Soviet Union only

gradually began to take hold. By the time Nixon and Kissinger were running US foreign policy from 1969, rapprochement with China was not only possible—as China looked to the US to balance the USSR—it also offered the Nixon administration a way out of Vietnam with some degree of dignity. China and the US set about normalising diplomatic relations, which saw a rapid expansion of exchanges and cooperation, including in highly sensitive areas such as intelligence activities against the Soviet Union along China's western frontier.[39]

Nixon's visit to Beijing in February 1972 marked not only rapprochement between, until then, two implacably opposed enemy states but China's first, and dramatic, step into the world of Westphalian international relations, where states align against another to balance the enemy's power.[40] Such was their common desire to contain the USSR, and their shared fear of its nuclear capability, that cooperation extended to areas that now would be unthinkable.

For example, by the late 1970s, China and the US agreed to operate joint spy stations along the Tian Shan mountains on China's western frontier in Xinjiang. In 1979, with the Iranian Revolution, the CIA lost the bases it used for monitoring Soviet nuclear weapons installations in Central Asia. The US and China had begun to look at cooperation over intelligence sharing on Soviet nuclear capabilities. During paramount leader Deng Xiaoping's visit to Washington in January and February of 1979, a secret visit was arranged to CIA headquarters at Langley, Virginia. In April 1979, senator Joe Biden, during a senate intelligence committee meeting visit to Beijing, asked Deng if he would agree to share intelligence facilities directed against the Soviet Union along the Xinjiang border. Deng confirmed this could occur, on the basis of China operating the equipment. Soon after, Project Chestnut was launched, which involved basing eavesdropping stations along China's western frontier, to collect intelligence on Soviet nuclear facilities and activities, especially testing.[41] By 1989, some ten stations were in place. But with the collapse of the Soviet Union, the common enemy disappeared, and the US no longer had an interest in maintaining the joint intelligence gathering facilities.[42]

Sino-Soviet relations deteriorated again, following the Soviet invasion of Afghanistan in 1979 and China's invasion of Vietnam in the same year. Vietnam was such a close ally of the Soviet Union that Beijing propaganda referred to it as 'Cuba of the East'. Views differ on Beijing's motivation for the short and ultimately costly invasion, but one outcome—intended or otherwise—was that China had demonstrated to Hanoi that, despite having a mutual defence treaty with the USSR, the Soviets could not be relied upon to come to their aid.[43] The retaliation from Moscow along the Xinjiang border that Beijing had feared, in return for its invasion of Vietnam, never materialised.

## Shifting Power Balance

Deng Xiaoping's ascendency as China's most powerful leader pivoted domestic policy towards pragmatism and economic growth. China's modernisation was at the top of the policy agenda, and for this Deng needed a peaceful international environment. Assessing that Moscow's invasion of Afghanistan and continued economic weakness, and growing discontent in Eastern Europe, had overstretched the Soviet empire, Beijing began to adopt a policy of equidistance between Moscow and Washington. Border negotiations that had briefly resumed in 1979, only to be abruptly stopped with the invasion of Afghanistan, were resumed in 1982. Trade expanded gradually from its minuscule base and cultural exchanges began again, after a break of some twenty years. In 1985, Gorbachev was appointed the new president and he soon set about clearing out the 'Sinophobes' from the Kremlin. Interest was also growing in China's market-oriented new economic model, which was clearly delivering impressive results, even in its early years of application.[44] Still, it was four years after Gorbachev's accession that he went to Beijing. Both sides, with no trust in each other, scarred by a history of mutual grievances, and with extant territorial and ideological antagonisms, were barely inching towards a rapprochement.

When Gorbachev visited Beijing on 14 May 1989, it marked the end of almost thirty years of China–Russia estrangement. While the visit was choreographed to put past territorial enmities and ideological contests behind them, Deng Xiaoping made it abundantly clear to his guest that Russian territorial expansion was the abiding source of conflict and tension between the two communist powers. Gorbachev received a 90-minute lecture on the history of foreign aggression towards China. Deng accused both Russia under the tsars and the Soviet Union under communism as being the most rapacious of the foreign predators, even more so than Japan. Gorbachev had to accept the lecture in good grace, although privately he was fuming. Even so, the visit restored normal relations—borders were to be opened, and trade and cultural exchanges began to flourish.[45]

What soon became clear to both sides, however, was how fundamentally the relationship had changed. In little more than a decade, China had transformed its economy from the old Soviet-style model, where shortages, especially of consumer goods, prevailed, to being export led, with surpluses to sell on global markets. Yet doctrinal disputes, never far below the surface, returned to prominence in the bilateral relationship. China's leadership was appalled at Gorbachev's policy of *glasnost*—or accountability of government—which was anathema to the hardline Marxism-Leninism of Deng Xiaoping and his colleagues. In late 1989, as the communist world of Eastern Europe shattered, Premier Li Peng felt he had to clarify China's position. He said that only state-to-state relations with the Soviet Union had been normalised during Gorbachev's visit in May, not the much more important party-to-party relations. In 1990, an internal CPC document leaked in Hong Kong labelled Gorbachev as a 'traitor to the socialist cause', with Deng, echoing Mao at an earlier time, warning of the 'danger from the north' (Russia).[46]

While Deng Xiaoping's wish to see off Gorbachev was fulfilled, when it happened, in 1992, with the collapse of the Soviet Union, the new Russian leader, Boris Yeltsin, sought closer alignment with the West. Hence, a new source of tension entered the relationship: it had gone from the older communist brother's patronising and bullying of China, to rejection of the Marxist-Leninist foundations of the CPC's rule, to now moving closer to the US-led liberal international order. Moscow began lecturing Beijing on human rights and, most alarming of all, pursuing closer ties with Taiwan.

Within Russia, during Yeltsin's faltering leadership and grasp on power, policy towards China was hotly contested between the 'Atlanticists', seeking ever closer alignment with the West, and the more China-friendly 'Eurasianists'.[47]

## End of the Eurasian Cold War

Russia's declining economy and China's rising economic strength, however, pushed these two Eurasian neighbours closer together. With Western sanctions on arms sales to China following the Tiananmen Square military crackdown, Russia became China's single biggest supplier of military equipment. For its part, in the 1990s, China's market for arms did much to support Russia's military–industrial complex. Meanwhile, and despite the West's enthusiasm for Russia's market-oriented economic 'shock therapy', little financial aid was provided by the West, compared with what was required to rebuild the Russian economy. As Russia teetered on the edge of economic collapse, NATO began absorbing former Warsaw Pact members and then the former Soviet-ruled Baltic nations.[48]

Now the Eurasianists in the Kremlin had something to work with, and Yeltsin sought closer and warmer relations with Beijing. Although furious with Gorbachev over the dissolution of the Soviet Union, and deeply suspicious of Yeltsin, Beijing had to respond to the suddenly changed geopolitical landscape, including the emergence overnight of newly independent states in Central Asia, and to do so before Taiwan did. Beijing also had to lock in territorial agreements reached in the dying days of the old Soviet Union. On the western border, China faced three new states—Kazakhstan, Kyrgyzstan and Tajikistan—and urgently needed to resolve border demarcations, especially as Beijing feared Islamic or Turkic influence entering the ever-troubled Xinjiang, and turbocharging demands for Eastern Turkestan independence. Consequently, outstanding issues were resolved relatively smoothly.[49]

Troop reduction along the western borders was another major Chinese objective. In April 1996, in Shanghai, a five-party agreement between China, Russia and the three Stans on China's borders was reached. It drastically reduced troop numbers, and involved confidence-building measures, including obligations to consult on troop movements and joint monitoring arrangements. This group formally constituted itself as the Shanghai Five. In 1997, the Reduction of Military Forces in the Border Regions Agreement was signed in Moscow, limiting Chinese and Russian troops, plus the Stans' troops, to 130,400 on each side; and creating a 100-kilometre buffer zone along the border.[50] In addition to Russia selling substantial quantities of arms to China, Beijing began to look to it as a secure source of energy to reduce China's dependence on seaborne oil and gas from the Middle East. Cooperation in science and technology, and especially regarding outer space, deepened.

In 1997, to mark the agreement on troop reductions, came the first joint declaration by Russia and China on foreign policy—a statement of their joint opposition to the US-dominated unipolar order of the time. After this, NATO's campaign against Serbia in 1999 and the bombing of the Chinese embassy in Belgrade drew Moscow and Beijing closer in opposition to the West. In 2001, the first treaty between Russia and China since the Valentine's Day Treaty of fifty years earlier was signed: the wordy Treaty of Good Neighbourliness and Friendly Cooperation Between the People's Republic of China and the Russian Federation. Neither side sought a formal alliance relationship via the encumbering obligations of mutual military support that it would entail. It was, rather, a statement of enduring friendship and of the wish to avoid again becoming enemies.[51] It was renewed on 28 June 2021, with both sides describing it as representing a model for a 'new type of international relations'.[52]

On 15 June 2001, the Shanghai Five signed an agreement to create the SCO. Uzbekistan joined what had become the first formal anti-Western multilateral political organisation.[53] Its unifying agenda initially was cooperating to fight against the spread of Islamic fundamentalism in Central Asia. Moscow was increasingly concerned about Chechens and Tartars in southern Russia, and Beijing about Uyghurs and Kazakhs in Xinjiang. An elaborate secretariat structure was quickly established, with its headquarters in Beijing. Many subordinate permanent bodies have since been created, including the

Regional Anti-Terrorist Structure. Joint military exercises between Russia and China commenced in August 2005. Under the auspices of the SCO, regular large-scale military drills are conducted on the Eurasian land mass, and these have since been expanded to include distant naval operations, as well as air force wargames over the Sea of Japan.[54]

In October 2004, during a visit by Putin to Beijing, the outstanding eastern border issues were finally settled. The remaining territory along the Ussuri River was formally handed back to China in 2008. By 2012, Russian policy spoke more formally of a 'Pivot to Asia'. This was primarily economically driven, to attempt to participate more in the rapid economic growth occurring in East Asia, although China was the principal focus. It was, though, also in response to growing tensions with the West, especially the US. These became acute following the annexation of Crimea in 2014 and the imposition of Western sanctions on Russia.[55] The pivot became a lifeline.

From 2012, with the ascendency of Xi Jinping, regular high-level contact became a distinguishing feature of the relationship. Inevitably, with this kind of regular contact and visits, bureaucrats need to devise inventive institutional arrangements, which their senior leaders can announce and, over time, they begin to add structure to relationships, even when substance initially is sometimes lacking. The new bodies that quickly followed the warming of relations between China and Russia included a Sino-Russian business council, a Sino-Russian research centre, and a Russian–Chinese commission on military cooperation.

The relationship between Russia and China that has emerged, while superficially looking like that between the two communist powers of the 1950s, is fundamentally different. It is based on Westphalian principles of the absolute sovereignty of the nation state and non-interference in the internal affairs of another state. For this reason, Russia's invasion of Ukraine in 2022 was a major shock to Beijing, as it was to most other countries. Moreover, China and Ukraine had until then enjoyed close economic and political relations, including a mutual security agreement, the only one China had signed with another country. China has not formally supported

Russia but, controversially, like India, neither has it condemned it. Similarly, the SCO has not supported Russia's position, as it did not support Russia's annexation of the Crimea: at the 2014 Dushanbe SCO summit, Putin failed to secure support for his 'interpretation' of the Crimean crisis.[56]

China and Russia are united in their opposition to the US's insistence on universal values and accountability for human rights violations. Accordingly, they back each other when challenged by the West. As permanent members of the UN Security Council, they regularly support each other exercising a veto. Beijing and Moscow are united in shared objectives to make the world a safer place for authoritarian regimes, and for authoritarian regimes to be influential in shaping and reordering the international system in their favour.[57]

But tensions in the relationship continued to surface from time to time. Following the 9/11 al-Qaeda attacks on the World Trade Center in New York, Putin supported the US deploying forces at former Soviet air bases in Uzbekistan, Kyrgyzstan and Tajikistan from which to attack Afghanistan. China was not consulted and did not approve of the Kremlin opening the door of Central Asia to the US. Beijing was also unhappy with Russia's 2008 invasion of Georgia—in what has become a familiar pattern for Moscow, to encourage provinces of one state to be ceded and join Russia. To Beijing, with its eyes firmly on Taiwan and Xinjiang, secession is anathema. Further, such actions are clearly against the Westphalian doctrine of the 'sanctity of borders' that Russia and China pledged to each other to uphold.[58]

Putin launched the 2008 assault on Georgia at the time China was hosting the Summer Olympics. He attended the opening ceremony in a blaze of publicity, with warm greetings from President Hu. That evening, he flew back to Moscow; the next morning, Russian troops were in Georgia, wiping from the front pages the grand opening ceremony and the CPC's ambitions to project itself globally. Throughout February 2022, when the Winter Olympics were in session, international attention was focused almost exclusively on Russia's preparations to launch a full-scale military invasion of Ukraine, and speculation on whether it would in fact occur. The

Chinese party-state devotes enormous effort, and expense, to choreographing such events as the Olympics, as part of its image management at home and abroad. Putin has shown no regard for China's face. Even if the resentment is unspoken, such slights will be remembered and added to the list of grievances still being nursed. Unlike in 2008, Putin may have delayed the Ukraine invasion until after the closing ceremony, in deference to the CPC's sensitivities, but this only shows how much relative power in the relationship has shifted in China's favour since 2008.

Over the intervening three centuries since the Treaty of Nerchinsk, the balance of power in Eurasia shifted from being somewhat in China's favour, to heavily in Russia's favour for nearly two centuries. Over the past forty years, it has shifted decisively back to China, in what has been the second major power shift after the power shift from the US to China over the past two decades. Although military power has been in Russia's favour, the Ukraine war has depleted its capabilities. In view of the absence of trust, and the long-standing historical grievances, outstanding territorial ambitions of nationalists on both sides, and their respective, incompatible approaches to achieving their security, the relationship is, and will continue to be, inherently unstable.

CHAPTER 7

# CONCERT OF CONVENIENCE

*'Putin has three advisers: Ivan the Terrible, Peter the Great, and Catherine the Great.'*
Sergey Lavrov, Russian foreign minister since 2004[1]

In 2016, when I was on a vacation in Vladivostok, and then Mongolia and Siberia, it was hard to imagine that China, with its 100 million residents in the northeast, was so near. It only takes about an hour and a half to fly to Vladivostok from Harbin, the capital of Heilongjiang province with a population of 31 million; and about double that from Seoul. But in Vladivostok, Korean businessmen were much more prevalent than Chinese ones, who were almost non-existent. South Korean businesses—including construction-related companies, hotels and restaurants, as well as retail stores—were ubiquitous. In contrast, Chinese businesses were notable by their absence. Whereas India is cut off from pervasive Chinese influence along its northern frontiers by the formidable Himalaya range of mountains, no such barriers divide the Russian Far East from Chinese Manchuria.

If the Putin–Xi concert of convenience holds fast, then all of that is about to change. In February 2022, their joint statement, made in Beijing on the eve of Putin's invasion of Ukraine, declared the Russia–China relationship to be based now on a 'friendship without limits' and that it was to be a new model of great power relations. Since that time, new commercial transport corridors and trade zones to deepen economic engagement have been announced. Historical, cultural and nationalistic headwinds will continue to blow, however;

and at times at gale-force levels. Despite formal treaties that were supposed to have settled long-standing border disputes, the vast, empty lands of Siberia and the Russian Far East are likely to continue to roil the relationship between Russia and China, as their relative strengths adjust and international forces shape their respective calculus of interests.

All these lands were once China's. They were lost under the 'unequal treaties' of the nineteenth century, and have every so often been the source of live grievances between Beijing and Moscow. Of all the lands China lost to foreign imperial powers during its 'century of humiliation', only those gained by Russia under the 'unequal treaties' have mostly not been returned. But Hong Kong, Taiwan and the treaty ports taken from China by the West and Japan are immaterial when compared with what Russia took and has not returned. These lands lie from the east of the Ussuri River to the Pacific Ocean, and north of the Amur River. Their loss continues to be deeply felt, injurious as it is to China's sense that its time has come.

## Amur Fault Line

The Trans-Siberian Express—the final word is used loosely—broadly follows the Ussuri going north, then turns west along the Amur to Ulan-Ude, the capital of the Russian Buryatia region, 138 kilometres from the eastern shore of Lake Baikal, Siberia. It takes three days to travel from Vladivostok to Ulan-Ude, which still honours Vladimir Lenin with giant socialist-realist statues brutally hacked out of granite. A shorter option west is the Trans-Manchurian train, but it is only on the longer route that the extent of the territory lost, and its remoteness and desolation, can be fully appreciated.

On the first day out from Vladivostok, the train threads its way north along the Ussuri River. Unannounced, it passes near Zhenbao/Damansky Island in the Ussuri River, where in March 1969 the PLA launched a surprise pre-emptive strike against the Red Army. The Ussuri forms the Russia–China border north of Vladivostok until the major city of Khabarovsk, where it becomes a tributary of the Amur. These riverine border demarcations were determined by the Treaty of Aigun (1858) for the Amur River, depriving China of large swathes of land to the north it had held for nearly two hundred years; and then extended by the Convention of Peking (1860), where China lost its territory east of the Ussuri River, and access to the Pacific Ocean.

The Ussuri is part of a broad, flat floodplain, which, ever changing, spreads out depending on the season, making borders at times indistinct and unreliable. Islands, then, are significant, as fixed points of demarcation between China and Russia. Otherwise, the landscape is featureless, disturbed every so often by scattered copses of fir and birch. No people seem to live there. No animals are grazing, nor fields being ploughed; perhaps they're off in the distant haze that rises in the direction of the great rivers that divide the region. The train moves slowly onwards against this vast background, the sense of progress along the route retarded by this great emptiness.

————————

Being in first class on the train made one worry what the other classes might be like. It had hard bunk beds—two up two down, with taut, slippery surfaces that sent bedding cascading to the floor with irritating regularity—and scratched sepia-stained windows, which added to the external gloom even on sunny days, as if the train were trying to trap the outdoors in its own past. Communal toilets and washing facilities were combined in a cramped stainless-steel pod, with something around the size of a small fire hose for cleaning. It was annoying being sprayed by its force; the tap required dexterity to adjust it, a feat that was beyond me. Later that evening, when all fifteen or so foreigners, the only passengers in the car, were tormented by food poisoning from the 'special first-class bonus meal' of 'fresh' fish, the hose's utility was at last understood and greatly appreciated.

Before that late-night post-prandial denouement, we stopped for forty-five minutes at Khabarovsk: long enough for me to get off the train, stretch and have a cigar. At the end of September, the air was already frigid. Khabarovsk is just east of where the Ussuri flows into the Amur on their now-combined course north to the Pacific Ocean, where the Amur's trans-continental journey ends in sight of Sakhalin Island. Khabarovsk is the largest city on the Amur. It has been navigable by steamers since the mid-nineteenth century, a major Russian commercial centre for facilitating east–west trade, linking Siberia and the Russian Far East.

The night stretched out to become an Orson Welles monochrome drama of contorted angles and positions: trying to brace against the swaying, bouncing carriage; guarding against soiling myself; trying to avoid icy spray from the black long-necked demon hose while it cleaned from ceiling to floor. Then, again, trying to stay steady for the waltz along the narrow corridor leading to the steel pod, the mounting anxiety that another traveller might already be there nearly too much to contemplate. And then, back in my compartment, slipping off my bunk, wondering if I would get any rest before having to dance again.

Exhausted though I was, things were calmer in the morning, as bright sunshine bathed Belogorsky station. One of the occupants of my compartment would hardly move for the next twenty-four hours; one was chirpy as ever. My photographs show one of our conductors, overcoat stiffly buttoned up, examining her watch in the sharp early light, waiting to give the signal to go. She seemed bliss-fully unaware of the drama that had engulfed the first-class carriage during the night. A compartment halfway down the carriage was still in darkness. Six young female students from Guangzhou were in a bad way from the food poisoning.

Belogorsky is the administrative centre of the Belogorsk district in the Amur Oblast region; just one of the twenty sparsely populated administrative districts in the area, which have seen their populations fall by over a third since the collapse of the Soviet Union. It is one of the closest stops on the line to another Russian city along the Amur, Blagoveshchensk; and its twin Chinese city on the west bank of the Amur, Heihe.

Today, in conformity with international law and practice, the navigable channel of the Amur (essentially its central point) marks the formal international boundary between China and Russia. It has long been a contested frontier between the two great Eurasian empires. A formal boundary demarcation between Russia and the

PRC was only finalised early in the 2000s, but emotionally, and in terms of nationalist feeling, it is far from settled. As the British travel writer Colin Thubron observed about the Amur, in his recent account of his journey along it from source to sea:

> I stare out ... remembering others of the earth's great rivers that carry no such tensions: the Nile, the Yangtze, the Ganges, the Amazon, the Indus ... they flow like lifeblood through their nation's heart. Only the Amur divides.[2]

Had we broken the train trip in Belogorsky and hired a car, we could have covered the 130 kilometres to Blagoveshchensk—formerly a Russian trading town with a dark history of anti-Chinese pogroms—in under two hours. In July 1900, during the Boxer Rebellion, Blagoveshchensk was the scene of a massacre by Russian Cossacks and army regulars of thousands of innocent Chinese. Boxer insurgents had fired a few rounds of artillery at the riverbanks of Blagoveshchensk and another nearby Russian town, Aigun (Aihui)—famous for the 1858 treaty that ceded all this territory north of the Amur to Russia. In response, the local Russian governor ordered the elimination of the Chinese, torching their villages and razing the town of Aigun. All the adult Chinese of Blagoveshchensk were engaged in market gardening, retail and domestic services, and 'coolie' transport—they were hardly the stuff of bloodcurdling revolutionaries. Somewhere between 5000 and 6000 died during a single incident, when Cossacks drove the entire Chinese population of the town into the powerful, fast-flowing Amur at the small downstream village of Verkhne-Blagoveshchensk. Another 7000 or so were hacked to death as the Russian army sacked villages along its banks.

Today, both governments are asking the curious to look away, saying there is 'nothing to be seen here'. As Thubron says, 'all knowledge of this slaughter has thinned into oblivion'.[3] However, a contemporary Russian account of the massacre on 16 July 1900 survives.

Some days afterwards, Aleksandr Vasilyevich Vereshchagin, a colonel in the Russian General Staff, was travelling on a steamer heading downstream from Blagoveshchensk.[4] He described seeing bloated, fish-eaten bodies bobbing along the river surface as his journey proceeded:

> Our steamer was fast overtaking a drowned man … [h]e floated face down as if immersed in deep thought … After this Chinaman we came across another one, then another one, and finally the whole width of the Amur was covered with floating bodies, as if chasing us. Clearly, these were those unfortunate ones who had been drowned in Blagoveshchensk. Having stayed a given amount of time on the bottom, they bloated and rose to the surface.
>
> 'Gentlemen! Gentlemen! Look how many of them are on the shore! Those are all Chinamen, too!' excitedly cried out a red-haired lieutenant … At this section, the left bank of the Amur protruded into the middle of the river, forming a wide and flat sandbar. And this is where the drowned corpses accumulated … It is hard to say even approximately how many floating bodies we passed that day. But based on the fact that on that single sandbar we counted a hundred and fifty of them, it is reasonable to suppose that their number was quite large.[5]

Attacks also occurred on the 'Sixty-four Villages' east of the Amur. The Sixty-four Villages had been recognised in the treaties of both Aigun and Peking. Retained by the Qing as a means of keeping its foot in the door of its former territories ceded to the Russians, and as a concession by Moscow, ethnic Manchu inhabitants were allowed to continue their hunting and fishing in the area without being subject to Russian taxes or military service.[6]

These anti-Chinese pogroms were justified at the time as reprisals for purported Boxer attacks in July 1900 on Russian infrastructure and buildings. But they were also a means for Russia to extend and strengthen its control over the region. Until July, Boxer activity had not reached Heilongjiang and the Amur, but reports of the uprisings further south had created a charged atmosphere of anxiety that, according to the often-exaggerated reports in Russian newspapers, would soon reach the Russian side of the Amur. The 'unequal treaties' of Aigun and Peking were still fresh in people's minds and feeding resentments. The extreme Russian reactions to their Chinese residents seemed also to be motivated by a sense of collective guilt, as if they were afraid of imminent revenge for taking Chinese lands.[7]

The disproportionality of the reaction also suggests embedded racism: fear and loathing of 'the Other'. As *New York Times* journalist Andrew Higgins concluded:

> the massacre was a calculated display of imperial power shaped
> by Russian attitudes at the time of racial and cultural superiority.[8]

These events are a challenge for propagandists on both sides now that the official emphasis has shifted to promoting good relations. On the Russian side, the instinct is to ignore the atrocities entirely, but this is impossible for the Chinese side, as the history is still too raw. Forgetting is simply not an option.

On the Russian side, the Blagoveshchensk Museum of Local History is silent on the massacre. On the Chinese side, the Aihui Historical Museum, just east of Heihe, displays a large painting showing Russians driving the Chinese into the river; but at the current time of cordial relations, the museum is closed to Russians, and no photos are permitted in case they are posted on social media sites. Curiously, however, explanations are in three languages: Chinese, Russian and English.[9] Its maps show Chinese territory to be deep inside Russia—the lands ceded under the Treaty of Aigun and the Convention of Peking, when more than 1 million square kilometres of territory 'were lost to Russia', according to the museum's narrative. This reality on the ground is far removed from the Chinese official position that, 'Beijing and Moscow see the evolution of their relations—from mistrust and competition to partnership and cooperation—as a model for how countries can manage their differences.'[10] The sanitisation for contemporary geopolitical needs is at odds with the locked doors of the Aihui Historical Museum.

Thubron describes its displays, when touring this museum, as 'building up into a mounting grievance against Russia'.[11] Towards the end of the display is an 'immense, accusing cyclorama', where those watching it gaze as if 'stunned':

painted in frenzied outrage … the Cossacks go heartlessly to work … the foreground, littered with corpses … blends into a vast canvas where struggling figures, as far as the eye can see, are being shot, clubbed, or hacked to death … women, men and children cringe and plead or battle vainly back … The Amur itself, awash with their heads and arms, blurs … to a horizon where the Chinese shore lies hopelessly out of reach.[12]

While Beijing today is much more concerned with directing attention towards Western imperial depredations than Russia's, historical memory of the events along the Amur is ever present. As recently as 2015, an official report by China's Ethnic Affairs Commission on Russia's expansion along the Amur River accused it of seizing more than 1 million square kilometres.[13] Chinese claims over the area of Outer Manchuria have a substantial historical basis. Until Stalin's mass deportations of ethnic Chinese from the area to Xinjiang in the 1930s, 41 per cent of the registered workforce was Chinese. It is thought the actual number would have been even higher, as many Chinese were itinerant and continually crossed the border for seasonal work.[14]

Historical grievances over lost territory continue to disturb the superficial calm around Sino-Russia relations. In July 2020, the threat that brittle nationalism would continue to bedevil the relationship became the focus of attention when Russia's embassy in Beijing naively blundered into creating a brief social media firestorm. To mark the 160th anniversary of the founding of Vladivostok after the Convention of Peking was signed, it posted a congratulatory message on Twitter. Enraged Chinese bloggers attacked Russia for having, in the nineteenth century, jumped on the 'bandwagon' of Western imperialists gobbling up Chinese territory.[15] The ultra-nationalist then editor of the *Global Times*, Hu Xijin, said the embassy's Weibo post was a reminder of the 'country's historical humiliation at the hands of foreign powers'. In response, he refused to use the customary Chinese translation of the Russian name Vladivostok, '*tongzhi dongfang*' or 'Ruler of the East', and instead used its historic Chinese name, Haishenwei.[16] The very nomenclature has a power of its own.

This approach has now become official policy. On 14 February 2023, it was decreed that for international maps to be recognised in China, they must have Chinese names instead of the more usual Russian ones: so, for example, Vladivostok became Haishenwai, and Sakhalin Island became Kuyedao. This policy will be applied to eight Russian cities in former Chinese territories in the Russian Far East.[17] By insisting on giving Chinese names to cities in certain Russian territories, Beijing is letting Moscow know that it has neither forgotten nor forgiven the loss of territories it regards as historically Chinese. It might be a stretch to suggest China is putting Russia on notice, but by putting its own stamp on the map, it is leaving little room for the outside world to doubt who sees itself as the rightful owner of these lands.

In August 2023, China's ministry of natural resources published the new official map of Chinese territory, which shows all Bolshoi Ussuriysky Island—the place where nuclear war between the Soviet Union and China was only just averted in 1969—as being part of Chinese territory. After decades of disagreement, China and Russia resolved the dispute in 2005, and the partition of the disputed island was completed by 2008. Under the deal, China received half the main island, along with some others nearby, and Russia kept the rest. Russia reiterated this when it rejected the new Chinese map in 2023. With this, it joined a long list of countries disputing territories with China. Moscow's reaction to the new official map was, however, more muted than that of other states.[18]

As it attempts to project an image of comity with the Kremlin, Beijing struggles to manage public opinion within China. In March 2023, ahead of Xi Jinping's visit to Moscow, a popular Shanghai blogger was shut down for reminding his followers of the 'unequal' treaties with Russia that ceded China's territory north of the Amur. Shanghai TV identity Zhou Libo was banned from social media platforms Weibo and Toutiao for posting that President Xi's 'Great Rejuvenation of the Chinese Nation'—the president's signature project—was incomplete for not including the recovery of lands lost to Russia in the nineteenth century.[19]

Xi has sought to make stronger relations with Russia a defining element of his foreign policy. To demonstrate this, his first overseas visit as China's president was to Moscow in March 2013, just one week after his confirmation as president. Xi's motivations were a mix of admiration for Putin's standing up to US pressures; the prospect of mutual support for authoritarian governments in challenging the existing dominant liberal world order; the need to reinforce Beijing's geostrategic interests in Core Eurasia; and, perhaps, some lingering nostalgia for the role the old Soviet Union played in establishing Communist China in the decade after 1949. He said Russia and China were 'most important strategic partners', who 'spoke a common language'.[20] While Putin responded by hailing Russia and China cooperation to fashion a more just world order, he demonstrated complete disregard for the history of the relationship and Chinese sensitivities in the state gift he had specially prepared for Xi. He presented him with a commemorative copy of the CPSU's official newspaper, *Pravda*, of 14 February 1950, announcing the signing by Stalin and Mao of the Sino-Soviet Treaty of Friendship, Alliance and Mutual Assistance. This was the Valentine's Day Treaty, so hated by Mao as an 'unequal treaty' for the concessions he had to make to Stalin over Xinjiang and Mongolia, hidden away in secret annexes.[21]

Consistency in grand strategy is not always to be expected. But the inconsistency between Beijing's endless recitation of nineteenth century grievances against the West, and its other territorial claims—such as regarding Taiwan, and with Japan over the Diaoyu/Senkaku Islands in the East China Sea, and regarding its frontier with India—serve to draw attention, by comparison, to the vastly greater territory China has 'lost' to Russia. The more Beijing rails about the former lost territories, the more this inevitably attracts attention to the Russian depredations, and the less convincing Beijing's dance with Moscow becomes. Beijing is at risk of being hoist with its own petard. At a dinner I attended in 2023 in Beijing, attended by retired and semi-retired Chinese professionals in their late sixties, it was striking how cynical they were about discussion of 'national rejuvenation' without including the lands occupied by Russia. Each participant knew to the square kilometre the territory ceded in the nineteenth century and sought its return. It was felt to be just a matter of time. Schoolchildren even today are taught that China

lost 1 million square kilometres of Manchuria to Russia, and that
Chairman Mao had said that one day China would 'present the bill
to Russia' for the territories it had stolen.[22] As has been observed
recently, the 'Sino-Russian partnership might have "no limits", but it
does have a shelf life'.[23]

Thubron, on his travels along the Amur, kept meeting ancient
visceral hatreds on both sides of the border, supported by ignorance,
prejudice and ill-informed stereotypes. Vladik, a local Russian driver,
tells Thubron that in his hometown of Mogoytuy, 'everyone gets
along okay—Russians, Buryats, immigrant Uzbeks, even Baptists—
but we all hate the Chinese'.[24] A Cossack descendant in Albazin,
Alexi, tells Thubron how Cossacks are needed to defend the borders
from China. When Thubron says the borders 'don't need guarding
now as Russia and China are at peace', Alexi replies, 'But we have to
be prepared. Always! The Chinese can't be trusted … We can never
be sure. Never!'[25] This is a fragile peace.

In 2015, a documentary called *China—a deadly friend* went viral on
the social media sites Russians use. The Russian-made movie played
on the locals' deeply held xenophobia about China taking over the
Russian Far East. Recent growth in Chinese direct foreign investment
in the area and the consequent influx of workers associated with this
have elevated anxieties. The apocalyptic documentary sensationalised
what was feared. It showed China preparing to invade, in its quest for
global dominance. Chinese PLA tanks were depicted ready to reach
the centre of the city of Khabarovsk within thirty minutes. Anxiety
that every Chinese immigrant 'might be a spy' is also regularly stoked
by 'alarmist' local newspapers.[26]

In 2010, when I visited Heihe on an official trip—and therefore
was unable to travel to Blagoveshchensk because of visa restrictions—
the Chinese city comprised mainly late-nineteenth and mid-
twentieth century buildings. Attesting to earlier Russian and Soviet
influences, it felt more European than Chinese, and the architecture
looked to be a poorer cousin to the more ornamental-style buildings
that could be glimpsed across the Amur in Russia. Typically of
commercial frontier towns, a mardi gras of ethnicities—Chinese,
Tartars, Uyghurs, Kazakhs, Koreans—paraded the streets. These cities

had long been a major commercial link between China and Russia in the otherwise isolated and sparsely populated northeast of China. Then, as now, goods from Russia were mainly natural and resource based—farm produce, fish, furs and skins—and goods from China were manufactured. Chinese family-owned trading firms provided the services infrastructure to support trade in both directions. During my trip, a deputy mayor put on a grand breakfast as an official welcome for me, with meat, fish, eggs, black bread, porridge, tea, fruit juices, milk and coffee, washed down with beer. He was in an expansive mood and his daughter was studying in Melbourne, my home city. He spoke enthusiastically of China–Russia friendship and the great commercial opportunities that improved relations would bring Heihe. Judging from Thubron's account of the city a decade later, it seems to have prospered as the deputy mayor had anticipated, having since transformed into a high-rise replica of larger southern cities in China. The first road bridge across the Amur connecting China and Russia only opened in June 2022; it is between Heihe and Blagoveshchensk. More are planned.[27] The obvious physical comparison of the city of Heihe leaving its Russian cousins behind would add to the prevailing Russian anxiety over China: a constant reminder of the ever-increasing disparities between the two countries and a cameo of the power shifts of recent times.

In the past, Stalin's fear of China saw the USSR constructing along this section of the Amur, from Chita in the west to Khabarovsk, the world's longest fortified border, comprising some 2000 kilometres of 'barbed wire and raked soil'. The latter was so that telltale footprints, warning of potential breaches of security, might be spotted.[28] Thubron felt as if the whole border with China was hermetically sealed, seeing 'steel watch towers [for] mile after mile [with] gibbet-like posts linked in barbed wire … snaking into the distance'.[29]

In 1891, Tsar Nicholas II, on his final tour of empire as heir to the throne, visited Albazin, which was the last Russian-controlled town on the Amur at the time of the Treaty of Nerchinsk, before the siege and obliteration of its fort by the Manchus in 1691. Albazin had taken on mythical dimensions as a place of Russian resistance to China. Further along the Amur, Tsar Nicholas II's visit is marked at Aigun, where all the land lost at Nerchinsk nearly two hundred years earlier was recovered by the eponymous treaty in 1858, with a plaque in old Cyrillic script on a big boulder 'confirming Russian power on the Amur.' [30] As if still uneasy and uncertain about their control over these lands, the plaque is in fact modern, dating from 2015; the Cyrillic script was used to create the illusion of permanent control since historic times. At nearby Blagoveshchensk, the tsar's 1891 visit is marked by a vaulting memorial arch, which declares, 'The Amur was, is and will always be Russian'.

Thubron summarises the mutual incomprehension along the Amur thus:

> Today's economic penetration arouses an old apprehension. The Chinese remain profoundly alien. Almost no local Russians learn their language or travel their hinterland. Yet the Chinese they see are no longer the flotsam of a failed empire, but the citizens of a formidable nation … although few people fear sudden invasion, an anxiety exists—a subdued fatalism—that in some unknown future Beijing will transform its economic ownership into political sovereignty, and that the Russia Far East will become a Chinese province. [31]

At the local level in Russia, the China Threat is alive and well.

## Never Mind the Rhetoric

By late next morning on the Trans-Siberian Express to Ulan-Ude, the condition of one of the young women from Guangzhou had become so serious that when we arrived at Karymsky station a Soviet-era ambulance and medical crew were waiting to board the train. She was given an injection of something, and her recovery was nothing short of miraculous. Her friends were delighted that, within an hour, she went from looking like death warmed up to her appetite showing signs of recovery.

The days on the train, though, were long and mostly boring. Apart from when we were seated in the first-class dining car, alcohol consumption was banned, and, even in the dining car, only drinks purchased there, and with food, could be consumed. Not only was everything outrageously expensive, but the offerings were limited to local beers served at room temperature, and Georgian red wines that had sugar levels hovering somewhere above either port wine, or a warm, sticky, fizzy white wine. My Australian travelling companions and I had loaded up with various wines and, being in Russia, we naturally had included a variety of attractively packaged local vodkas in our stash. So, it was with some dismay that we discovered the train was mostly dry and the rules policed, although we never quite learned the punishment. To avoid detection, one of us would linger in the passageway outside the compartment door—deflecting the odd local drunk who wandered by, looking to engage the foreigners with his unintelligible rant—and give the warning of 'Red fox': that one of the babushkas was on the way. This helped pass the day, as did regular visits to the dining car. These were not about eating, as we had ample provisions in our bags aside from the smuggled alcohol, but to have fun with the babushkas and break the monotony of the trip. On our last night, we finally purchased the local 'champagne', which they had been urging us to do, and shared it with the stout, peroxided, and heavily made up and perfumed babushkas, who enjoyed the fun and distraction as much as we did.

During that fog-blanketed evening, we would have gone near but not through Nerchinsk, missing out on seeing the location where the treaty achieved geopolitical stability along the Russia–Manchu frontier for nearly two centuries. As the sun rose, we slowed to pass the junction with the Trans-Manchurian branch line, a 900-kilometre shortcut from the much longer Trans-Siberian line that we were on, through what had formerly been Chinese territory. In 1902, the tsar forced this concession on the feeble Manchu empire.[32]

The morning also brought relief from the tedium of days travelling through flat, marshy taiga country. The train was beginning to ascend lush valleys in the Dauraky Mountains. We stopped at Chita long enough for a stretch and to smoke a cigar. We had covered from Vladivostok to Chita in three days and nights of constant movement; clacking, rocking, swaying and the banging of steel on steel for some 2800 kilometres. Chita was where, in 1945, Puyi was taken when the

Soviets abducted him at Mukden (Shenyang) airport as he attempted to flee China for Japan.[33] Ulan-Ude was our last stop, before driving south to Mongolia for a two-hour border crossing, which gave ample time to see, but not comprehend, the bureaucracies of both countries.

Lake Baikal is the world's deepest lake, a cornucopia of rare wildlife and abundant natural beauty. Next to the lake, a sprawling, abandoned and semi-ruined dream of a Chinese luxury tourist resort lies, seemingly as a monument to Russian and Chinese mutual incomprehension; a forlorn statement of just how far removed the people of China and Russia are from each other, despite being neighbours. Built in the early 2000s by an ambitious property developer, the hope was it would attract large numbers of wealthy Chinese to Lake Baikal. But they did not come, and the business eventually folded. Since then, the lake has become the focus of renewed Russia–China tensions, as well as now facing severe environmental challenges from surrounding land use, lack of sewerage systems, and chemical discharges.

On the opposite shore of Lake Baikal, in the small town of Listvyanka, dissension has arisen regarding Chinese investments in real estate and other businesses. In 2019, for example, a proposal by a Russian company to build a Chinese-funded water bottling plant led to anti-Chinese protests and an online campaign, which attracted over 1 million signatures, opposing the plant. The local courts eventually stepped in and suspended the project, which has since been cancelled.[34]

Recent initiatives may one day revive the fortunes of the Chinese-funded Lake Baikal resort village. In May 2023, as part of the political leaders' attempts to forge a closer relationship between the two countries, it was agreed that a transport corridor would be opened between Jilin province in China's northeast and Vladivostok, and that Vladivostok would be classified as a domestic Chinese transhipment port for goods bound for Zhejiang province in China's south. When it is operating, this will be the first time China's northeast has had access to a Pacific port since Russia annexed the territory east of the Ussuri River in 1860, with the Convention of Peking after the Second Opium War. It signals that Russia will more actively engage with China in developing the Russian Far East. Post the invasion of Ukraine, political constraints on Japan and South Korea arising from US-led international sanctions will curtail their commercial involvement there, leaving the Russian Far East even more dependent on Chinese trade, investment and entrepreneurship.[35] While this is certainly a noteworthy development, what sticks out is just how modest the initiative is, especially when it is stood against the soaring rhetoric of the leaders on both sides.

The opening of the Jilin–Vladivostok transport corridor is likely to expand trade flows only gradually. By road, Dalian is still the closest major port for much of Jilin province, and its cities and towns, unlike in Russia, are linked by modern six-lane freeways and high-speed trains. The distance from the capital, Changchun, is 677 kilometres, compared with 803 kilometres to Vladivostok. When the corridor is eventually extended to Heilongjiang province, as is inevitable, it will almost halve the road distance from Harbin to Vladivostok (508 kilometres), compared with Harbin to Dalian (930 kilometres). Over time, economic integration between Chinese and Russian Manchuria can be expected to spread and deepen. In view of the potential complementarities between the Russian Far East's natural resource-based industries and northeast China's manufacturing, the commercial opportunities are substantial. Whether they are realised or not will depend on how well those things that for so long have dragged on the relationship are managed: local animosities, nationalism, and strategic suspicion by Moscow, and how third countries view the geoeconomics of the region. Again, though, these measures to open the Russian Far East to China are still modest at best, especially in light of proclaimed ambitions.

Yet, already, Moscow is displaying its unease about deepening China's involvement in the Russian Far East. To balance China's potential for exercising outsized influence in the region, it has begun courting greater Indian presence there. In 2019, Russia and India signed a memorandum of understanding to establish the Vladivostok-Chennai Maritime Corridor. Since 2019, India has been investing in gas supplies from the region, which will go through Vladivostok. In 2021, an agreement was reached to build jointly in Vladivostok large vessels suitable for the gas trade.[36] Prime Minister Modi's first overseas visit after his 2024 re-election was to Moscow. Among the high-priority isues for discussion was the Vladivostok-Chennai Maritime Corridor. Both New Delhi and Moscow were signalling to Beijing that they were intent on balancing China.[37]

The VCMC was formalised in an agreement on 23 June 2023. While it involves construction of dedicated port infrastructure in Vladivostok, other aspects of how exactly it will expand trade beyond existing shipping arrangements remain vague. It does, however, underscore the determination of both governments to deepen commercial engagement between India and the Russian Far East. The VCMC is foreshadowed to be an arrangement for transporting metallurgical coal, gas and agricultural products from Russia to India. It will also mean greater Indian shipping through the South China Sea, raising strategic sensitivities between India and China in this region. But, for some time, the significance of the VCMC will mainly be its strategic messaging to Beijing by both Russia and India. Despite China's enormous natural advantages in the Russian Far East, and Russia's need for Chinese investment and markets, expansion of China's influence there will be contested.

China will inevitably become the dominant influence in the Russian Far East through trade, investment, immigration and large-scale infrastructure projects. How far and deep Moscow permits this to go will have a significant impact on the strategic balance for the northwest Pacific. So far, however, Putin's rhetoric about welcoming China to develop the region has not been matched with action. Most likely, because of local sensitivities and resentments, Moscow will continue to hedge its bets on Chinese engagement there.

# CHAPTER 8

# CHUSSIA'S FEET OF CLAY

*'China needs to dissolve itself in Eurasia the way Germany dissolved itself in the EU—*
*otherwise, we'll have problems.'*

Sergei Karaganov, leading academic proponent of the pivot to the East and
senior policy guru for Putin, 2022[1]

Beijing essentially sees Russia as an inherently expansionist power, and racist in its attitudes and reflexes towards China. Moscow has existential anxieties over vast numbers of Chinese occupying the expansive, productive but empty lands of the Russian Far East. Their respective approaches to achieving security—buffer states versus client states—are also at odds.[2] Yet recent geopolitical realities have drawn China and Russia closer together—especially their desire to push back against the US and reshape the liberal international order.

With relations being closer between Russia and China, a school of thought—which has found support in the White House—has emerged that there is a single theatre of strategic competition: liberal democracies versus autocracies. It is easy to see the appeal of this formulation, both in its simplicity and its powerful invocation of the binary ideological struggle of the Cold War. But viewing the world order as a struggle between might and right, without acknowledging the nuances and subtleties between different countries, runs the risk of increasing the chances of conflict. This 'new Cold War' is giving rise to the very same kind of reductionist geopolitical thinking as its predecessor.[3]

Ambitions for a new strategic alliance between China and Russia, as a counterweight to the US-led West, gained momentum after

Xi Jinping's elevation in 2012. Deng Xiaoping's policy of 'biding time, concealing strengths'—that is, not to confront the US—would always have a limited shelf life. It would only be a matter of time before China, with its economic growth, would feel strong enough to assert itself forcefully in its foreign policy. Xi Jinping, by virtue of his background in the Party and his own attitudes, was the person to reset China's relations with the West, and challenge the Washington Consensus of a perpetually politically liberalising and economically globalising world.[4]

The globalising assumption once held by influential sections of the US policy elite found its fullest expression in then deputy secretary of state Robert Zoellick's call in 2005 for China to become a 'responsible stakeholder' in the international system. This was inspired but fundamentally flawed. Zoellick saw China participating in the US-led international system as a constructive, helpful member, essentially sustaining the post–World War II Bretton Woods order. For China, and especially Xi Jinping, this meant supporting a system it had no role in shaping, and doing so as a junior partner. It was naive to think that as China grew more powerful it would accept this position.

With Xi's elevation to CPC general secretary and president, all that changed. China's time had come, and Beijing was determined to shape the international system in its own interests. Soon after Xi's elevation, China's diplomacy became more muscular and assertive, especially in the 'near-abroad': Taiwan, Japan and the South China Sea.[5] The anti-Western narrative plays out well in China, by emphasising its material success, independence and, most importantly, the respect it has earned. When it comes to the advanced countries of the world, China also wants to be seen as first among equals.

At around the same time, Putin came to the view that the West was determined to contain Russia, especially with the eastern expansion of NATO's membership. This was a shift by Putin, from Russia acting more as a status quo power to being more of a revisionist one. In 1998, Russia had become a fully participating member of the G7, which then became the G8, and, in 2006, hosted its summit in St Petersburg. Also in 1998, it became a member of the APEC grouping, although it was not until 2012 that it joined the WTO.

Early in the 2000s, Putin backed the US-led 'war on terror' under President George W Bush. As noted earlier, following the 9/11 attacks on the World Trade Center, and despite Beijing's displeasure, Putin supported the US deploying forces at former Soviet air bases in Uzbekistan, Kyrgyzstan and Tajikistan, from which to attack Afghanistan. Putin's embrace of the West ended in 2014, when Russia annexed Crimea, although tensions with the West had been rising since its invasion of Georgia. Russia was permanently expelled from the G8 and the West imposed limited sanctions on Russia. The message was clear: Russia and the liberal West were now in conflict. Putin then turned 'east' and Xi was waiting to welcome him.[6]

## Putin's Pivot to the East

Since 2012, when Putin announced his 'pivot to the East' and Xi Jinping ascended to the top of the Chinese leadership, China and Russia have uneasily accommodated each other. Bilateral cooperation has been extended and expanded across many spheres, including joint military and naval exercises, and extensive training and exchanges between internal security services. Outside these areas, Russia has grudgingly accepted something of a junior-partner role, recognising the size of the Chinese economy, and China's importance as a market for Russian energy exports, and as a source of investment in the energy and transport sectors. Post the Ukraine invasion and consequent imposition of Western trade sanctions, their previously modest trade flows have soared. For its part, China has been generally supportive of Russia when it comes to sanctions or its ambitions in the Middle East; although, more recently, China has begun to play a larger role, as it did when it brokered the Saudi–Iran diplomatic agreement of March 2023.[7]

## 'Friendship without Limits'

In February 2022, twenty days before Russia's invasion of Ukraine, Putin was in the Chinese capital for the opening of the Beijing Winter Olympics but also, and much more importantly, for a bilateral meeting with Xi. The Chinese leader would not have realised quite how historically significant that meeting would become.

Xi was at the height of his anti-Western antagonism in foreign policy, and hubris domestically. At that moment, seemingly against the odds, China gained control over Covid-19. While China was closed to much of the outside world, it was largely business as usual within it. The economy was beginning to recover, while the West was either still comprehensively locked down or, as in the UK and US, having relaxed many restrictions, needing to manage large numbers of cases. Xi had also prevailed in what had been, throughout 2020–22, a titanic public relations struggle over the origins and causes of Covid-19: in short, the lab-leak theory versus the wet-market theory, with the former implying secret biological weapons programs—or even deliberate intent on Beijing's behalf, as some would have it.[8] A year earlier, the US (by the narrowest of margins and in an election that was still contested by the defeated Trump forces) installed in the White House an elderly gentleman whose first major foreign policy action was the unilateral withdrawal of the US, and consequently NATO forces, from Afghanistan. NATO was increasingly divided against itself and adrift in terms of its mission after the Trump years, to the point that the French president, Emmanuel Macron, described it as 'brain dead'.[9]

In an *Australian Foreign Affairs* article, commissioned soon after Putin's invasion and published in October 2022, I described the 4 February Putin–Xi statement that the relationship between Russia and China knew 'no limits' as merely a concert of convenience. I compared it with the 1939 Molotov–Ribbentrop Pact, signed by two powers that understood their divergent strategic interests would, at some time, draw them into conflict. In the West, the Putin–Xi statement was widely misinterpreted. The surprise and dismay with which their statement was met ignored the fact that China and Russia, like Nazi Germany and the Soviet Union in the 1930s, are strategic competitors. Putin was seeking China's complicity in his intended criminality in Ukraine, and, if needed, the security to cut his massive forces in the east, directed at China. He achieved both, but the price has been Russia, over time, assuming a role of junior partner to China.

The China–Russia joint statement also sat comfortably with Xi's anti-Western narrative. This had become much more pronounced in the run-up to the crucial twentieth party congress in October 2022, when Xi's term in office was to be extended. The close relationship with Russia, and the publicly projected personal rapport between the leaders, would have been seen as a plus for Xi among conservative elements in the CPC. That Xi could be seen to be forging a unified anti-Western partnership with Russia had wide appeal, especially among China's numerous social media nationalists. Elites beyond CPC conservatives, however, had misgivings that Xi was positioning China as being too close to Russia and against the US. The subsequent heightening of geopolitical competition with the US and, increasingly, forceful US-led sanctions on high-tech trade with China have led to further misgivings about Xi's adroitness in handling great power relations.[10]

The eye-catching headline statement that the China–Russia friendship knew 'no limits' was predictably presented in China as a great diplomatic achievement for Xi. It meant the existential threat that Russia had always posed to China was postponed indefinitely, allowing China more time to consolidate and extend its dominance over Central Asia and, ultimately, its power over Russia. That was until 24 February 2022. China was then forced to choose awkwardly between its newly minted special relationship with Russia, and the cornerstone of its foreign policy: non-interference.[11]

## The Ukraine Invasion

In 2014, Russia's annexation of Crimea was a key geopolitical event. For the first time since the Soviet Union collapsed, there was a direct challenge by a rising power against the dominant powers of NATO. Russia had been applying increasing pressure on Ukraine; nationalists had never accepted its independence after the dissolution of the Soviet Union. Putin has said that the breakup of the Soviet Union was the greatest tragedy ever to befall Russia. He was putting it above the 'heroic' losses of World War II, making this the new organising principle of his nationalist appeal for broad support. In March 2007, his speech in Munich to the annual Organization for Security and Co-operation in Europe conference, as much as it shocked Western observers, was a defining moment for Russian foreign policy and relations with the West. This address, in which Putin criticised the US's dominance in global relations, has come to be seen as foreshadowing the 2022 invasion of Ukraine. Washington and NATO continued to ignore Putin's warnings about extending NATO to Russia's borders.[12] As British historian of modern Russia, Mark Smith, observed, years before the invasion, this reinforced Russia's view that international organisations and the 'complicated and institutionalized successors of the Concert of Europe … simply do not accept Russian interests as legitimate'.[13]

Putin's February visit to Beijing took place against the backdrop of his amassing invasion forces along Ukraine's borders. Notwithstanding the White House releasing intelligence that showed an invasion would in fact occur, the enormity of the action, were it to happen, engendered a sense of disbelief among most capitals. The reaction of Beijing to the invasion suggests strongly that it too was caught short, again, by Putin's audacity. At the time, it was asserted that at Beijing's request, Putin delayed the invasion until after the closing of the games. He met Xi in Beijing on 4 February, their thirty-eighth bilateral meeting, but these were more often on the margins of other international meetings. The closing ceremony of the games was on 20 February; on the following day, Putin ordered more troops into insurgent controlled areas of eastern Ukraine; and then, on 22 February, according to the *New York Times*, he made a 'furious' speech about Ukraine, in which he said it should be part of Russia. By early on 24 February, the full-scale invasion began, under the rubric 'special operation'.

As China–Russia relations expert Bobo Lo argued, Beijing was taken by surprise; at least at the scale of the attack, as demonstrated by its 'haphazard public diplomacy' immediately afterwards, and that it had made no prior preparations to remove over 6000 Chinese students who were stranded by the invasion.[14] Despite some initial speculation in the West, it is unlikely that Putin confided in Xi as to his plans to invade, especially the timing. Westad's assertion that Xi 'gave Putin a green light to invade' so long as it was after the Winter Olympics is without foundation.[15] A detailed survey of intelligence sources conducted by the *New York Times* soon after the invasion was inconclusive, but found no evidence to support the suggestion that

Xi was aware an invasion was imminent. That Putin was marshalling his assets for an invasion was known to all. Like many European governments, Beijing was sceptical.[16]

The *New York Times* reported some speculation that lower-level Chinese officials may have requested through diplomatic channels that Putin not invade before the conclusion of the Beijing Winter Olympics on 22 February, to avoid repeating the embarrassment caused to Beijing by Putin's invasion of Georgia at the start of the 2008 Summer Olympics. This does not itself support the view that at least some Chinese officials knew in advance. Rather, since it was being widely speculated that an invasion would occur, it would be prudent for officials to ensure that Putin understood the sensitivities on the Chinese side over precise timing and to avoid a clash with the Olympics.[17]

The invasion by Russia was both symptomatic of the changed order and a product of it. Russia did what it did because it could. Moreover, it has not flinched despite massive coordinated Western sanctions. With the rise of China, and authoritarian states being more assertive in the face of declining US influence, a form of multipolarity has returned. Whatever its outcome, the war in Europe is likely to leave China in a stronger position than it was before Putin's invasion.[18] It is also changing China–Russia dynamics and will continue to do so for some time. It reinforces the trend that had long been underway of China's ascendency over Russia; and, also, the direction of change in the world order that China has been determined to bring about by challenging US primacy.

Xi, like Putin, would have been alarmed at the solidarity, sense of purpose and determination the West found following the invasion of Ukraine. European states had long accommodated Putin's malicious behaviour: from poisoning adversaries on foreign soil; to Russia's aggression in Georgia, Crimea and eastern Ukraine. As Putin was amassing troops on the Ukraine border, the West was acrimoniously at odds over the Afghanistan debacle.

Against this background, the speed, coordination and forcefulness of the West's response would have emphatically reminded Xi of China's own vulnerability to coordinated action by it. The energy and financial sanctions demonstrated that the West was prepared to bear substantial costs in defence of basic international norms.

For China's leadership, this is especially worrying, as it is much more deeply integrated in the international economic system than is Russia: from trade and investment flows, holding of foreign government bonds and integration of global supply chains; to elite family fortunes stashed overseas, Chinese families resident in the West, reliance on Western education and research, and much more. Unlike Russia, China also faces a significant strategic vulnerability. Among other things, it is the world's biggest importer of crude oil, liquefied natural gas (LNG) and iron ore. These are shipped mainly via the Strait of Malacca—one of the world's most vulnerable transport choke points—and the South China Sea. A concerted effort by the West to block these transport routes would, in a heartbeat, deny China access to the raw materials and energy it needs, and bring the country's economy to its knees.[19]

China's attitude to Putin's invasion of Ukraine was further complicated by having a rare, for China, security pact with Ukraine, and a 'special relationship' with Kyiv, with substantial commercial underpinnings.[20] Military cooperation between the countries was also substantial. China's first aircraft carrier, the *Liaoning*, for example, was purchased from Ukraine. Beijing, rather awkwardly, has been attempting to play both sides of the conflict, while its failure to condemn the invasion unequivocally has also brought China into direct discord with the West. China was, however, in good company with the West's new ally, India, which also continued to trade with Russia, benefit from its cheaper energy and buy arms. India, it seems, may have gone significantly further than China in supporting Russia against Western sanctions, including processing Russian crude oil and selling it on to third parties, among them the US. As reported by CNN, this would be hugely embarrassing for Washington, as it has gone to great lengths to court India as a counterweight to China.[21] To emphasise the importance of Russia to India, and underline India's determination to remain aloof from the West, Prime Minister Modi's first overseas trip after his re-election in June 2024 was to visit Putin in Moscow.[22]

By late 2023, China's share of Russia's crude oil exports had risen from 5 per cent to 45–50 per cent. India's share had similarly risen, and accounted for 40 per cent in 2023. By the end of 2023, China and India together accounted for around 90 per cent of Russia's oil exports, compared with Europe's 4 per cent, down from 45 per cent pre-2022; thereby helping Russia circumvent Western sanctions on its main export.[23] In 2023, bilateral trade rose some 30 per cent. Both Moscow and Beijing congratulated themselves that they had reached a year early the target set by leaders in February 2022 of $US200 billion total bilateral trade. Putin attributed this to the close friendship he had with Xi. At the same time, Xi Jinping's ambitions to 'de-dollarize' the international payments system received a boost, with 95 per cent of trade between China and Russia conducted in each other's currency, but predominately settled with Chinese yuan. By the end of 2023, about 40 per cent of Russia's forex reserves were held in renminbi (RMB).[24]

Russia's imports from China are also diversifying rapidly, especially autos and advance manufacturing machinery. China's exports of vehicles have increased fivefold since sanctions were applied in 2022, and by the end of 2023 accounted for 20 per cent of China's exports to Russia. Chery and BYD vehicles are beginning to replace BMWs and Mercedes on the streets of Moscow, reflected in the 44 per cent fall in German exports to Russia in 2023. Despite this diversification in the composition of trade, hydrocarbons will continue to dominate and remain the major component of China's imports from Russia. LNG imports are forecast to expand substantially in the coming years, as several major transcontinental pipelines are completed. In December 2023, at the conclusion of the twentieth meeting of the bilateral high-level China–Russia Energy Cooperation Committee, both sides committed to deepening and expanding cooperation.[25]

Although China and India are throwing Putin a financial lifeline by purchasing hydrocarbons that have now been substantially barred from the formerly major European market, it is entirely in their respective economic interests to be doing so, whatever the geopolitics suggest. Putin has hailed the growing energy trade between Russia and China as an expression of the close bilateral relationship between the two, and while the public rhetoric is effusive, the commercial considerations are hard-headed. As a result of Western sanctions, according to a detailed Reuters analysis of price data, China saved $US4.34 billion in the first nine months of 2023, by importing Russian crude oil. In December 2022, Russia's crude oil export price was capped at $US60 per barrel under Western sanctions. LNG is transported to China by the Power of Siberia pipeline, but this is not part of, nor connected to, the western network, so cannot be used to divert surplus gas from Europe to China. A second pipeline— Power of Siberia 2—which would connect the western and eastern networks, has been under discussion between Russia and China for years, with little progress on terms and threshold issues such as equity shares. During Putin's February 2022 visit to Beijing, an agreement was signed that Russia would supply China with 10 billion cubic metres of LNG per year for thirty years. Again, the devil is in the detail, and negotiations over prices and other issues are continuing.[26] During Putin's visit to Beijing in May 2024, his first overseas trip after his re-election, the Power of Siberia 2 was once more said to be a priority issue for him, but progress was still not made.[27]

China's efforts to balance its interests between Russia and the West in the light of the Ukraine invasion have come at a cost to its foreign relations, especially with Europe. At its 2022 Madrid summit, NATO was careful to distinguish China from Russia, by not naming it an 'adversary', while for the first time classifying China as a 'strategic challenge to its security and values'. Because of China's unwillingness to condemn Russia, its bullying diplomacy and military assertiveness, and ongoing commercial antagonisms, NATO now believes it has entered an era of strategic competition with China. NATO has expanded and deepened its outreach activities with countries such as South Korea, Australia and India.[28] Although China's ambivalence over the invasion of Ukraine is not the sole reason, Xi's foreign policy management, especially with respect to Ukraine, finds China facing a far more hostile international environment than it did at the beginning of Xi's term. At the July 2024 NATO Summit in Washington, the leaders' communique significantly hardened its language on China's support for Russia's war in Ukraine, calling China 'a decisive enabler' because of the equipment it is accused of supplying.[29] It also said that developments in the Indo-Pacific directly affected Euro-Atlantic security, a declaration aimed squarely at China.

Unwittingly, the CPC also now finds itself riding the tiger of Russia politically. From the China leadership's perspective, where the CPC is the institutional mechanism through which power is maintained and exercised, Putin's singular leadership supported by a cabal of oligarchs must look to be a high-wire act, replete with risks and uncertainties. The brief rebellion in 2023 by the leader of the Wagner mercenary group, Yevgeny Prigozhin, and his subsequent assassination via the blowing of up his aircraft, would have confirmed the Chinese leadership's view of the inherent instability of Putin's rule. This would make them increasingly nervous and uncomfortable about hitching their foreign policy and strategic interests to his clique.[30] As Bobo Lo puts it, Putin's 'personalised authoritarianism' is very different from the CPC's institutionalised bureaucratic rule.[31]

For now, however, China will support Putin publicly. Nevertheless, Beijing will see that Putin has been weakened by his ill-judged invasion of Ukraine and its flawed execution; and the internally led revolt against his leadership by a close lieutenant whom he created, albeit a revolt that was short lived. Meanwhile, as Russian analyst Alexander Duben writes:

> As a consequence of the Ukraine war, a relatively isolated Moscow has already become unprecedentedly dependent on China, especially in economic and technological terms, a process that is increasingly turning Russia into something resembling a Chinese client state. In the aftermath of the abortive Wagner revolt, Russia will likely become even more structurally dependent on China than it already was.[32]

### Chussia and its Contradictions

China and Russia's embrace is both opportunistic—involving trade, investment, energy and arms—and strategic, to refashion the international order to make it accommodate authoritarian states.

Regime security is paramount for both Beijing and Moscow. They share an existential fear of 'colour revolutions' like the democratic movements in some former Soviet republics after the collapse of the USSR, which they see as US-sponsored attempts at regime change. Their obsession with regime security binds them together, despite many differences. Although his revolt was not a 'coloured revolution', Prigozhin's incandescent arc over several days before flaming out alarmed Moscow and Beijing equally, highlighting potential regime instability and vulnerability. Both China and Russia are also sanctioned by the West, and their diplomatic relations with it are in urgent need of repair. Both leaders are also drawn together by a sour antipathy towards the US. Talk, accompanied by actions, from both Beijing and Moscow of forging a new, fairer world order resonates well with the Global South.[33] For its part, the West is alarmed at the prospect of authoritarian China and Russia working in concert against it. This is what I call the 'Chussia anxiety' in the West: China and Russia working hand in glove against liberal democracies. To whatever extent the current leadership also believes this to be possible, it is the triumph of hope over experience in the Kremlin and Zhongnanhai.

In view of the history of mistrust, populist nationalist territorial ambitions on both sides, and China's deep engagement with the West, Beijing required a narrative to explain the new frothiness in its relationship with Russia, but one that would not alarm the West. This was supplied by former senior diplomat Fu Ying, then chairwoman of the Foreign Affairs Committee of the 12th National People's Congress, a ministerial-level appointment. In a *Foreign Affairs* article in 2016, which would have been personally approved by Xi Jinping, she explained that the relationship between China, Russia and the US was that of a 'scalene triangle' of great powers, but that the side connecting China and Russia was shorter than the one connecting either the US and China, or the US and Russia. So, in this official world view, China and Russia were closer to each other than either was to the US. Fu argued that China and Russia would 'work together on areas of agreement in ways that supported global order and decreased the chance that the world would descend into great power conflict and war'.[34]

This official account sought to position China as something of a balancing element between Russia and the US. The West was unconvinced by this; moreover, when the time came, China's failure to condemn Russia's invasion of Ukraine made its position of being a 'friend to all and enemy of none' much harder to sustain. Fu's conclusion that Beijing and Moscow's relationship provided a model of how the world can avoid descending into great power conflict looks especially hollow following the invasion. Putin's tanks rolled over the cornerstone of China's security and foreign policy: non-interference. With this, Putin has seriously harmed the trust so essential to building a close relationship. Just as the Brezhnev Doctrine justified Soviet military intervention in communist states, including Afghanistan at the time, so Putin's imperial ambitions alarm former Soviet republics and challenge China.

Fu's scalene triangle was intended to present a benign world view, to salve anxieties in the West about an emerging authoritarian Chussia. It also posited China and Russia as co-equal powers, which, by 2015, was already no longer the case: Russia faced increasing sanctions and isolation from the West, and its economy massively underperformed China's. Moreover, Chussia becoming a stable reality in great power relations would require high levels of trust between China and Russia, and a strong convergence of interests. The former is tenuous at best, while the latter is fractured.

Rather than stand side by side with its comrade gainst Western sanctions following the Ukraine invasion, China has in fact adopted a cautious approach, distancing itself from Putin's actions, especially after Russia's early military setbacks. Beijing is extremely wary of being sanctioned by the West for undermining its actions against Russia. Chinese firms that were suspected of contributing, albeit indirectly, to Russia's war effort were quickly identified, and punished or threatened with sanctions. Although the West is upset that China has not done more to put pressure on Moscow, which it could clearly do, as could India and other major states such as Turkey,

Beijing's actions have been far less than Putin would have expected from his closest friend, Xi Jinping.

Since 22 February 2022, Beijing has signed no new long-term hydrocarbon purchase contracts; it has not invested in the upstream sector to maintain and expand production capacity as Western firms have exited; and, although it has increased oil imports, benefiting from the price cap, this trade has been conducted via third parties or non-state-owned Chinese firms. It also has not used its state-owned tanker fleet, and neither has it provided alternative shipping insurance.[35] As would be expected from a rational actor, Beijing has sat on the fence, taking a wait-and-see approach, accepting the benefits of cheaper hydrocarbons, while balancing this with its self-centred interests regarding the West. All the while, the longer the war drags on in Europe, power shifts to Beijing and strengthens its negotiating position with Russia on all these vital energy matters.

A third, but seldom discussed, perspective on Chussia's prospects is that China's ambitions far exceed managing a stable relationship with Russia in support of a more authoritarian world order. China is a Eurasian power and, historically, Eurasia has mostly been dominated by a single major power—it will seek its security by becoming the pre-eminent Eurasian power. China's land frontiers have been its key vulnerability. Its history of territorial loss to Russia and the domestic pressure that will mount to recover lost territories mean that Chussia is structurally inherently unstable: equilibrium then becomes the exception rather than the norm. China is playing a long game with Russia, which has nowhere else to go. Russia's recent dealings with North Korea only highlight its isolation (and that of the Democratic People's Republic of Korea (DPRK))—and China has all the forward momentum in the relationship, with its relative economic performance, technological advancement and military catchup.

The notion of an 'authoritarian' troika of Russia, China and North Korea has attracted some speculation in the West, but a short reflection on what this might involve shows how fanciful the notion is in fact. The Korean War is a bitter memory for both North Korea—abandoned by the Soviet Union when fighting began—and China, as Stalin suckered Mao into committing more than half a million troops and possibly giving up forever the chance to overrun Taiwan. At the time, Mao was assembling his forces in Fujian for a large-scale, much-anticipated assault on Taiwan. Moreover, neither Moscow nor Beijing will forget how Pyongyang played one off against the other during the long Sino-Soviet split.

For Kim Jong-Un to make his first post-Covid visit to Russia and describe the relationship with Russia as North Korea's 'most important'—despite China's continuing to be the economic bulwark of the DPRK—was a calculated offence aimed at Xi Jinping. Putin returned the favour in June 2024, when he visited Pyongyang. During that visit, a mutual defence treaty was signed and Kim agreed to sell Russia large quantities of munitions. The visit served to remind Beijing that Moscow has options in East Asia other than China and it is prepared to act in an area traditionally regarded as China's primary sphere of influence. Expanded North Korean arms sales to Russia will make Pyongyang less beholden to Beijing.[36] Stability on the Korean Peninsula is Beijing's overriding security concern and adventurism by Kim the greatest risk to it. Putin's meddling will make Beijing worry that Kim may come to feel as if he has a backer in the Kremlin. The reality is that this troika has no shared ideology, some overlapping interests, and a sour history. The same can be said of Chussia.

The Ukraine invasion has changed Beijing's calculus in its favour. With the war continuing to deplete Russia economically and in manpower, China need do no more than bide its time. It is emerging as the dominant power in Eurasia by Russia's own hand. If Russia were to prevail and integrate Ukraine into the Federation, then, as Zbigniew Brzezinski argued in the mid-1990s, Russia would again have the wherewithal to become a powerful imperial state. It would then have the capacity to turn its attention to Central Asian states; China would once more face Russian competition in Central Asia.[37] On one view, China's interests would therefore be best served by Russia's failure in Ukraine—again, Chussia's internal strategic interests lie in different directions. On another view, however, their interests converge around regime survival. The loss of Putin's regime would focus attention externally and internally on the authoritarians in Beijing. What would replace Putin's regime would also be of major concern to Beijing—a colour revolution in Russia would be a disaster for Xi and the CPC. Having aligned itself so closely with Putin, Beijing faces a serious conundrum that brings to the fore an underlying tension between regime survival, and foreign and strategic policies.

Beijing cannot base its long-term security on Putin's Russia. As a Eurasian power, it must consolidate its position to ensure that Russia can never again become the dominant power in Eurasia. In this way, Beijing not only achieves long-term security of its borders, which it feels it has been denied by foreign powers for centuries, but also refashions the global order in its own interests, if not image.

Snow's magisterial study of 400 years of the Russia–China relationship is the most recent word on the subject. While avoiding firm judgements, the weight of his conclusion after 500 pages is that, on balance, these two historically competing great powers are likely to enter an extended period of geopolitical comity.[38] This view is based largely on his understanding that following the signing of the Treaty of Nerchinsk, the Manchurian and Mongolian borders were largely undisturbed for the next 200 years. Of course, this overlooks the ongoing instability on the Qing's western borders; Russia's involvement in repeated attempts to provoke Xinjiang's secession, and the elevated insecurity this caused the Manchu court; and the loss of some 300,000 hectares of territory along the western frontier, besides land lost to Russia in Manchuria.

For much of this period, the lands to the north and northeast of China were so remote from Moscow and Beijing as to lack strategic value for either empire. Yet when the relative power balance changed in the second half of the nineteenth century, following the Opium Wars, Moscow moved decisively to stake its claims from Siberia to the Pacific Ocean. Taking a long-term view, temporary equilibria, rather than structural stability, characterised the relationship.

Structural stability is, however, the premise of the current public presentation of Chinese policy towards Russia. The policy seeks to set aside historical differences and identify explicitly common interests of Russia and China in opposition to the West, while seeking to calm fears that Russia and China might craft an alliance relationship where mutual obligations, especially in defence, would be involved. China wants to amplify its common interests with Russia while seeking not to alarm the West that it is facing an 'alliance of autocracies'. China also wants to avoid taking on possible military obligations that could entail commitments to a potentially unstable or unreliable partner. Putin's invasion of Ukraine would only have reinforced these anxieties.[39] Westad has argued that:

> China condoning Putin's war of aggression ... will create a Russia evermore dependent on China, as will Western sanctions. By saying very little and blaming the West, Beijing expects a positive outcome for itself.[40]

Far from being an 'axis of authoritarians', then, the relationship is best understood as a 'traditional great power relationship' based on strategic calculations of national self-interest.[41] Both empires, which for so long were outside the Westphalian system of power balancing, are now deeply engaged with it. In this system, alliances shift and change according to alterations in relative power. As the old cliché has it, there are no permanent friendships, only permanent interests. Rather than China dissolving itself in Eurasia, it is more likely Eurasia will be sinizised.

# CHAPTER 9

# SOVIETSTAN TO SINOSTAN[1]

*'We, you and I, witnessed how the Soviet Union collapsed. Then, like now, not enough attention was paid to the small republics … Where did we offend you? What are we? Foreigners or something?'*

Tajikistan president Emomali Rahmon publicly rebuking Vladimir Putin, October 2022[2]

In October 2017, I was nearing the end of a trip across the Stans, from the Aral Sea to Kashgar in China, with a couple of friends.[3] For a good part of our trip, we followed the Amu Darya river in Uzbekistan, and then in Tajikistan, where it creates a border with Afghanistan. With his book detailing travels overland from Europe to Afghanistan, *The Road to Oxiana*, first published in 1937, Robert Byron brought this area along the northern border of Afghanistan to popular attention in Britain. At about the same time, Peter Fleming and Ella Maillart were setting off on their epic travel adventure from Peking to Lahore. Eighty years later, my route along the Amu Darya shadowed Byron's in places. Legendary British travel writer Bruce Chatwin, in his introduction to the 2004 edition, described Byron's book as 'sacred text, beyond criticism'.[4]

Until the Soviet invasion of Afghanistan in 1979, this was the furthest southern extent of the Russian Empire in Central Asia. It was through this region—and across the ironically named 'Friendship Bridge' spanning the Amu Darya river—that Moscow launched its invasion of Afghanistan, and it remains one of the most heavily landmined areas in the world. To the northeast, Russia's Central Asian empire extended then to the frontiers of Xinjiang and Mongolia.

From the Amu Darya, we turned north for two days and followed the Wakhan Corridor, which once formed a buffer zone between Imperial Russia and British India. This was the only road across the region. Until the 1930s, it had been a camel track and was then made into a road for vehicles. It was not paved until 1979, when the Soviets needed to supply their forces in Afghanistan. Today, it is a rutted, potholed, bone-shaking endurance test. To reach the border of Tajikistan and Kyrgyzstan, we travelled through the Marco Polo Valley in the Pamir Mountains, the 'roof of the world'. This was Great Game country, where Russian and British agents and adventurers, including Sir Francis Younghusband, travelled between the British and Russian consulates in Kashgar and the high Pamir passes, collecting intelligence. Later, Bolshevik troops marched along these tracks as the Soviets sought to quash local rebellions and reclaim tsarist territories momentarily lost to jihadist uprisings in Central Asia.

Beside the deserted crumbling stone caravanserais dotted along this ancient trunk route of the old Silk Road is a rusted single-wire fence erected by the Soviet Union during its estrangement with China in the 1960s and 1970s. It was intended to prevent a Chinese invasion but would barely stop a Marco Polo sheep, which are native to this valley, from straying across the border. It runs for almost 1500 kilometres to Kazakhstan and took twelve years to erect—such was the fear then of Chinese incursions along the border.[5] If the fence had any benefit at all, it would have been psychological, assuaging far-distant anxieties over an open Central Asian frontier. It smacks of inefficient Soviet central planning and mindless defence expenditure. From a desk in Moscow, it may have seemed like an inspired idea. On the ground, in these rugged, dry hills, it is something of an exotic aberration, offering no more defence than a laser beam.

Beyond the Marco Polo Valley, along a muddy, unsealed road, lies a two-hour crossing of 18 kilometres of no-man's-land between the two countries before reaching Kyrgyzstan. We were passing through Gorno-Badakhshan, which had seen a violent Islamicist insurgency flare up intermittently for years before finally being brutally supressed in 2015. Tajikistan and Kyrgyzstan also fought a bloody border war there in 2022. In every direction were the white Pamir Mountains.

On the valley floor, as a further reminder of the lost Soviet Empire, stood two giant, faded green domes—like something out of the old US Cold War propaganda TV series *Jet Jackson, Flying Commando!*— which were part of its nuclear defence command against China. The absolute remoteness of these two, now-abandoned, lonely sentinels, standing guard on the frontier, was deeply disturbing: the imminent threat of nuclear war had been so present in the minds of those in the Kremlin.[6]

Our last day in Tajikistan was coming to an end. We headed to Sary-Tash, a border town in Kyrgyzstan. To the west, the majestic Lenin Peak (7134 metres) was gilded by the setting sun. We stayed the night, with drug dealers from Afghanistan prowling the broken, grey, dusty streets outside our lodgings.[7]

We were just 140 kilometres from the border with China. Next morning, the trip to the Chinese border followed a high-altitude valley, with the Pamirs to the south, where they join the Tian Shan mountain range, which runs north between China and the Stans, to Russia and Mongolia. The crossing into China took hours and included a 7-kilometre hike through the Torugart Pass in the no-man's-land between Kyrgyzstan and China. As we tramped up to the second Chinese border post, I counted fifty-two big lorries, most loaded with coal, heading towards China. This was despite Kyrgyzstan's own energy shortages.[8]

The security was extreme, reflecting both Beijing's neurotic anxiety about ensuring 'stability' in Xinjiang and controlling its ethnic Uyghur population, and the timing of our return to China, which coincided with the Communist Party's 19th National Congress. In all, we passed through four border and customs checks, involving searches of our backpacks; and much time wasted queuing and having passports checked repeatedly, bags being X-rayed, and then unpacked and repacked. My box of cigars often facilitated the process slightly, as the guards seemed more obliging after having helped themselves to one or two Cuban coronas.[9]

## Russian Imperialism in Central Asia
In the 1820s, the extent of Russia's eastern expansion was marked by outposts along the Ural and Irtysh rivers. A century later, nearly

2.5 million square kilometres and some six million subjects had been added. By then—as UK historian of Central Asia Alexander Morrison writes—Russian Central Asia:

> stretched from the Altai and Ala-Tau mountains in the east of what is now Kazakhstan to the deserts of Transcaspia (Turkmenistan) in the west, with a southern frontier which ran through the lofty plateaus of the Pamirs and along the Amu-Darya, the Oxus of antiquity.[10]

Russia's conquest of Central Asia had less to do with geopolitical competition, as is often claimed by Great Game historians, and much to do with acquiring status and respect for Imperial Russia through colonisation. Nor were economic considerations paramount. Instead, as other major European powers were assembling colonial maritime empires, the tsars looked east across the vastness of Eurasia to create theirs. Morrison explains that:

> the Russians saw Central Asia's states not as rational, sovereign polities open to the usual niceties of diplomacy and negotiation, but as savage, backward, unreliable, and amenable only to force. And like the British [with their colonies] they aimed above all to maintain Russia's status and prestige as a great power, both in the eyes of these 'Asiatics' and in those of its European rivals.[11]

It was vital for the tsars to sustain what he calls the 'myth of conquest', which helped Russia assert its great power status in the nineteenth century, and attracted both respect and fear from rivals, serving to bolster their authority. And, like other powers of the nineteenth century, Russia saw its imperial expansion as a civilising mission, bringing high culture and Christianity to the newly conquered subjects.[12] Russia's national power and security were believed to flow from its relentless nineteenth century expansion eastwards. The statesmen who pursued such policies were from a generation that had come of age during the war against Napoleon, and had come to be convinced of the need for Russia to find territories that would be defensive buffers against foreign aggression.[13]

In its expansion across Central Asia, Russia had to overcome powerful states in Oxiana and the Ferghana Valley (parts of today's Uzbekistan and Kyrgyzstan). In successive campaigns during the middle decades of the nineteenth century, as discussed in Chapter 2, Russia finally established its dominance over Central Asia after the capture of Tashkent in 1865 and the establishment of the administrative region of Turkestan.[14] Russian colonisation of Central Asia was a continuous process, punctuated at times by discrete campaigns. Unlike in Afghanistan, Russian expansion, although violent, met relatively little resistance. Colonisation proceeded with the creation of protectorates, associated bureaucracies, systems of taxation, administration of justice, and the introduction of settler immigrant communities into formerly nomadic lands.

The Russian Empire soon found itself ruling a vast territory that was almost entirely Muslim. In contrast with earlier Asian conquests in Siberia, these subjects would turn out to be 'largely unassimilable to the Russian core'.[15] Consequently, in terms of maintaining regional identities and cultures, Central Asia would remain outside the main administrative structures of the empire. This in turn encouraged Russian statesmen to keep thinking of the region as colonial territory, and perpetuated the distinction between metropole and periphery.

The arrival of the Bolsheviks after the October 1917 revolution upended all of this. Bringing European ideas of nation-building, they embarked on an unprecedented program of reshaping Central Asia. New Soviet republics were arbitrarily drawn on the map, often with little regard for their local ethnic composition and mix. In the Soviet period, Russian colonialism was replaced by an 'extraordinary experiment' in nation-building.[16] Soviet colonialism rewrote the history of these subjugated territories, redrew, and then redrew again, the borders of ethnic groupings. Further, it redefined ethnic identity and cultures, and propagated the new myth that they had always been part of the greater Russian fatherland. Russian language and education were imposed from above, and local languages tossed aside; local traditions and cultures were marginalised. These dispersed ethnic minorities were required first and foremost to be proud Russians, loyal to this new idea of 'greater Russia'. Ethnicity was an embarrassment and a bar to an individual's social progress.[17] This colonial integration of Central Asia with Russia remained in place until the Soviet Union collapsed.

## Post-Soviet Central Asia

Of the Central Asian Soviet republics that emerged from the wreckage of the Soviet Union, Kazakhstan, Kyrgyzstan and Turkmenistan belonged to the Turkic world, joined by linguistic, cultural and historical ties from before the time of Genghis Khan. Xinjiang similarly belongs to this Central Asian Turkic corridor. Tajikistan's and Uzbekistan's major cultural influences came from Persia.[18] At a much earlier time, Alexander the Great had established fortified towns in parts of the Amu Darya valley. His first and favourite wife, Roxana, came from what today is Tajikistan.

With the establishment of the Soviet Union, then the onset of the Cold War, and the breakdown in relations with China from the early 1960s, Central Asia was isolated from its ethnic, cultural and economic links, in both the west and east. The collapse of the Soviet project left the newly independent states with Soviet-style authoritarian systems of social and political organisation, and a ruling elite closely tied to Moscow—itself in turmoil. The imposition of the Soviet system on these states, however, had left them with a legacy of relatively high levels of education, of Russian language, and of health care and social services.

In all, except Tajikistan, the incumbent first secretary of the Communist Party became the president in elections that were neither free nor fair. Corrupt sales of state assets, especially those involving mining, energy and metals processing, and controlling of licences for services, such as media and telecommunications, resulted in highly concentrated incomes for the ruling elites, which have served to perpetuate their grip on power. The transitions in these states, unlike in other former Soviet republics, such as the Baltic states, did not occur in response to popular uprisings demanding democracy. Rather, they came from the collapse of centralised power in Moscow. Since then, political successions in Turkmenistan (2006), Uzbekistan

(2016) and Kazakhstan (2019) have been carefully managed by those within the ruling elite.[19]

While the initial economic collapse that each experienced following the demise of the Soviet Union was sharp and deep, during the 2000s their economic performance benefited considerably from the resources boom of that decade; and, especially in the case of resource-poor Tajikistan, from strong flows of remittances from workers who had migrated to Russia. These factors helped to sustain older patterns of economic specialisation as carryovers from the former Soviet colonial era. Leadership transitions across the region, except in Tajikistan, have seen a change from having in charge a generation entirely brought up under Soviet central planning to one that has only experienced market economies and private ownership. By 2001, the transition was largely complete and has since changed little: sustainable national economies had been established.[20]

With the ending of the resources boom in 2014, all looked to diversify their economies by relying more heavily on international trade and attracting foreign investment. The governments of each finally had to overcome suspicion of foreign trade and globalisation. In the late 1990s, Kazakhstan was the first to apply to join the WTO, becoming a member in 2015. Tajikistan's accession was speedier and it joined in 2013, one year after the Russian Federation. Uzbekistan and Turkmenistan's accession negotiations are still in progress; in 2021, Turkmenistan was the last of the Central Asian states to apply for membership.[21]

Table 1

| Country | Area (km2) (m) | Population (m) | GDP ($USbn) | GDP per capita ($US) |
|---|---|---|---|---|
| Kazakhstan | 2.8 | 20 | 226 | 11,492 |
| Turkmenistan | 0.5 | 6 | 57 | 8,800 |
| Uzbekistan | 0.4 | 36 | 80 | 2,255 |
| Kyrgyzstan | 0.2 | 7 | 12 | 1,655 |
| Tajikistan | 0.15 | 10 | 10 | 1,054 |

All data are for 2022

Leaders in the emerging states looked to craft a new post-imperial nationalism to unite their people and legitimise their rule, and in doing so became staunch critics of the system that they once served. Simultaneously, they embraced Islam as part of the new national identity, unlike in Soviet times when Russian nationalism was the glue that held the multi-ethnic state together. Leaders promoted and endorsed a secular form of Islam, free from politics—distinguishing between 'good' Islam, which is apolitical, and 'bad' Islam, which is foreign derived, rejects the ruling powers, and promotes jihadism, as in Afghanistan. Good Islam has its roots within the region: specifically, a brand of Sufism based on ancient religious schools emanating from Samarkand, whose teachings seek to promote harmony between the devout and the ruling authorities. In case any doubt should arise, religious activities are overseen by committees for religious affairs in the different states.[22]

Table 2

| Russia's trade with Central Asian markets, 2016–23 (US$bn) | | | | | | | | |
|---|---|---|---|---|---|---|---|---|
| | 2016 | 2017 | 2018 | 2019 | 2020 | 2021 | 2022 | 2023 |
| **Kazakhstan** | | | | | | | | |
| Export | 9.0 | 12.3 | 13.0 | 14.0 | 14.0 | 18.5 | - | - |
| Import | 3.6 | 5.0 | 5.3 | 5.6 | 5.0 | 7.1 | - | - |
| **Turkmenistan** | | | | | | | | |
| Export | 0.6 | 0.3 | 0.3 | 0.5 | 0.6 | 0.7 | - | - |
| Import | 0.3 | NA | 0.2 | 0.2 | 0.3 | 0.1 | - | - |
| **Uzbekistan** | | | | | | | | |
| Export | 2.0 | 2.6 | 3.3 | 4.0 | 5.0 | 5.0 | - | - |
| Import | 0.8 | 1.0 | 1.0 | 1.2 | 1.2 | 1.7 | - | - |
| **Tajikistan** | | | | | | | | |
| Export | 0.7 | 0.7 | 0.8 | 1.0 | 1.0 | 0.8 | - | - |
| Import | NA | NA | NA | 0.08 | NA | NA | - | - |
| **Kyrgyzstan** | | | | | | | | |
| Export | 1.0 | 1.4 | 1.6 | 1.6 | 1.5 | 2.2 | - | - |
| Import | 1.7 | 2.0 | 2.5 | 3.2 | 2.4 | 3.5 | - | - |

Source: Trade Map, ITC, trademap.org/bilateral_ts.aspx; NA = <$US100m; data not available for 2022, 2023

Table 3

| China's Trade with Central Asian markets, 2016–23 (US$bn) | | | | | | | | |
|---|---|---|---|---|---|---|---|---|
| | 2016 | 2017 | 2018 | 2019 | 2020 | 2021 | 2022 | 2023 |
| **Kazakhstan** | | | | | | | | |
| Export | 8.2 | 11.6 | 11.3 | 12.7 | 11.7 | 14.0 | 16.3 | 24.7 |
| Import | 4.7 | 6.3 | 8.5 | 7.9 | 8.6 | 10.3 | 14.9 | 16.3 |
| **Turkmenistan** | | | | | | | | |
| Export | 0.3 | 0.4 | 0.3 | 0.4 | 0.4 | 0.5 | 0.9 | 1.0 |
| Import | 5.6 | 6.6 | 8.1 | 8.7 | 7.7 | 5.1 | 10.3 | 9.6 |
| **Uzbekistan** | | | | | | | | |
| Export | 2.0 | 2.8 | 4.0 | 5.0 | 5.1 | 5.9 | 7.5 | 12.4 |
| Import | 1.7 | 1.5 | 2.3 | 1.1 | 0.9 | 1.4 | 2.3 | 1.7 |
| **Tajikistan** | | | | | | | | |
| Export | 1.7 | 1.3 | 1.4 | 1.6 | 1.0 | 1.7 | 2.2 | 3.7 |
| Import | NA | NA | NA | NA | NA | 0.2 | 0.4 | 0.3 |
| **Kyrgyzstan** | | | | | | | | |
| Export | 5.6 | 5.3 | 5.5 | 6.2 | 2.8 | 7.5 | 15.4 | 19.7 |
| Import | NA | NA | NA | NA | NA | NA | NA | NA |

Source: Trade Map, ITC, trademap.org/bilateral_ts.aspx; NA = <$US100m

## Russia's Economic Presence in Central Asia

Russia's close historical ties with and geographical proximity to Central Asia, together with mobility of labour and capital for those states participating in the Russian-led Eurasian Economic Union (EAEU), have resulted in a strong commercial presence. It is estimated that some 100,000 Russian firms and joint ventures with local partners are doing business in Central Asia. The most important and substantial economic tie is, however, through remittances of workers from Russia. In 2022, remittances accounted for 11 per cent of Uzbekistan's GDP and 26 per cent of Kyrgyzstan's. For Tajikistan, they accounted for 51 per cent of GDP, or $US5.3 billion.[23] Compare this with the Philippines, which is widely acknowledged to depend heavily on remittances from its workers abroad, where remittances accounted for just 10 per cent of GDP.

Today, Russia's economic engagement with the region does not reflect its past deep integration with the Soviet Union's economy, in which it was encompassed. Since the Soviet Union's collapse, trade has shifted from Russia to China and the EU, in addition to countries such as Turkey, the US and Iran. As can be seen from Table 2, Russia's traditionally close ally in Central Asia, Kazakhstan, has also been overwhelming its biggest trading partner. This has been based narrowly on hydrocarbons and natural resource-based products from the mining sector. Trade with the other four Central Asian states has been minimal. In 2021, Russia's total trade with all Central Asia amounted to $US40 billion, compared with some $US47 to $US50 billion with China, depending on the data source. The EU ranks third behind China and Russia, with total trade of $US16 billion, with exports and imports roughly balanced. Since the invasion of Ukraine, China's exports to Central Asia (Table 3) have increased significantly, especially to Kazakhstan, Uzbekistan and Kyrgyzstan. This is attributable both to the trade diversion that has occurred in response to sanctions, and to the use by Chinese exporters of Central Asia as a corridor through which to subvert Western sanctions on Russia.[24]

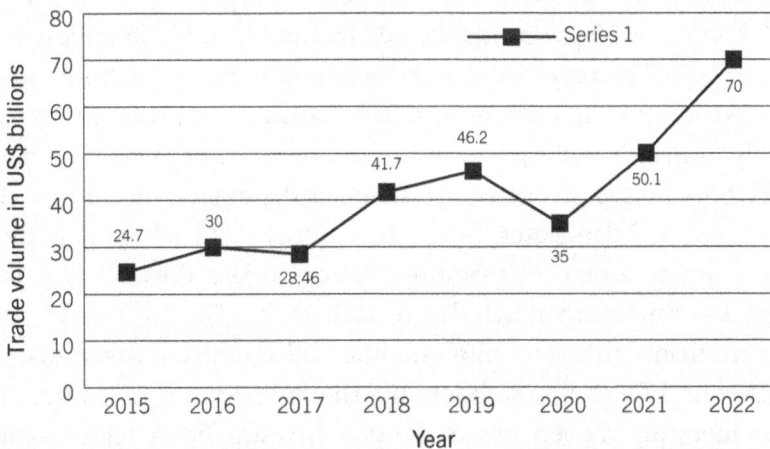

Figure 1: Trade volume between China and Central Asia, 2015–22 (US$bn)

Source: OECD, *Weathering Economic Storms in Central Asia: initial impacts of the war in Ukraine*, 2023

Russia's trade with Central Asia is dwarfed by China's. In 2021, the last year for which comparable figures are available, China's total trade with Central Asia was over 20 per cent greater than Russia's; China had become Central Asia's largest trading partner.[25] By 2023, China's total trade with the region topped US$90 billion, receiving a substantial lift from sanctions-busting trade diverted through Central Asia since the invasion of Ukraine. Remarkably, for a country with limited manufacturing capacity, Kyrgyzstan's exports of machinery to Russia increased 2500 per cent in 2023, compared with the previous year. Uzbekistan, Kazakhstan and Kyrgyzstan have all seen a big increase in the value of the same goods imported from China as exported to Russia since the war began.[26]

By 2023, China had replaced Russia as Central Asia's major source of foreign direct investment (FDI).[27] In 2023, China invested $US221 million, or 28 per cent of the region's total for the year; Russia's FDI was next at $US147 million, and Kazakhstan's was next at $US67.3 million. Of China's stock of FDI in Central Asia and Russia between 2016 and 2023, 52 per cent was invested in Kazakhstan, mainly in hydrocarbons. China has also invested $US10 billion in Turkmenistan, mainly in pipelines to transport natural gas.[28]

FDI in Kazakhstan, however, is dominated by the EU. In 2022, the Netherlands was the single largest investor, accounting for $US8 billion, or 35 per cent, followed by the US at $US5 billion, or 21.5 per cent. This reflects the overriding importance of Kazakhstan's rich reserves of hydrocarbons. In 2022, Russia and China's FDI was roughly similar, accounting for just over 6 per cent, or $US1.5 billion and $US1.4 billion, respectively.[29] China is the biggest investor in all other Central Asian states, other than Kyrgyzstan, where it is the second-largest source of investment after Turkey. Russia's FDI in Kyrgyzstan was less than half that of China's.[30]

Apart from Turkestan and Tajikistan, all countries saw a sharp increase in FDI inflows following the invasion of Ukraine, as major investors moved out of Russia. Investment in Kyrgyzstan and Uzbekistan jumped 104 per cent and 38 per cent respectively, albeit from low bases. Inflows into Kazakhstan increased 17 per cent.

In 2022, Kazakhstan attracted forty-one foreign firms from Russia, including US, European, Chinese and Australian companies.[31]

## China's Debt Diplomacy

China has emerged rapidly as the major source of foreign debt for the region, with total lending having increased over four times, from an estimated $US40 billion in 2010 to $US180 billion by 2021. Much of the debt is expensive, compared with lower interest rates available from the International Monetary Fund (IMF), World Bank or Asian Development Bank (ADB); or bilaterally from Paris Club members, who cooperate to assist poorer countries restructure and manage their debt obligations—China is not a member of the Paris Club. During the pandemic, Central Asian states had to renegotiate $US52 billion, or almost a third of their total debt obligations, with China. Most of the loans are made under BRI auspices, and are heavily concentrated on energy, resources, and transport infrastructure. Regarding the latter, the focus is especially on the various transcontinental corridors.[32]

According to the Organisation for Economic Co-operation and Development (OECD), actual debt exposure of individual Central Asian states to China is unclear. It does, however, vary widely. The latest estimates by the OECD show that in 2017 Kyrgyzstan and Tajikistan were the most heavily indebted, amounting to around 30 per cent of their GDP. An official 2022 estimate for Kyrgyzstan increased this figure to 42 per cent of GDP.[33] Both have relatively few natural resources compared with the other Central Asian states and are therefore under greater debt stress. International commodity markets have generally remained strong since the pandemic, and so have favoured the resource and energy exporters. Another estimate shows the level of indebtedness to China is increasing among all Central Asian states, with Tajikistan's debt rising to 52 per cent of GDP and Kyrgyzstan's to 45 per cent of GDP. At these levels, the OECD finds, their debt is unsustainable and will need further rescheduling and refinancing. In such cases in the past, Chinese lenders have sought to recover part of the interest owning by taking over assets such as gold and silver mines, and power stations. The debt exposure of

Turkmenistan, Uzbekistan and Kazakhstan to China is much lower, and regarded as sustainable and without causing any repayment stress.[34]

## Debt Sustainability in Central Asia

Tajikistan has the highest level of debt distress risk in Central Asia, indicated by a higher debt-to-export revenue ratio (DER as % GDP, rhs), closely followed by Kyrgyzstan.

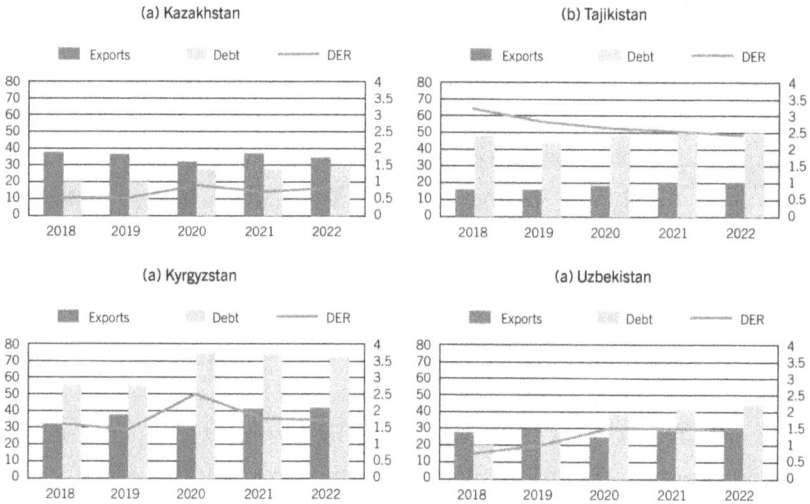

Notes:

1  Exports refer to total exports of goods and services, expressed as % of GDP based on the nominal GDP of the given year.

2  Government debt refers to all government or publicly backed liabilities, both internal and external, and is expressed as % of GDP.

3  The debt-to-export revenue (DER) is a commonly used indicator of sustainability of debt (rhs), expressed as a simple ratio of export earnings to outstanding debt; a lower number indicates that outstanding liabilities can be settled more quickly using export earnings.

4  The assessment of debt distress is taken from debt sustainability analyses compiled by the IMF in its most recent country reports for Kyrgyzstan, Tajikistan and Uzbekistan.

Source: IMF, 2022; OECD, 2023

In the most indebted nations, popular resentment and anger have resulted in (sometimes violent) demonstrations against Chinese interests, especially when Chinese firms have taken over previously nationally owned or controlled assets. The spread of the use of Chinese private security companies to protect Chinese-owned assets has stoked concerns over what is often seen as Chinese heavy-handedness. Since 2016, some 150 demonstrations in Tajikistan and Kazakhstan combined have been attributed to local reactions to Chinese debt behaviour. The situation is often inflamed by what locals perceive as the remoteness and strangeness of Chinese involvement in their economies. Chinese creditors usually insist on using only Chinese workers, and sourcing parts and equipment only from Chinese firms. The Chinese workers live in compounds, usually on construction sites, and have minimal interaction with locals. In Kyrgyzstan and Kazakhstan, Beijing's treatment of its Uyghur minorities in Xinjiang has stoked considerable ill feeling. The 2016 bombing of the Chinese embassy in Bishkek has been attributed to this toxic mix.[35]

Corruption arising from the lack of transparency regarding Chinese-funded projects has created a politically influential social stratum built around the awarding of contracts, and sale of land and other resources. China has also been supporting leaders of authoritarian regimes by supplying surveillance technology to assist them in maintaining political control. It is not surprising, then, that there is popular disquiet over China's increasing presence and influence in Central Asia. At the same time, elite opinion—for obvious reasons, because the elites have skin in the game—has become increasingly favourable towards China and more distanced towards Russia.

Despite the costs, disaffection and corruption involved, China's investments and loans can also be strongly positive. It is building infrastructure that, most likely, would not have been built otherwise, or at least for a long time; it is developing new industries, and giving some of these countries more diverse export profiles, all of which continue to support economic growth and rising living standards. China's expanding security footprint also helps maintain a more effective united front in resisting Islamic fundamentalist terrorism in the region.[36] The headline-catching negative sentiments about China's presence do need to be carefully balanced against the benefits of its deeper engagement in the region.

### Russia's Institutional Atrophy

With the collapse of the Soviet Union, former Soviet republics led by Russia created the Commonwealth of Independent States (CIS) to oversee, manage, regulate and coordinate relations via a new regional forum. The bonds between the ruling autocrats who emerged from the rubble of the Soviet Union were strong. Although everything had changed almost overnight, it was as if they believed a virtual Soviet Union could somehow be pulled from the wreckage. Other than the Baltic states, all former Soviet republics joined CIS, with Turkestan an associate member. Since then, Georgia, Ukraine and Moldovia have left. Under the authority of the CIS council of member-state leaders, its two most important functional bodies were established: the Collective Security Treaty Organization (CSTO) and the EAEU.

When CIS was established, its ambitions were well beyond what it could achieve practically. Intended to coordinate foreign and domestic policies under the leadership of the council, its members soon looked beyond the CIS coterie of states. Russian dominance grated on these newly independent rulers, and domestic politics led to relationships developing among members bilaterally, rather than regionally. At Russia's urging, it has, unsuccessfully, tried to have Russian adopted as an official language in all member states; so far, only Kazakhstan and Kyrgyzstan have done so. CIS has come to be seen as an example of failed regionalism.[37]

Geography and Russia's historical sense of vulnerability to invasions have led it to adopt strategies to insulate itself from attack. Accordingly, in 2009, Russia and its Eurasian partners, other than China, upgraded their military ties to create the CSTO, with Russia's largest overseas base located in Tajikistan. A 25,000-strong multilateral command was created to deal with 'low level security threats', such as counter insurgency and terrorism. It had its first test in January 2022 in Kazakhstan, with civil unrest following an increase in LNG prices after a government-enforced price cap was lifted.[38]

The CSTO, which has, since its inception, been the institutional expression of Russia's security guarantee for Central Asia, is also starting to fray and lose internal cohesion. Of its members, Belarus was the only one to support the invasion of Ukraine. Kazakhstan, Tajikistan and Kyrgyzstan have either been neutral or started to distance themselves. None has recognised Russia's annexation of Donbas, Kherson and Zaporizhia. In October 2022, Bishkek cancelled participation in joint military exercises, following the Tajikistan–Kyrgyzstan conflict in 2022. Kazakhstan and Kyrgyzstan have begun seeking greater military cooperation from Turkey. In May 2023, Kazakhstan and Turkey signed an agreement to manufacture drones. With a stalemate in Ukraine, the CSTO's identity and sense of purpose recedes further.[39]

Kazakhstan president Kassym-Jomart Tokayev has probably been the most dismissive of Putin's invasion of Ukraine, openly defying the Russian leader on several occasions. When Kazakhstan opened an emergency aid centre near Kyiv, its foreign minister dismissed a 'please explain' from Moscow, saying 'it was there because it was there'. He also stated that his country would not be part of circumventing Western economic sanctions. In June 2022, at the St Petersburg International Economic Forum, he said he would not recognise 'quasi-states', just as he did not recognise Taiwan or Kosovo. He declined to accept the Order of Alexander Nevsky, an eighteenth-century tsarist Russian honour for bravery. In June 2023, he told Putin that the Wagner Group mutiny was an 'internal affair in Russia' and none of the CSTO's business. Tokayev is not pro-China: rather, he is fixated on maintaining Kazakhstan's independence and agency, as he tries to navigate a multivariant foreign policy through which to advance his country's interests by balancing regional powers, or having them compete for influence.[40]

Tokayev has some reason to be concerned about the limits of Putin's territorial ambitions if Moscow were to prevail in Ukraine, or even perhaps if it does not. The northern regions of Kazakhstan are vulnerable to Russian invasion, and third-country military

support is practically non-existent. These areas also contain significant Slavic minorities. Putin has asserted that Russians outside of
Russia's formal borders are still essentially part of the motherland.
Alarmingly, he has also spoken of the desire of 'millions of Russians'
living outside their country to return to their 'historical homeland'.
In 2010, Putin claimed that Kazakhs never had 'statehood' and that
it was in their interests to 'remain in the greater Russian world'.[41]
Russian revanchists, such as Alexandr Solzhenitsyn, once called for
their reincorporation into Russia; in 2020, Russian nationalists hung
a banner on the Kazakh embassy in Moscow, declaring Kazakhstan
to be 'Russian land'. Nonetheless, in January 2022, President Tokayev
was prepared to take the risk and seek CSTO, mainly Russian, troops
to quell the violent demonstrations in Astana.

The western front holds some stark warnings for a country in
Kazakhstan's position. Putin used local separatist groups to stir up
trouble in Georgia and Ukraine, for example, before sending in
regular troops. These 'grey-zone' conflicts were used to provide the
justification for Russia's overt, direct interventions. This could be
repeated in Central Asian states that are seen to be drifting too far
from Russia's orbit.

The CSTO's counterpart in the economic sphere is the EAEU,
which remains an incomplete institutional innovation by Russia.
Created in 2014, after Russia's annexation of Crimea and Donetsk,
it comprises Kazakhstan, Kyrgyzstan, Armenia, Belarus and Russia.
Three of the Central Asia five—Uzbekistan, Turkmenistan and
Tajikistan—have refused to join, despite the Kremlin's pressure on
them to do so. While it embraces a free-trade zone, which has been
helpful for the circumvention of Western sanctions, probably its most
valuable aspect for regional members is free movement of labour
within the bloc.

Before the 2022 invasion of Ukraine, Russia was the main destination for labour flows within the EAEU. Movement is less free,
however, than the official rules of the EAEU suggest. Russia requires
foreign workers to go through often complicated local registration
and residency procedures, intended to restrict immigration as well
as exercise political control. Meanwhile, large numbers of workers

from non-EAEU countries, notably Tajikistan, still access Russia's labour markets. Since its inception, the EAEU has seen frequent disputes between members over the use of non-tariff barriers, as different members seek to protect local industries, and extract rents through 'unofficial' charges and levies. Also, it has attracted no new members. In 2020, Uzbekistan became an observer; but Tajikistan has made it clear it still has no intention of joining.[42]

The Eurasian Development Bank (EDB) was established in 2006 by Russia and Kazakhstan, with a capital commitment of $US7 billion, of which $US1.5 billion was paid up. Russia contributed 66 per cent and Kazakhstan the balance. Since then, membership has expanded. It now includes Armenia (which joined in 2009), Tajikistan (2009), Belarus (2010) and Kyrgyzstan (2011). As with the EAEU, Uzbekistan and Turkmenistan, despite pressure from Moscow to do so, have never joined. Its total loan portfolio is a paltry $US6.1 billion.[43]

The EDB also manages the Eurasian Fund for Stabilization and Development. This was set up in 2009, amid the global financial crisis (GFC), to assist members with regaining financial stability in times of crisis. The fund's capital base is around $US9 billion. It extends concessional finance to assist with members' short-term financing difficulties, and is involved with balance of payments support, infrastructure loans for poorer members, and government expenditure on smaller members' social sectors. Its membership comprises Armenia, Belarus, Kazakhstan, Tajikistan and Russia.[44]

This blizzard of institutions and accompanying alphabet soup of acronyms have all been part of Moscow's efforts since the dissolution of the Soviet Union to buttress its deeply held belief that these territories, collectively, are its natural and historical sphere of influence, power and prestige. They are intended to hold Central Asia tightly to the Russian core. None has proved effective in this enterprise—particularly as much more powerful forces are attracting these states in terms of economic interests and, increasingly, security towards the east.

## Connecting Eurasia

It was a warm late spring day in May 2007 when I made my first official call on the deputy mayor of Chongqing, Huang Qifan. Although I had only been ambassador for three months, I wanted to establish early links with this major western city of 30 million people that was booming at the time. Huang was the person driving the growth, and Australia had a great interest in exporting iron ore to Chongqing Iron and Steel Company, whose works stretched out along the side of a valley, high above the Yangtze River. Huang was a big, bear-like man, with a direct, gruff manner. He was clearly someone in a hurry but took time to meet with the embassy delegation. A few years later, in 2010, he was promoted to mayor. As it turned out, Huang was also a great survivor of the Chinese political system. He would not be tarnished by the ousting of Chongqing party secretary Bo Xilai, nor by the defection of his deputy police commissioner Wang Lijun to the US consulate in Chengdu, both occurring in 2012.

Huang was keen to brief me on new development plans for Chongqing, which had only recently been approved by China's State Council in Beijing. He explained that Chongqing, which had grown so large that in 1997 it was separated from Sichuan province and made a provincial-level city, would become the locus of a new central-government-sponsored western development strategy. Astonishingly, he said that an overland goods freight line would be built from Chongqing to Duisburg in Germany, and that this would be the first of several new overland freight corridors going west to Europe and emanating from Chongqing. This was to become the Eurasian Land Bridge, which began operating in 2011, via Khorgos, a dry port in Kazakhstan on the border with China.[45]

Deputy Mayor Huang's briefing to us was detailed, in terms of costs per tonne, distances involved, time of transit and expected economic returns. He got straight to the point, and his presentation was without bravado and the usual puffing up by officials of ambitions or achievements. Upon leaving the meeting, however, I was confronted with a serious professional dilemma: how to report all of this to Canberra, as I needed to, without creating the impression that in my first three months in the job I had come down with *localitis*: a

made-up name for the condition of having succumbed to the blan-
dishments of one's host country, which is not uncommon among
diplomats. On this occasion, heavy scepticism had to flavour my
report, as Huang's scheme seemed at the time to be so far-fetched.
Yet Canberra needed to learn of these plans and take them seriously.
This may have been the first time anyone in Australia, or just about
anywhere else outside of China's political leadership, had heard of
what, six years later, would become known as the One Belt, One
Road Initiative, eventually to be the BRI.

Huang explained that train connections across Central Asia
would open the city much more to international trade. Chongqing
was 1700 kilometres from Shanghai, requiring that goods navigate
the Yangtze River, including the complicated system of locks at the
Three Gorges Dam. They would take up to eight to ten days to make
the journey, before then being offloaded and transferred to ocean-
going ships for a six-week voyage to northern European ports. The
train to Duisburg would then take fourteen to sixteen days.

For higher-value-added goods, the economic benefits of the new
overland freight line were obvious. But the plan's success seemed
improbable. China would have to negotiate and secure access for
transit across four countries—Kazakhstan, Russia, Belarus and
Poland—before reaching Germany. This would require extensive
regulatory, bureaucratic and administrative coordination, which in
turn needed a great level of political agreement and support. As
China would be the main beneficiary of the scheme, it would be
expanding its reach and influence across Eurasia; especially as the rail
transport networks were expected to multiply.

This extensive trans-continental transport system is now called the
China–Europe Railway Express. It has expanded to cover 120 cities
in China, and reach 219 cities in Europe in twenty-five countries.
In the first two months of 2024, freight volume increased 10 per
cent over the previous year, partly in response to Houthi attacks on
shipping in the Red Sea. By February 2024, 85,000 journeys had
been made. With its usual chutzpah, the *Global Times* declared it to
be the 'cornerstone of Eurasian trade'.[46]

### China's Belt and Road Initiative

More efficient access to markets in wealthy countries and developing the western regions of China were not the only reasons for Beijing's opening these land-based transport routes. It has long been aware of its dangerous strategic vulnerability from so much of its trade having to transit the South China Sea and the Strait of Malacca. Much of China's crude oil, gas and other resources for its fast-growing industries pass through these waters that are controlled by the US and could be blockaded in a heartbeat.[47] Just as world geopolitics changed in 1497 after Vasco de Gama rounded the Cape of Good Hope at Africa's southern tip and became the first European to reach India by sea, China's modern trans-Eurasian corridors are changing geopolitics again.

By the time the BRI was formally announced by Xi Jinping in Astana in October 2013, many connectivity projects had been started. The development and upgrade of the Karakoram Highway, as part of the CPEC, was just beginning when I drove through the Hunza Valley in September 2006, although the official commencement date was said to be 2008.[48] Plans for major Eurasian pipeline projects, such as the Central Asia natural gas pipeline from Turkmenistan and the Kazakhstan–China oil pipeline, were well advanced. The Myanmar–China natural gas and oil pipelines were commissioned in 2013, and stretch from the Bay of Bengal to Kunming in Yunnan province; the oil pipeline was completed in August 2014 and reached full capacity in 2017.[49]

Following the Third Belt and Road Forum for International Cooperation in October 2023, China announced a recalibration of its approach to BRI infrastructure projects, to focus more on financially sustainable and better-targeted ones. Infrastructure connectivity, especially involving Chinese-owned digital networks, will continue to be given high importance by Beijing. In 2015, Xi Jinping, at the Second Belt and Road Forum, announced the Digital Silk Road (DSR),[50] which was intended to promote the digital economy—high-speed networks, e-commerce, quantum computing, AI and nanotechnology. It has opened Eurasia to China's major communications firms, such as Huawei and ZTE. China now dominates critical digital networks from Beijing to Warsaw, with DSR having become steadily more important in expanding its influence across Eurasia.[51] China has also increasingly emphasised green, sustainable, low-carbon investment priorities. While elite opinion in recipient countries has tended to welcome Chinese infrastructure investment, the broader popular response has been decidedly mixed. This has been the experience in Central Asia as well. The recalibration of BRI investment is in part a response to this and an attempt to widen its appeal to recipients.

The BRI also involves institutional mechanisms; not only to support specific investment activities, but also to develop new norms and regulatory arrangements, to reinforce connectivity, integration among participants and interdependencies. The BRI encompasses a broad range of working groups, covering all manner of areas such as intellectual property, standards, customs procedures and dispute settlement. At its core, however, it remains focused on promoting infrastructure projects, and often ones that are strategically beneficial to Beijing. At the Third Belt and Road Forum, Xi Jinping stated that the main priority for the next phase of the BRI was to strengthen Eurasian connectivity, saying that:

> The country will speed up high-quality development of the China–Europe Railway Express, participate in the trans-Caspian international transportation corridor, and host the China–Europe Railway Express Cooperation Forum … [and] together with other parties, will build a new logistics corridor across the Eurasian continent linked by direct railway and road transportation.[52]

## Russian Soft Power

Since the invasion of Ukraine, Russian imperialism and Soviet totalitarian subjugation are increasingly being questioned in Central Asia. Where speaking Russian was once a mark of high culture, and was necessary to having successful bureaucratic and business careers, in these former colonies it is now becoming identified with colonial repression. There is increasing interest in the traditional languages of the various ethnic groups from the areas that comprised the former empire, especially in urban places. People are starting to ask, 'Why do we speak Russian and not our native languages?'[53] Cultural self-determination is in a period of proud reassertion. Even so, while 'Russified Central Asia feels the pain of the Ukraine war' and identifies with Ukraine's plight, attitudes are mixed.[54] For example, public opinion polls of people in Kazakhstan and Kyrgyzstan show less than half condemn the invasion of Ukraine. Nevertheless, the questioning of Russia's colonial past is gathering momentum. As an important cultural change, it is likely over time to contribute to altering further Central Asia's relations with Russia.[55]

Migration to Russia has been a major source of its continuing influence over Central Asia. Some 10 million migrants work in Russia and send much-needed remittances back home. While hundreds of thousands of Russians fled to former Soviet republics when the Ukraine war broke out—to avoid compulsory military service or harmful economic effects, especially of Western sanctions—Russian military recruiters have, by both fair and foul means, been able to enlist recruits to fight on the western front. The movement of people under the EAEU's mobility rules is not only a major source of Russian influence over the region but one that cannot readily be replicated by other powers. It is estimated that over 1 million Tajiks are working in Russia and that hundreds of thousands have taken up Russian citizenship since the late 1990s. This trend has been growing rapidly in recent years: in 2016, 30,000 Tajiks became Russian citizens; in 2021, 103,000 had done so. The invasion of Ukraine is expected to reverse this trend temporarily. In Russia, at the same time, rising nationalism, weaker economic performance and concerns over terrorist threats are leading to greater stigmatisation, discrimination, police harassment and deportation of immigrants. Discrimination against Tajiki immigrants, especially, is reported to have become significantly elevated following the 22 March 2024 terrorist assault on the Crocus City Hall in Moscow.[56]

In the past, education and scientific exchanges have been major contributors to Russia's soft power in the region, facilitated by, and perpetuating, the widespread use of the Russian language.

The Kremlin still demands of regional leaders that their TV and radio channels broadcast Russian-language media. In 2022, 185,000 students from Central Asia were studying in Russian tertiary institutes, of whom one-third were from Kazakhstan, despite its having only the second-biggest population in Central Asia.[57] In the longer term, however, over half the region's population is under thirty, born well after the collapse of the Soviet Union, and have looser political and cultural ties to Russia than do older generations. Many of these people are likely to have concerns about the negative effects of the war in Ukraine.[58] Russia's isolation will also prevent it from continuing to be a regional hub for knowledge, with access to technology and modern business practices. The ADB, in a major report on the consequences of Putin's invasion of Ukraine, concluded that to catch up with the productivity of more advanced economies, 'Central Asia will need to build relationships elsewhere other than with Russia'.[59]

The big influx of Russians into the region following the invasion of Ukraine has fuelled local nationalism, stoking anti-Russian sentiment and raising ethnic tensions. The CSTO and Russia's inaction during the 2022 border conflict between Tajikistan and Kyrgyzstan 'discredited Russia's image as regional sheriff', and led to Kyrgyzstan refusing to participate in CSTO exercises called 'Indestructible Brotherhood—2022'. Russia has also transferred forces from its base in Tajikistan to Ukraine.[60]

Meanwhile, as Russia faces turmoil at home, on the frontline in Ukraine, and in Central Asia, China has stepped up its diplomatic activity. A recent Royal United Services Institute (RUSI) report concluded, however, that China has neither the means nor intention to replace Russia in the region, preferring 'cooperative hegemony'. This was written, however, before Putin's military misadventure became such a costly and intractable mess, and China has since sought to take advantage of Putin's travails. It is a view heard less frequently now as Putin's Ukraine quagmire deepens.

**'Unequal Equals'**

Even before Ukraine, Russia's influence across the region was waning. It is itself instructive that Erika Fatland's book about the five former Soviet republics was titled *Sovietstan* in 2014—to highlight Russia's continuing imperial embrace and dominance of Central Asia—and, just eight years later, in 2022, Pantucci and Peterson's book on the same subject was called *Sinostan*. This title cleverly draws attention to how much China expanded its regional presence and gained influence over Russia in a short period. This trend has only accelerated, although certain specifically war-related developments, such as trade flows run—for the time being, at least—in the opposite direction.[61]

Recognition of the power shift towards China was also reflected in academic writing before the invasion of Ukraine. For example, a leading US expert on Eurasia, the late Jeanne L Wilson, in two major academic articles, substantially changed her assessment over a period of five years. Writing in 2017, Wilson saw the Russia–China relationship as being essentially stable and enduring, based on a 'division of labour', whereby Russia provided security to, and China economic support for, Central Asia. She concluded that 'Russia is destined by virtue of geography alone to exercise a prominent role in the Eurasian region'.[62] China's presence and engagement received scant mention, other than the noting of Chinese-led initiatives such as the SCO, AIIB, and the group of emerging economies known collectively as the BRICS (since 2010, comprising Brazil, Russia, India, China and South Africa; and since January 2024 it includes Iran, Saudi Arabia, the United Arab Emirates, Egypt and Ethiopia).

By 2021, Wilson had changed her assessment, concluding that geographical proximity was by itself insufficient and that:

> Russia does not possess the material capabilities to contest China in Central Asia. Russia is also dependent on the Chinese leadership's willingness to maintain the fiction that the two interact as equal partners … Russia seems likely to adopt a policy of *de facto* but unacknowledged band wagoning towards China in Central Asia.[63]

This has turned out to have occurred, with Russia, at just about every point, talking up its cooperative relationship of equal partners with China.[64]

From the time of Russia's financial crisis in the late 2000s, it has become the conventional wisdom to talk of a 'division of labour', or 'division of influence', or 'cooperative hegemony', between Russia and China in the region, with the former responsible for security and the latter for economic development—that they are the regional 'sheriff and banker'.[65] This 'division of labour' or 'division of influence' took shape after the GFC, which slashed Russia's capacity to fund development in Central Asia, and allowed China to step in to finance major hydrocarbon projects. In 2009, China wrested control of Turkmenistan gas supplies from Russia, when it invested $US3 billion in additional gas fields and sent the pipelines east to its markets, rather than to Russia. In the same year, it supported Kazakhstan banks, to the tune of $US10 billion, to fund the Central Asia–China pipeline. With this financing, China 'broke Russia's control over the export of gas' from Central Asia.[66] The division of labour that then emerged helped to assuage concerns among Russian elites about becoming the junior partner of China in the anti-Western club.[67] Yet, as early as 2019, this relationship was being referred to as 'an equal partnership of unequals'.[68]

Russia has a 'sense of entitlement' over Central Asia. It has declared these areas as being of 'privileged interest' and as its 'near abroad'. The primary assumption is that they remain firmly ensconced within Russia's sphere of influence. Since the 1990s, it has been an obsession among elements of the Russian elites to restore their country as a great power, which, since 2022, has been played out with tragic consequences in Ukraine. Central Asia is not the only region where Russia can seek to fulfil its great power ambitions, but it has had great difficulty reconciling itself to the fact that these states are now independent entities and should be treated as equals.[69]

President Rahmon's public rebuke of Putin, cited at the outset of this chapter, captured the built-up resentment from years of Russian indifference. At a summit meeting, in front of all the leaders of Central Asian states, he attacked Putin verbally for treating them as if they were still part of the Soviet Union. That he felt he could do so without any adverse consequences was deemed to be a clear sign of Russia's declining influence in the region. It was also interpreted as a signal to others (China) that might want to come in and take Russia's place.[70]

China avoids declarations of regional ambitions, and instead seeks to advance its interests in functional ways: mainly related to economic matters and targeted assistance, such as during the Covid-19 pandemic. It takes a long view: mindful not to challenge too openly, it is ultra-sensitive to preserving face among Russia's elite, is confident of the long-run trends, and has time on its side while playing the long game of growing its influence and prestige in Central Asia. Aware of Russia's sense of strategic vulnerability, China has tried to calibrate its involvement carefully, while venturing into the region via the SCO and the BRI, as well as bilaterally.

The BRI has an open, undefined political role and so is non-threatening. Even so, Russia was ambivalent about, if not suspicious of, the BRI, joining only in 2015, and on the condition that a BRI–EAEU joint statement of cooperation between the two bodies be issued. In the end, a statement was released but signed only by Russia. In the SCO, Russia and China are ostensibly co-equal leaders, but China's economic weight lends it greater authority and respect. Russia has consequently sought to restrict the SCO's activities expanding into economic matters, while seeking to widen its membership to dilute China's influence. It was Russia, against China's wishes, that pushed for Indian membership of the SCO, as part of its efforts to use it to balance China in Central Asia. These included proposing, but failing to achieve, a free trade agreement between India and the EAEU.[71]

As China's power has grown, both absolutely as well as relatively, its relationship with Russia has come to be described as one of 'competitive hegemony'. But this conceptual framing denies Central Asia agency, which it has successfully sought to exercise, as demonstrated by trade and investment flows from beyond the regional hegemons, such as with the EU and Turkey. It has also welcomed cooperation with the EU and Japan on infrastructure projects.[72] Nevertheless, the major powers of Russia and China will continue to exercise the main influence over the region. This has especially been the case since the US and NATO abandoned Afghanistan to the Taliban in 2021.

## China's Imperial Underreach

China has never telegraphed its intentions for Central Asia. It is for this reason that the words in *Sinostan*'s subtitle, 'China's inadvertent empire', are a misdescription.[73] China and Russia both continue to stress that theirs is a new form of 'great power relationship', one based on cooperation without competition.[74] However, their relationship is looking more like one of 'silent competition'.[75]

Beijing is becoming more overt in its ambitions for regional hegemony. A key development came in May 2023, with Xi Jinping's hosting of a regional summit of the five leaders of the Central Asian states, without Russia; held in Xi'an, the terminus of the ancient Silk Road. Hosting this meeting in the same year as the tenth anniversary of the BRI, about which Russia had always been, at best, lukewarm, further added to the symbolism of the event. C+C5 was chaired by China, and attended by all five presidents, who agreed on the Xi'an Declaration: a far-reaching proposal for 'substantially expanded and deepened relations in all fields'. Beijing used the summit to expand strategic cooperation with the Central Asian states, each of which backed Xi Jinping's four major foreign policy initiatives: namely, the BRI, Global Security Initiative, Global Development Initiative (GDI) and the Global Civilization Initiative (GCI). Echoing Xi Jinping's key foreign policy concepts, it promised to:

> foster a closer China–Central Asia community, with a shared future and contribute to building a community with a common future for mankind.

In language that could readily be seen as critical of Russia's invasion of Ukraine, it stressed the central importance of:

> independence, territorial integrity … and firmly opposed interference in internal affairs by any force or under any pretext.

It then went on to vow to uphold:

> the principles of the UN Charter, uphold multilateralism and the universally recognised international laws and norms governing international relations.

The meeting established a formal China–Central Asia Mechanism, which would hold biannual meetings—the next will be in Kazakhstan in 2025. A permanent secretariat is to be established in China.[76]

China has made Uzbekistan a particular focus of attention. It has the largest population of all Central Asian states, accounting for 40 per cent of the total. Uzbekistan is also the country where the population has the most favourable opinion of China. Some 70 per cent held such a view of China in 2020, compared with only 27 per cent in Kazakhstan. The Chinese auto industry has also begun to invest in manufacturing there, with Chery and BYD having both opened plants to build electric vehicles for export. As well, Uzbekistan is closely aligned with China's Central Asia connectivity strategy,[77] and the China–Kyrgyzstan–Uzbekistan railway (CKU) is a high priority for both countries. While the Trans-Afghan Railway is facing financing, security and governance challenges, Uzbekistan has made it, too, a high priority, which China supports.[78] These projects open Central Asia to Chinese railways, while diversifying trans-continental railway links away from Russia. With the Houthi attacks in the Red Sea, Central Asia's importance as a transport corridor between Europe and China has been elevated.

In January 2024, just eight months after he attended the C+C5 Summit, Uzbekistan's president, Shavkat Mirziyoyev, visited Beijing and Shenzhen. While he was in Beijing, there was an agreement to upgrade the bilateral relationship to an 'all-weather comprehensive strategic partnership'. Agreements were also reached on green energy, including the construction of two photovoltaic 500-megawatt power stations; on the sale of a fleet of Chinese electric buses to Samarkand; on the establishment of a BYD joint venture to manufacture autos; and on cooperation with Huawei regarding facial recognition monitoring systems. China also committed to expediting the CKU railway, with a further promise of funds.[79]

China has the economic weight, and more targeted, deliberate foreign policy directed at securing greater influence. It is proceeding to build its influence while being mindful of Moscow's sensitivities, also aware that there is little Moscow can do about it. It has been incrementally and persistently elevating its own security involvement in the region. Its interests have mainly been shaped by its concern over the security of its western borders, especially with Afghanistan, dating to before the US and NATO withdrawal. China's second overseas military base, after Djibouti, was secretly established inside Tajikistan around 2016. It was only in 2019, following the international release of satellite imagery, that China acknowledged its existence. Located 12 kilometres from the strategic Wakhan Corridor and 30 kilometres inside Tajikistan, it has also raised sensitivities with New Delhi, as it is close to the disputed Gilgit-Baltistan area of Pakistan-controlled Kashmir.[80]

Beijing initiated a series of security activities with its Central Asia neighbours, without involving Russia. In 2003–16, bilateral military drills were conducted between China and Tajikistan (eleven times), Kyrgyzstan (ten times), and Kazakhstan (sixteen times).[81] In 2013, it installed in Dushanbe, Tajikistan, its 'Safe City' face recognition surveillance system. In 2014, following Russia's annexation of Donbas and Crimea, it commenced providing military aid to both Kazakhstan and Kyrgyzstan, and began formal cooperation with Uzbekistan's military academy. In 2015, it initiated the Lianyungang Forum, with Kazakhstan, Tajikistan, Uzbekistan and Kyrgyzstan, as a working-level body for discussing law enforcement and security operations; in 2016, the Quadrilateral Cooperation and Coordination Mechanism for counter-terrorism coordination, involving Pakistan, Afghanistan and Tajikistan; and in 2019, launched 'Cooperation 2019', involving exercises to deepen inter-operability between China's and Central Asia's paramilitaries. Since 2020, there have been C+C5 foreign ministers' meetings; and since 2023, a biannual summit process. In addition, as China's investments in Central Asia continue to grow, Chinese private security companies are becoming more prevalent.[82]

Economic opportunity and counter-terrorism/insurgency inevitably draw China more and more into assuming the role of sheriff, as well as that of banker, in the region. For as long as possible, Beijing will seek to do this in ways that do not seem to be challenging Russian primacy, but that, inevitably, will be undercutting it all the time. China will not support Russia in Central Asia if its actions conflict with its interests. Central Asian states, however, will not want to replace Russia's hegemony with China's, but will seek out other relationships as they try to build a multivector foreign policy, though one that is, unavoidably, of greatly unequal parts. The era of two great powers' 'cooperative hegemony' in Central Asia has ended.[83]

## China's Coming Pre-eminence

Russia used to stride across Central Asia with seven-league boots, and, under the USSR, Moscow's iron heel pressed down heavily.[84] A major geostrategic consequence of Putin's invasion of Ukraine has been a pivot by the five Central Asian states away from Russia. China is not yet the main beneficiary, as the states seek to involve multiple actors—including Turkey, the EU, Iran, Japan, South Korea, India and also the US—in regional affairs. As discussed, Russia is now a minor investor in the region and eclipsed by China as the largest trading partner. The EU also has a significant presence, as a source of FDI, as the third-largest trading partner, and as a backer of cooperative infrastructure projects such as the Transcaspian International Transport Route.[85]

Russia's influence in Central Asia has been on a course of long-run decline, while China has increasingly turned its attention to the region as a key strategic priority. It also has a powerful security imperative regarding its western frontier between Xinjiang and three of the Central Asian states. The return of the Taliban to power in Afghanistan further complicates Beijing's security challenges along this frontier, and draws it further into Central Asian security concerns by sharpening their identity of interests.

Sinostan is an advanced work in progress. But Russia and China will continue to look to each other for support in their contests with the US, and this will remain a strong point of convergence in their relationship. The fiction of a 'division of labour' or 'cooperative hegemony' served its purpose well until Russia's invasion of Ukraine, but Russia's greater dependence on China has opened up a bigger space for China to advance its interests. Putin's invasion has become a defining moment in great power relations in Central Asia. Not only has it weakened, possibly fatally, Russia's role as the guarantor of the region's security—by loss of capacity, intent and trust—it has also accelerated public discussion in these lands about Russian colonialism, with a rethinking of the Soviet past that will invariably change Central Asia's relations with Russia for the long term.[86] The European Policy Centre observed that:

> the Kremlin is unhappy about China's success, but it cannot be vocal about it. The importance of Chinese aid and indirect support for [its war in] Ukraine takes precedence for Moscow and will shape its approach to Beijing as long as the confrontation with the West continues.[87]

China has time on its side to complete the Sinostan project. Meanwhile, the trends in geopolitics are running in its favour. China will be happy to play mainly to its strengths through the power of its market, investments and, increasingly, technology, while opportunistically but consistently expanding its activities in the security area of the region. Sinostan has been a deliberate project for Beijing for a long time, with complex interlocking policies involving trade and, especially, infrastructure investment; crisscrossing transport corridors; a mesh of regional institutional arrangements involving the SCO, the BRI, the China–Europe Railway Express, and, more recently, a C+C5 Summit mechanism and parallel foreign ministers' meetings; together with an ever-thickening network of bilateral relations that tie elites more closely to China, even while popular opinion ranges from ambivalent to antagonistic, depending on the country. Meanwhile, the invasion of Ukraine challenges both Russia's capacity for and commitment to regional security, and raises suspicions about its future behaviour towards former Soviet republics, including in Central Asia.

Fatland, in her travelogue of a journey around the Stans, emphasises their shared Soviet heritage and autocratic governments. She concludes that:

> it is impossible to understand the five new countries of Central Asia without taking into consideration the way in which their past as Soviet republics has shaped them. During the seventy years of Soviet rule, Central Asia was forced to leave the Middle Ages and step into the twentieth century ... Internal borders were drawn up, external borders were sealed with barbed wire fences, and five nations were born.[88]

But, nearly thirty-five years since then—and with Kazakhstan and Uzbekistan having each managed leadership transitions, and a representative system of government having been sustained in Kyrgyzstan—the outlook for political stability and economic development appears somewhat better than it did when Fatland made her trip more than a decade ago. The Stans have since moved out of Russia's shadow and into China's, a process accelerated by Putin's invasion of Ukraine. In Central Asia, the future looks more and more like it will belong to China.

# CHAPTER 10

# NEXT GREAT GAME

*'Right now there are changes in the world—the likes of which we haven't seen for*
*100 years—and we are the ones driving those changes together.'*
Xi Jinping to Vladimir Putin, 22 March 2023, Moscow

In early 2020, when writing my previous book, *China's Grand Strategy and Australia's Future in the New Global Order*, it seemed bold, almost audacious, to be arguing that with China's rise the old US-dominated order was already over.[1] Then, political leaders were locked in a Goya-like nightmare of confusion and panic, with the onslaught of the Covid-19 pandemic. The US-led Western alliance was profoundly unsettled by the policies of the Trump administration. Washington had formed a new consensus: China's rise had to be resisted. It was now the adversary. Strategic cooperation with it had become strategic competition, and, in many cases, a reprise of Cold War–style containment. The greatest power shift in history had occurred across the Pacific and now, Canute-like, the US was, with its remaining allies—such as the UK, Australia, Japan and a few European states—trying to preserve its primacy in the global order. Like a thief in the night, for these US allies, the old order had slipped away, unnoticed.

By then, the unipolar moment was no more than a relic of a previous age, when, following the end of the Cold War, a historically aberrant period of a single hegemonic power prevailed. Many had made the mistake of assuming that such an order would be permanent.[2] This ahistorical view shaped foreign, security and trade policies globally, especially among the democracies. Globalisation and the so-called 'Washington Consensus' of liberal economic and trade policies, were still articles of faith for a majority of the world's policy elites. A new species of human life had emerged, now largely extinct: 'Davos man'. 'And while Davos man was not interested in geopolitics, geopolitics [became] very interested in him ... The geopolitics takeover of globalisation is almost complete.'[3]

This was before the US and its Western allies were defeated in Afghanistan, leaving Eurasia to Russia and China. And it was before Putin's audacious invasion of Ukraine put a knife through the heart of the old order. War has returned to the European continent, and the US, guarantor of European security, has struggled to prevail and may yet lose interest in doing so. The illegality of Putin's action was also not condemned universally. UN motions on the matter did more to highlight global divisions, with major powers such as India and China refusing to join the criticism of Russia's actions. Draconian sanctions have been applied, but Russian trade and financial flows have continued, including with Europe.

## Bounded Order

The emerging order at the time described in my book comprised two bounded orders. One was a US-led order of states that mainly have competitive political systems (the term 'democracy' is so ideologically loaded that it is best to set it to one side). The other is more loosely configured, with less convergence in values and political systems, but distinctly led by China. At the time, the international order had not yet formed itself into these two bounded orders, but this shape was emerging from the haze.

The concept of 'bounded orders' was drawn from the work of realist international relations theorist John Mearsheimer.[4] He had suggested as a theoretical possibility that the bounded order would be led by two dominant powers and those within each group would have generally similar values and forms of political and social organisation: representative political systems would be lined up against authoritarian political systems. Each order would have its own transnational institutional arrangements that would provide definition and structure. By 2020, through active institutional innovation, China had already created layers of new bodies that reinforced its leadership of its order. In addition to its BRI, these included the SCO (principally concerned with Eurasian security); AIIB (infrastructure investment); the New Development Bank (finance); and the BRICS, whose membership has substantially expanded to BRICS Plus (policy coordination). States from both orders would still participate in multilateral fora such as the UN, the Bretton Woods institutions, G20, and arms control agreements, and other functional arrangements. The global order would be shaped by degrees of competition and cooperation between bounded orders.

As early as 2016, reflecting on China's multilateral and regional institutional innovations, Brazilian international relations authority Oliver Stuenkel argued that China had set about crafting a 'parallel order' of international institutions and norms, rather than directly challenging existing ones.[5] No one in the West seemed to care to take any notice of his analysis. By the 2023 BRICS summit, applications to join were accepted from Egypt, Ethiopia, Iran, Saudi Arabia and the United Arab Emirates. They became members on 1 January 2024. So far, some forty countries have applied to become members. One of the BRICS Plus's highest policy objectives is to develop alternative financial instruments that are not based on either the US dollar or the euro, and the group has launched its own digital currency.[6] Malaysia, which has become a strong proponent of creating an Asian Monetary Fund and of de-dollarisation, is the most recent applicant for BRICS Plus membership.[7]

For Mearsheimer, the emergence of bounded, or parallel, orders was initially treated as a theoretical, possible alternative to the inevitability of war between the dominant and ascendent power. But as he argued in *The Tragedy of Great Power Politics* (2001), the balance of probability was heavily weighted towards war. In an interview in May 2023, his thinking about a world of bounded orders had moved beyond being just a theoretical possibility. He suggested, in fact, that a world order comprising US-led and Chinese-led bounded orders was emerging.[8] It was already apparent by 2020, but its shape has since crystalised, as China's economic and military power has continued growing, relative to that of the US. Over the past four years, China has also started to present itself as a leader of the Global South. In this world of bounded orders, China—by virtue of its superior economic performance, multilateral and regional institutional innovation, and well-funded and disciplined diplomacy—stands alone at the head of its order. As we have seen, China and Russia's divergent strategic interests and, as a result, history of mutual mistrust and hostility, would prevent Chussia becoming an enduring stable leader. Russia will continue to be China's junior partner; this would have occurred with or without Putin's invasion of Ukraine. In the words of former US president Bill Clinton's famous 1992 election message, 'It's the economy, stupid', but on a continental scale in the case of China.

China is increasingly being recognised as having become an established alternative to the US-led order. In 2024, the US international affairs specialist Elizabeth Economy argued that a China order is now an established fact of life in the international system.[9] She sets out the essential elements of China's order:

> built not just on multipolarity but also on absolute sovereignty; security rooted in international consensus and the UN Charter; state-determined human rights based on each country's circumstances; development as the 'master key' to all solutions; the end of U.S. dollar dominance; and a pledge to leave no country and no one behind.[10]

Within China's order, the most widely supported institutional initiative has been the BRI, in which some 150 countries, and multilateral and regional institutions, have become active participants. More recently, Beijing has sought to give greater expression to its leadership of the Global South, with several new initiatives. The GDI, inaugurated in 2022, aligns with the UN's Global Development Agenda, and emphasises China's strengths when it comes to digital and green technologies suitable for poorer countries. The Global Security Initiative (GSI), also introduced in 2022, is based on absolute sovereignty and non-interference, rejecting unilateralism and bloc security alliances. In May 2023, the newly announced

GCI was endorsed at the C+C5 summit. It emphasises diversity of civilisations and defines human rights as relative to a particular country's conditions, rejecting the primacy of the values of liberal democracies and the universal application of human rights norms. China claims that more than 100 countries participate in its GDI and a similar number support the GSI. In the security field, China has stepped up its bilateral training and technical assistance programs, in addition to arms sales. It has linked these activities to the BRI and GSI, with Africa becoming a particular focus of attention. Together, these activities help build a 'collaborative security system' centred on China.[11] They are all intended to underpin Xi Jinping's vision of a world order based on his principle of a 'global community of shared future'.[12]

## China's Grand Strategy

Analysis of China's consolidation of power in the Eurasian heartland usually lacks any account of its own grand strategy. Powerful structural factors relating to China's search for security are seldom addressed explicitly; the thirst for primacy is taken for granted. It has been argued in this book, however, that this has not been driven by a need for imperial conquest, as in the case of Russia, whose empire project was carried forward by competitive visions of grandeur, hunger for status, and colossal racial conceit. Rather, it has come from China's deeply embedded need to find security and stability along its frontiers in continental Asia.

China's grand strategy has been based on weakness, not strength. This reflects the historical circumstances of the founding of the People's Republic: the CPC took charge not of a country or a unified state but of shards of territory. Its primary focus has been securing and maintaining territorial integrity, and protecting its frontiers. Possibly the only action that went beyond this was China's invasion of Vietnam in 1979, which saw the PLA defeated.[13] Sulmaan Wasif Khan, in his brilliant book on China's grand strategy, summarised it as follows:

Mao took a broken colossus, made it whole, and stood it up on its feet. Deng dragged it to reason and strength; Jiang and Hu nurtured the still-wounded giant and ensured that it continued to grow. Now, as Xi Jinping emerged to take mastery of it, great China strode the world, a behemoth whose time had come. But though the colossus was whole, it still felt fragile. It was hobbled by the memories of how difficult safety had been to achieve, and it was terrified that it would fall apart again.[14]

China has attained its leading, but not yet globally hegemonic, position by commerce and investment; expanding technological capacity; and, mostly, skilful and determined diplomacy—bilaterally, regionally and multilaterally. It has also been by luck. Had China's economy faltered for an extended period, or if America and NATO had not been defeated in Afghanistan, or if Putin had not invaded Ukraine, the story might be quite different.

## From Heartland to Rimland

China's rise to pre-eminence in Eurasia conjures the ghosts of Mackinder and Spykman, who themselves sound like participants in the Great Game. In the contemporary setting, some analysts view the strong parallels between China's BRI and Mackinder's theory as 'proof' that China is pursuing a global strategy of world domination based on its securing primacy over the Eurasian heartland. Eloquent assertions by Mackinder make it plain why so many fall into this trap:

> Trans-continental railways are now transmuting the conditions of land-power, and nowhere can they have such effect as in the closed heartland of Euro-Asia.[15]

Or by Spykman:

> Whoever controls the rimland also controls the heartland, and so, by virtue of such colossal power, threatens the Americas.[16]

But beyond geography, competition for global primacy has become increasingly centred on technology and the cyber world. The influence of technology on geopolitics is fast eclipsing geography's. Joshua Walker, a leading expert in the field of the geopolitics of technological competition, claims that geography is becoming much less important in geostrategy compared with cyber and digital technologies. In Beijing and Silicon Valley, two distinct 'online ecosystems' are emerging, which, he emphasises, is becoming the greatest source of conflict between the US and China, and it is here that 'China is, today, a true superpower'.[17]

In mid-2024, the *Economist* described China as a 'scientific superpower'. Quoting an OECD report on the publication of 'quality research', it said that by 2022 China had overtaken the US in spending on applied research and experimental development, and was fast catching up on spending on basic research. Meanwhile, China now leads the US and EU in the share of 'high impact' papers in eight out of fourteen disciplines surveyed, and was not far behind in the other categories.[18]

China's consolidation of Eurasia is not complete, and will never achieve the extent of direct colonial control envisaged by Mackinder in his horror scenarios for the West. It is very much a work in progress and without a defined end, as it derives from China's search for security, not a vision of a Sinocentric world. Nonetheless, just as power shifted from the US to China in the first two decades of this millennium, so it has shifted from Russia to China over the past decade. Freed from continental insecurity, other than the ever-present threat of Islamic fundamentalism, China is connecting its land power with its emerging sea power.

Australian historian of China Wang Gungwu argues that continental threats from nomadic invaders saw Ming China move defensive resources, from maritime protection to building the Great Wall of China. In the end, it failed, and the nomadic Manchu–Mongolian invaders came from the north and established the Qing dynasty. Until the nineteenth century, the Qing remained focused on threats from the interior of Eurasia. Now, according to Wang, China is able to build maritime power. In this respect, argues Wang, it is becoming more like the US.[19]

The US will continue to be a great power, and one with the capacity to balance China globally if it has the will to do so. While the Biden administration has worked assiduously to strengthen and expand the US alliance system, doubts remain about the US's will to provide global leadership. These doubts are significantly elevated under a Trump presidency. The country is deeply divided by domestic politics; its economy has areas of great strength but also of weakness; its national debt is stratospheric; the US dollar, as the global reserve currency, is under increasing challenge; and US continental security is not directly threatened by China's rise. Already, the great champion of globalisation has turned inward and away from deeper international engagement. There is little to suggest that the US will return to Eurasia to contest China in its heartland.

For some time now, China has been viewed as the West's greatest strategic competitor. The US and Australia were early to this view; Europe was later, reflecting the range of commercial and political interests among its members. In 2019, the EU changed its strategic assessment of China from being a 'strategic partner' to a 'systemic rival' to the EU, in terms of values and interests. Nonetheless, it has remained committed to cooperation and engagement with China, refusing, unlike Australia, to be overtly drawn into Washington's great power rivalry with Beijing and its policies of containment.[20]

### China and Russia, or Chussia's Feet of Clay

Despite its economic challenges, Russia has, through single-minded determination and ruthlessness, and substantial military—especially nuclear—assets, been able to play itself back into the role of a world power. Putin set out to regain Russia's international influence and has succeeded in doing so. He has shown his people a Russia that is once again an important actor internationally and that can, as in the Middle East, exercise real power and influence.

Isolated internationally and sharing with Xi Jinping disdain for the US and the remnants of the liberal international order, Putin has increasingly aligned himself with Xi, even if that means accepting a junior-partner role for Russia. Both leaders are keen to stress how past differences between Russia and China have been resolved; that they present to the world a new model of great-power relations; and that they seek a 'fairer', more inclusive international order, which is responsive to all countries' needs for development and security, especially those in the Global South. As shown in previous chapters (especially Chapters 7 and 8), theirs is a 'concert of convenience' for the present time. Already their respective different interests have begun to mute the enthusiasm spruiked in the statement that it was a friendship 'without limits'. Wariness is creeping back, as China's relative power and influence keep rising and it acts independently of Russia's interests. As argued in this book, and despite shrill warnings of a Chussia aligned against the West, Chussia has feet of clay for reasons to do with Russia and China's history, geostrategy and interests.

The Russian Far East, or the former lands of Chinese Manchuria, need to be watched carefully, as an emerging area of tension between Russia and China. Nationalist grievances in China, so wantonly cultivated by the CPC, and the desire to right the wrongs of the 'century of humiliation', may turn to focus on recovery of the vast swathes of its former territory now held by Russia. As controversial historian and Russian authority Alexander Etkind wrote in 2023:

In 2014, Russia took Crimea back, launching the conflict that continues today. Talking to Xi, Putin hoped the Chinese leader would understand his actions in Ukraine but would not apply the same logic to the lands that the Russian Empire annexed from China. Such an asymmetric, egocentric aspiration does not have a chance in great-power politics.

Could the Chinese use their northern troops in a battle for Taiwan? Probably yes, but this would be a tragic mistake. The immense and undefended spaces of southern Siberia and Russia's Pacific coastal provinces would be an easier target. For a rational nation … reaching the strategic goal of colonizing Siberia in a peaceful, profitable manner would be more desirable than engaging in a bloody, complicated battle for Taiwan.[21]

While the likelihood of China seeking formally to recover these lost northeastern territories must be for some time considered to be low, the fact that official names on maps were revised in 2023 to show prior Chinese occupation, and the occasional flare-up on social media over the continuing injustice of Russia holding on to these territories, are instructive straws in the wind. The nationalist sensitivities in China are so pronounced that no leader can simply sweep them under the rug. Meanwhile, Beijing's influence will expand at Moscow's expense, due to the vast population imbalance between China and Russia in the Far East; the existence of extensive underutilised land and resources; labour shortages; growing cross-border mobility, taking place with official blessings; and a creeping colonisation of these territories by Chinese businesspeople and workers.[22]

## Islamic Fundamentalism

Brzezinski distinguished between 'geopolitical players' and 'geopolitical pivots'. The former have the capacity to exercise power beyond their borders and shape the geopolitical situation. 'Geopolitical pivots' derive their importance from the sensitivity of their geographical locations and their potential for destabilising geopolitical players. While Brzezinski identified Russia and China as key players, looking west, rather than east, he picked Ukraine and Azerbaijan as key pivot states. Writing in the mid-1990s, these now seem to be prescient choices, especially considering Ukraine–Russia relations since the 2000s.[23]

In this book, with its focus on Core Eurasia as the principal theatre of contest, the key pivots on the chessboard are Afghanistan and Xinjiang. Afghanistan's geopolitical position ensured it has always been critical to Eurasian stability. Xinjiang is not, of course, a state, but its culture, history, ethnicity, and the competition for it between great empires, locates it geopolitically more as a part of Central Asia, rather than of China.[24]

With the heightened threat of the spread of Islamic fundamentalism, both Beijing and Moscow will want to work with Central Asian states to reinforce them. China's concerns led to a military base being established in Tajikistan in 2016, well before the US retreat from Afghanistan. China has sought out its own relations with Afghanistan, and its strategy and actions will be shaped mostly by its concerns over Xinjiang. The SCO will likely grow in importance as the main regional security vehicle, leading to higher levels of cooperation between Chinese, Russian and Central Asian security services, covering military, anti-terrorism and policing activities. The common threat of Islamic militantism will be a constant point of convergence between all Core Eurasian states.

## Great Game Over

Empires and great powers' competing imperial projects for primacy across Eurasia have, after centuries, come to an end. China has emerged as the pre-eminent power, something that was almost unthinkable when, in the mid-nineteenth century, Yaqub Beg established the Khanate of Kashgaria, and the Qing court was forced to concede vast territories in Siberia and Manchuria to the Russians, with the treaties of Aigun and Peking.

For the first time in Chinese history, its rulers can feel secure about its inner Asian borders. The persistent threats to its land-based frontiers and loss of territory to neighbouring states have ended. It is fast approaching a moment akin to that the US experienced from the late nineteenth and early twentieth centuries, when it secured its borders, and then established hegemony over the Western Hemisphere. This epochal process had been given its policy legitimisation as early as 1823 with the Monroe Doctrine, which declared that the Americas were off limits to the European powers. Once the west of the United States was consolidated, the US continued to expand across the Pacific and from there to become the global hegemon.[25] China is now free to project power globally, in direct competition with the US.

China may or may not choose to do this. Even if it does, as I have argued elsewhere, China is a constrained superpower—*Prometheus Bound*—in a way the US was not when it sought security beyond its neighbourhood.[26] China is constrained by its history, and continuing territorial threats from within its border: namely, Xinjiang, Tibet, and also Taiwan and Hong Kong. But, more than anything else, it is constrained by its utter dependence on world markets for all the resources it needs to keep its economic engines turning and to buy much of the things it needs for what it produces. While it has begun to reduce its dependence on seaborne trade, it still has massive strategic vulnerabilities, with the bulk of its energy and resources transiting narrow global choke-points, such as the Strait of Malacca and the South China Sea.[27]

China is also much more deeply integrated into the international economy than is Russia. The sanctions regime Russia has faced following its invasion of Ukraine would be far more damaging to China, which is substantially more dependent on foreign markets and would be hurt badly by the type of financial sanctions the West has imposed. The comprehensiveness of these latter measures has, since the invasion of Ukraine, spurred Beijing to double down on expanding the use of the yuan in competition with the US dollar, and to develop alternative international payments systems, including digital ones.

An effective Central Asian Monroe Doctrine could see China being the final arbiter on political leaders in the region: basing its military in different locations to deal with terrorist insurgencies; and expecting, and receiving, unified support for Chinese positions in regional and multilateral forums, including within the UN. Over time, this could extend deep into the cultural sphere of ordinary life, with Chinese replacing Russian as a second language, and a shift in preferences to Chinese cultural products.

Of course, should China's economy falter and its internal politics fracture, then even Chinese territorial integrity may come into question. Xinjiang independence may emerge as a serious challenge to the remnant Chinese state; Islamic fundamentalists may find in Xinjiang a relatively soft target without the presence of a strong centralised Chinese state. The spread of militant Islam across Central Asia may gather momentum. These are, admittedly, distant possibilities at this time, but are nevertheless worth considering—they put into perspective what could happen in this dynamic and inherently unstable region, in the absence of dominant great powers ensuring stability.

## Implications for India

As China's primacy over Core Eurasia consolidates, other states will look at hedging, if not balancing, or containing China. Central Asian states are themselves exercising agency by pursuing 'multivariant' foreign policies, which seek to attract the involvement of those outside the region, such as Turkey and the EU, both of which are keen to expand their influence there.

India would seem to be an obvious balance for China in Core Eurasia, in view of its size and proximity. Russia and India's relations have historically been close and remain so today. In the early 1960s, as we saw in Chapter 5, Moscow moved closer to New Delhi and away from China, at a time when its relations with Beijing were dire. Moscow's failure to support China in its conflict with India during the 1962 Sino-Indian War contributed substantially to Beijing's ire with Moscow and the public Sino-Soviet split that froze relations between them for twenty-seven years.

India was restrained in its comments on Putin's invasion of Ukraine and abstained from key UN votes condemning Russia. It has maintained normal trade relations, despite the West's sanctions, and Russia has been a major source of arms for India. Unlike China, India has largely managed to avoid US criticism of its continuing closeness with Russia. Despite the war in Ukraine and India's acquiescence in Putin's invasion, the US's strategic objectives are better served by India contributing to balancing China in the Indo-Pacific.

Putin has sought to balance China in Russia's Far East, to some extent. India and Russia have agreed on a number of projects to develop shipping infrastructure, to promote greater Far East–India trade, as discussed in Chapter 8. Historically, geography has kept India apart from the Eurasian security system; this remains the case in the modern world. In the past, India's connection to Eurasia was through the Afghanistan corridor, but this was when Pakistan and India were part of a single imperial system: first the Mughals, and then British India. Since 1949, and the separation of India and Pakistan, this has been closed off.

Apart from specific points of potential conflict along the China–India border in the high Himalaya, India's security is not greatly threatened from the north. While border disputes could develop into serious military clashes, the topography of the area and India's ramping-up of its military presence, capabilities and transport infrastructure in the area will most likely ensure that conflict remains localised. Since the violent clashes in June 2020, in which troops on either side brawled, but without shots being fired, at the line of actual control in Ladakh, India has done much to build infrastructure and pre-position forces and matériel.[28]

It has also taken steps to raise the costs for China of what New Delhi views as Beijing's bad behaviour. A notable example of this was when, following the skirmishes in 2020, India set aside its doubts and ambivalent attitude towards the Quad and embraced it wholeheartedly. Since then, it has become an active participant and supported its elevation to a summit-level mechanism. It also invited Australia to participate in the annual Malabar naval exercises, something it had long resisted, despite Australia's repeated requests to join. New Delhi, as well, substantially recalibrated its relations with Washington, strengthening cooperation across civilian and military fields. All these actions demonstrated to Beijing that Delhi was prepared to act if its interests were challenged.

India's greatest security risk is on its northwest frontier, where it continues to be in dispute with Pakistan over Kashmir. Both are nuclear-armed states. Pakistan has at times supported terrorist interventions in India; and is also a close ally of China, with which it could coordinate to destabilise their contested border areas. Despite the obvious tensions in the relationship, New Delhi also has to tread carefully with Beijing. It joined the SCO and is also one of the leading lenders to China's AIIB. Both Delhi and Beijing undersand fully where their interests converge and also diverge, and so, at most times, manage the sensitivities in their relationship carefully.

India has an unbeatable advantage in the Indian Ocean. Besides the northwest frontier, this is its primary area of security interest. Geographically, India is a wedge cleaving the Indian Ocean into two halves. It is required to project power only over relatively short distances, compared with any likely adversary. It also controls numerous islands and reefs across the area.

While China has shown some interest in expanding its naval presence in the region, whatever Beijing's ambitions might be, practically it will always be at a substantial strategic disadvantage in the region as compared with India. The US also maintains considerable naval and air assets at the British military base on Diego Garcia. Along with Guam, it is one of two critical US strategic-bomber bases in the Indo-Pacific.

India has limited commercial interest in Central Asia. Its nationals account for only about 20,000 out of a population of 75 million, and its bilateral trade with the region is just $US2–3 billion. Half of this is with Kazakhstan, which is India's largest trading partner in Central Asia, but total trade is small and heavily in Kazakhstan's favour. In 2018, Kazakhstan exported goods worth about $US1 billion to India and imported $US300 million of goods. In 2018, Indian residents in Kazakhstan numbered around 6000, of whom some 3500 were students.[29]

In January 2022, the Indian prime minister, Narendra Modi, convened the first India–Central Asia Summit, attended by all five heads of state. Held virtually, participants agreed to institutionalise it with biannual leaders' gatherings, along with ministerial-level meetings covering specific areas. It was, however, mainly focused on security, especially with regards to Afghanistan. India has also, from time to time, conducted some limited joint anti-terrorism exercises with Central Asian states. In July 2023, it hosted the SCO summit but with few outcomes.[30] Overall, India's approach to Central Asia contrasts unfavourably with China's, as being half-hearted, piecemeal, and constrained by events external to the region.

India's Connect Central Asia policy, seeking to strengthen political, security, economic and cultural connections, has also failed to gain traction. It has sought to cooperate with Iran and Russia on a new overland transport corridor, but this has been frustrated by the state of its bilateral relations with Afghanistan, Pakistan and China. Beyond high-level interactions and rhetoric, however, the major challenges for India in increasing its footprint in Central Asia are how to match China's deep pockets, and the China–Pakistan axis. With the Taliban back in Kabul, the situation has become more

complicated and less conducive to India's asserting influence in
Central Asia. Its options to improve linkages through Iran and Russia
are also severly restricted because of the West's economic sanctions
on both countries.[31] All of these create favourable circumstances for
China to continue expanding its influence at the expense of both
Russia and India. New Delhi will have to seek out new avenues of
engagement, but it is likely that India's relations with the region will
continue to be based mainly on a few narrow security areas closely
tied to counter-terrorism.[32]

## Implications for Australia

The European occupiers of Australia have always benefited from
having a single major power—first the UK, and then the US—
with which their values and political systems were closely aligned,
providing security for the small population occupying the big
continent. It had long been an article of faith that it was necessary
for one of these powers to guarantee Australia's security against
the prospect of the teeming Asian masses to the country's north
overrunning this lonely outpost of Western civilisation, and that this
could be relied on into the future.[33] The end of the US-led order and
the arrival of a multipolar order directly challenged the foundational
assumption of Australia's security policy. A multipolar world was
beyond Australian policy makers' experience—their response had
been denial and to double down on the continuing US alliance.
Unlike in 2020, however, when *China's Grand Strategy and Australia's
Future in the New Global Order* was written, it is now recognised
that the world of Australian foreign policy and security has changed.
Ironically, one of the clearest recent statements on this has been made
by the Australian treasurer, not its foreign minister. In that speech,
the treasurer described a 'world of churn and change', and how with
the return of multipolarity, economic and security policies were
now inextricably linked.[34] Australia now faces a dystopian future in
a multipolar world; one in which there are no good choices, only
least bad ones.

Under Anthony Albanese's Labor government, elected May
2022, the perilous downward spiral in relations with China that had

taken place under the previous Liberal governments of Malcolm
Turnbull and Scott Morrison was arrested. Foreign Minister Penny
Wong liked to refer to the relationship as having been 'stabilised',
rather than 'normalised'. This is a distinction without a difference.
High-level visits have resumed on a regular basis in both directions,
and egregious bilateral Chinese trade measures against Australia as a
means of economic coercion have mostly ended.

The importance for Wong and the government in emphasising
'stabilisation' over 'normalisation' lies in the commitment to ramp
up further Australia's military enmeshment with the US in East Asia.
Australia, together with Japan, has become one of the staunchest
defenders of the rimland. In addition to its eye-watering financial commitment to AUKUS, Australia is likely to accept more US
military personnel to be located here, and to be a third base for
the US strategic bomber force. Interoperability of forces has now
reached unprecedented levels, to the extent that the defence minister, Richard Marles, boasts of the two forces being 'interchangable'.
All this is in addition to Australia's long-standing support for the US
nuclear defence system, via its hosting of the Pine Gap communications facility. Analysts such as Hugh White doubt that Australia has
retained an independent defence capability as it seeks to uphold,
over China, US primacy in East Asia. The challenge for the Albanese
government, then, is to nurture and expand commercial relations
with China, while working more closely with the US, than perhaps
any other state, to thwart China's ascendency in the region.[35]

Wong has explained that AUKUS, together with the overall
elevated commitment to US military strength in East Asia, is intended
to contribute to 'strategic equilibrium' in the region. Essentially,
this amounts to preserving in aspic the existing status quo. It does
not address the fundamental shifting power dynamics that prevent
such an equilibrium being achieved. For Wong, it is premised on
the US continuing to be the dominant power in the region and to
retain global primacy. This does not recognise the extent to which
the order has changed.[36] AUKUS is perhaps the most profound
expression of Australia's having surrendered its foreign and strategic
policy independence to China's competitor.

Wong's vision for the East Asia region is one where 'no one country dominates', and where individual states have agency and can choose their own strategic relationships. While Australian strategic policy thinking is maybe moving closer to that of its major South-East Asian partners, it still has some considerable way to move before it is aligned with that of its neighbours, as Evelyn Goh, from the Australian National University, points out.[37]

The Association of Southeast Asian Nations (ASEAN) has been clear-eyed about the changed strategic realities of East Asia as China's power has continued to grow. ASEAN, to which Australia needs to lean for its regional security, has for some time made it a pillar of its foreign policy not to put itself into a position where it has to choose between either great power, the US or China.[38] Recent opinion polling in the region suggests China is beginning to emerge as the preferred regional partner if a choice has to be made.[39] Australia's choice diminishes its influence with its neighbours, precisely in the areas where it should be investing most of its efforts. James Curran, international editor of the *Australian Financial Review*, summed up the contradictions in Australian foreign policy for the region:

> ASEAN by its nature is allergic to ... nailing its colours to the mast in the great power struggle between the US and China. This also means Australia speaks with something of a forked tongue in the region. There's ASEAN centrality, then there is AUKUS.[40]

More directly, Malaysia's prime minister, Anwar Ibrahim, during a recent ASEAN summit in Melbourne, warned Australia not to make its China problem ASEAN's problem. He said Malaysia had 'no problem with China', and urged all countries in the region to work with both the US and China, to ensure peace and security.[41]

## Avoiding the Tragedy of Great Powers

The realist view of where these big shifts in power end, as propounded by analysts such as Mearsheimer, is that they must result in tragedy: namely, war. In an anarchic world, great powers are inevitably set on a collision course as they seek to ensure their security and survival, by first becoming regional hegemons and then global ones. This is essentially a restatement of the Thucydides Trap.[42] Other historians draw heavily on the experience of Wilhelmine Germany and Britain before World War I.[43] This has found various expressions—most recently, as China's rise has begun to challenge US pre-eminence in the Asia-Pacific (a region the US has declared to be of vital interest to its own security) and may threaten its primacy globally. While rejecting the inevitability of war between the rising and dominant power, Graham Allison—Harvard professor and author of a much-acclaimed study of China's rise, *Destined for War*—concluded that 'the defining question about the global order is whether China and the US can escape the Thucydides Trap'.[44]

There are alternatives to the tragedy now unfolding. One that is frequently cited is the way Great Britain accommodated peacefully the rise of the US from the late nineteenth century and into the twentieth century. Armed conflict had been at hand on some occasions but, in the end, the dominant power, Great Britain, ceded strategic space to the emergent great power. This often-cited example, however, is also seen as exceptional because the dominant and ascendent powers shared values, and broadly similar forms of social and political organisation. As such, it might be of little help in identifying how relations between the US and China could settle without conflict into some sort of stable order.[45]

A more relevant historical example of accommodation between great powers can be found in Eurasia itself, as discussed in Chapter 2. To recap: in the early years of the twentieth century, after some sixty years of great power rivalry—most of it played out across Central Asia from Xinjiang to the Caspian Sea, and south to Afghanistan—Britain and Imperial Russia brought the Great Game to an end. In 1904, Russia was militarily crushed by the rising power of Japan in faraway Port Arthur (Lvshun) in China; meanwhile, Britain was becoming increasingly preoccupied by the rise of Germany, closer to home. Russia too was concerned about Germany's increasing power. In 1907, agreement was reached on the Wakhan Corridor being a buffer zone between them in Central Asia. Consequently, Britain ceded strategic space to Russia in Central Asia, and Russia did not threaten British India. The latter was, as we have seen, a case of policy catching up with the facts on the ground.

A closer reading of the history of power shifts suggests that rising powers have pursued a variety of strategies when dealing with a declining power—from support to predation, depending on the possible strategy's perceived value on the spectrum from accommodation to conflict.[46] Great powers can find a strategic accommodation without going to war with each other. With nuclear war off the table because of the risk of mutually assured destruction, and little idea of what victory in more conventional warfare would look like for either China or the US—other than involving exorbitant costs—options for finding strategic stability between their respective bounded orders are still worth exploring.

## A New Grand Bargain

With China's emergence as the primary Eurasian power, the issue for the West is how to respond to this new and evolving power distribution. States manage their relationships through forms of Westphalian balancing of power. Alliances and coalitions of states form and dissolve, as their relative power changes, and when interests align or diverge. States find an identity of interests in the need to balance one that is becoming too powerful and acting without regard to the interests of other states. But their judgements in doing so often involve the seeking—naturally enough—of a military or strategic advantage over their rivals; and so, in the longer term, they prove to be inherently unstable.

The US remains secure in its hemisphere as being the dominant rimland power while also commanding a continent. It will deal with China as a peer competitor and leading power in their respective orders. The lines of competition are already abundantly clear: notably, trade, investment and especially technology. Areas of cooperation are also apparent. The most important and urgent of these are climate change, cyber and AI regulation, pandemics, control of narcotics, outer space and the polar regions, as well as perennial concerns over arms control and terrorism. Across all these issues, it should be possible for diplomacy to prevail.

No state will be strong enough in the new order to impose its will on all others, even if it constantly manoeuvres to do so. To avoid anarchy, a grand bargain will have to be struck between the US-led West and China. As with any accommodation between great powers, this will require acknowledging the legitimacy of China's position in the world order and affording it strategic space, while seeking ways to hedge against bad behaviour. Specifically, this will also involve, as distasteful as it may be, Washington's forswearing the fostering of regime change in China, an intent that still has some powerful advocates within the Washington beltway.[47]

It will be necessary to respect, consistently and credibly, China's territorial integrity and not seek to destabilise the regime through fomenting instability in places such as Xinjiang, Tibet and Hong Kong. Taiwan will continue to be a vexed issue. The best that can be hoped for is a return to strategic ambiguity and the status quo ante on actual application of the 'one China policy'. At some point, however, the US may no longer be prepared to guarantee Taiwan's security. As far as the eye can see, the US will still be the dominant military power and China will continue to be an ascending military power, but if relative economic performance continues as it has over the past decades, China would become a peer, if not dominant, military power. The US can't 'wish away' its main competitor; 'peak China' is still far in the distant future.[48]

If the new order, based on managed competition and cooperation between the bounded orders, is to be less anarchic than any other alternative, China will need to be balanced in Eurasia. China's ascendency over Eurasia, to become the unchallenged pre-eminent power of this vast land mass, raises enormous questions of geostrategy and how best the liberal world should adjust. Europe, as the Russian invasion of Ukraine so abruptly reminded everyone, is directly affected by events in Eurasia. It does not have the luxury of withdrawing from the world in isolation, like the US has done in the past, and may do again—indeed, this is one likely outcome under another Trump presidency. Europe, then, is left with its own need to find a Westphalian response to China that does not rely solely on the US.

In the 2010s, China's emerging pre-eminence increasingly saw European states, individually and as the EU, move closer towards the US. And although the first Trump presidency created the impression that they were swimming towards a sinking ship, the rise of China as an ever-bigger presence globally pushed them closer together, while forcing them to minimise their differences with the US over technological competition, domestic industrial policies and climate change. The return of the Democrats to the White House helped manage the differences less fractiously, thereby permitting a sharper focus on the common threat of China. Putin's invasion of Ukraine and the Putin–Xi brotherhood added further weight to this. The Madrid NATO Summit in 2022 was the culmination of these events, with discussion of a 'single theatre' of strategic challenge to the West from Chussia. If not quite stillborn, the single theatre has stalled, as divergent national interests did not support such grandiose—and so clearly prematurely adorned—architecture.[49]

Europe is confronted by a historic choice. It can let Russia drift closer and closer to China and become integrated in its tributary system, or it can seek to do a 'reverse Kissinger' (that is, using Russia to balance China) and re-Europeanise Russia. In view of the long-term historical animosities, and strategic differences and outlook, between Russia and China, as has been shown here, the West has an opportunity once again to draw Russia closer to balance China.

The possibility of a 'reverse Kissinger' has been dismissed by some, but still merits being explored as a policy option. The East is not Russia's natural place. It has cleaved itself there because of frustration and failure finding a workable accommodation with the West. The invasion of Ukraine has made it more dependent on the East. The invasion has also, understandably, hardened views against Russia within Europe and the US-led Western order. But, no matter how difficult and unlikely it seems now, the West, through Europe, will need to use Russia to balance an ever more powerful China. The challenge for Europe will be to work out how to re-Europeanise Russia in a post-Putin world. Inevitably, stability in the global order requires a balance of power between states.

The expression 'reverse Kissinger' is often used to refer to the US once again exercising great power geostrategy but this time establishing an alliance directed against China. The concept has been around since at least 2017. US strategic analysts have suggested that if Nixon could 'play Beijing off against Moscow', today's Washington could play Moscow off against Beijing.[50] But as Putin and Xi have become over the years more openly and closely set against the US, it has generally been dismissed as a naive and therefore unworkable strategy. For example, Alexander Gabuev, Russian expert at the Carnegie Russia Eurasia Center in Berlin, dismissed the idea out of hand, arguing that Putin and Xi need each other, and are so like-minded in their stand against the US that 'western policy makers should abandon the idea that they could drive a wedge between Beijing and Moscow'.[51] Certainly, the war in Ukraine, and the expansion of NATO, both before and after Putin ordered the invasion, make any Western strategic realignment with Russia in the foreseeable future almost unthinkable. But, then again, so was Washington's rapprochement with Beijing, until it happened.

While those who would rule out a 'reverse Kissinger' generally acknowledge the historical, structural, economic and cultural divergence between Russia and China—and, consequently, the inherent fragility of the relationship and potential for mutual mistrust—they assert that the Putin–Xi bromance prevails over these differences. But neither Putin nor Xi will be around forever and, as early chapters of this book have shown, in modern times the relationship has been highly sensitive to changes in the individuals in charge. Geostrategy is often the work of decades, so preparation needs to begin for the post-Putin, post-Xi world. Moreover, it is not only up to the US to bring this about. In the new multipolar order, other actors can have an important role to play.

Europe should start thinking through what would be required for a grand project to 're-Europeanise' Russia. As previous chapters have shown, 'Chussia' is a thin reed via which China can project geopolitical power. Russia's tilt to the East also runs against Russian history, culture and traditions. So, there is fertile ground with which to work. Moreover, Russia can no longer dominate in Central Asia, so it will never feel secure in Eurasia. Inevitably, it will seek ways to move out of China's shadow, which Russia cannot do by itself. History also shows that seemingly impregnable orthodoxies can collapse overnight. While a 'reverse Kissinger' may seem remote in the current strategic moment, that does not mean that the hard brainwork required to achieve it should not be started. It will, however, require from European leaders statecraft of the highest order—of the sort that led to the creation of the EU itself.

Preparing for a post-Putin Russia will also involve working now to show the Russian people what this would look like. Europe should stop following the US, and framing the conflict with Russia as a contest between 'democracy' and 'autocracy'. Instead, it should be continually stressing its cultural and civilisational affinities with Russia. Belligerent speech and posturing play directly into Putin's hands. His invasion of Ukraine commands popular support in Russia because it is seen to be a defence of the country's civilisation against foreign predators.[52]

Europe can offer Russia so much in terms of investment and technology to rebuild the country, and provide an attractive alternative to China. This is the promise that needs to be constantly held out to Russia; with a firm commitment to actually deliver, unlike in the 1990s. Credible security guarantees must be provided, and there must be an end to eastern expansion of NATO. It will all require patient, clever work over the years, just as Putin's health or grip on political power starts to weaken. Political change in Europe may also assist this. If the broad trend across the EU to more right-wing governments continues, the gap in values between many European states and Russia will begin to shrink. Some of Europe's right-wing parties that have the potential to raise significantly their political influence over the next five years, or longer, are not overtly hostile towards Russia. Some would be prepared to accept post-2014 borders between Russia and Ukraine, and even Putin's territorial gains so far, as the price for ending the conflict. For Russians, this is a far more attractive prospect than becoming a long-term vassal of China.

## The New Great Game

After the dissolution of the Soviet Union, Zbigniew Brzezinski argued that the US had to become the dominant power over Eurasia. At the time, he had an inkling that China could become that, but it was still a long way off. No one could have imagined what has happened in the first two decades of the twenty-first century and the geopolitical power shifts that would occur, and in such a short historical period. Writing in the mid-1990s—in the afterglow of, and hubris at, the end of the Cold War, the ascendency of the 'Washington consensus', the opening of China under Deng Xiaping, the strengthening of US alliances and expansion of the EU and US-led NATO—he asked what could go wrong. His answer: the US could neglect Eurasia and thus not control, in MacKinder's words, the world's geopolitical 'heartland'. Brzezinski warned that if one country, especially if that country were to be China, gained control over Eurasia, the US would face the first serious challenge to its global leadership.[53]

With China becoming the dominant power in Core Eurasia and securing its borders, the implications of it becoming a global maritime power are immense. Freed from its continental constraints and security anxieties, it could shift its assets towards miliary operations against Taiwan before seeking to project maritime power globally, just as the US did with its annexation of the islands of Hawaii, some 3800 kilometres from the continental US.[54] China's ascendency to pre-eminence over Eurasia raises huge questions of geostrategy and how best the liberal world should adjust to this historically unprecedented event.

This is the new Great Game, in which the US and China are already engaged. It is being played out across all areas of diplomacy, technology, trade and investment, development assistance, infrastructure, health, outer space, financial settlements, intelligence, digital and cyber. In all areas, the US and its allies are being challenged by China. The world has entered the most intense phase of global competition, short of outright military conflict, ever experienced. The Great Game has shifted from being a contest within the heartland, to a struggle between the heartland and the rimland. It continues, but now on a truly global field.

# NOTES

## A Note on Eurasia

1 Khalid, Adeeb, *Central Asia: a new history from the imperial conquests to the present*, Princeton University Press, Princeton and Oxford, 2021.

## Chapter 1   Eurasian Hinge of the Global Order

1 Kaplan, Robert D, *The Return of Maroc Polo's World: war, strategy, and America's interests in the twenty-first century*, Random House, New York, 2018, p. 260.

2 Smith, Mark B, *The Russia Anxiety: and how history can resolve it*, Allen Lane, London, 2019.

3 Central Asia is commonly used to include Kazakhstan, Uzbekistan, Tajikistan, Kirgizstan and Turkmenistan, which is a political usage based on these states having been former Soviet republics, which became independent from 1992, after the collapse of the Soviet Union. But an older and geopolitical definition would also include Afghanistan and, although it has long been part of China, Xinjiang because of its religious, cultural, linguistic and historical affinities with the other Central Asian states. This broader usage is adopted here. While 'Eurasia' is often used to describe the territory from the Sea of Japan to the Vistula River in Poland, and even land further west, this study is concerned with the area east of the Caucasus mountains, which is sometimes referred to as 'Core Eurasia', comprising the five Stans, Russia, China, Afghanistan and Mongolia.

4 Sheik, Salman Rafi, 'Afghan–Pakistan border tensions grow', *Asia Sentinel*, 17 December 2022.

5 Roberts, Sean R, *The War on the Uyghurs: China's campaign against Xinjiang's Muslims*, Manchester University Press, Manchester, 2020, pp. 63–95.

6 Kelemen, Barbara, 'How the rise of the Islamic State of Khorasan in Afghanistan feeds Uyghur militancy', *The Diplomat*, 17 February 2022. It is important to note that broad concepts such as 'Afghan Uyghur-based militancy', 'militant Islam' and 'fundamentalist-inspired violence' are preferable to 'terrorist', as there is no internationally settled definition of the term 'terrorism'. Members of Hezbollah in the Arab world are 'freedom fighters', while to the US, Israel and the West, they are part of a 'terrorist' organisation. This lack of definition has plagued discussion of Uyghur terrorism. Beijing has been keen to tag all violent action against the state as 'terrorism', partly to gain international support and recognition for its

claims that Uyghur separatists are terrorists. This didn't matter much until after the 9/11 attacks, when George W Bush launched the global war on terror. China undertook a strenuous diplomatic effort to have the UN declare the East Turkestan independence movement a terrorist organisation. Its campaign was helped by some Uyghurs captured in Afghanistan having ended up in Guantanamo Bay. Sean Roberts, in his careful study of Uyghur 'terrorism', draws a clear distinction between violent attacks on innocent civilians, non-state actors, which he defines as 'terrorism', and violent acts against state actors, which he defines as guerrilla war. A potential weakness in this approach is that it casts 'terrorism' too narrowly and can define away the problem. In this study, 'terrorism' will be used sparingly but will occasionally include acts of violence against both non-state and state actors. When viewed from the perspective of the state, violent political acts are acts of terrorism whatever the target. For a discussion of the definition of 'terrorism' and its application in Xinjiang, see Roberts, ibid., pp. 10–15.

7 'Wang Yi meets head of the Afghan Taliban Political Commission Mullah Abdul Ghani Baradar', Ministry of Foreign Affairs, People's Republic of China, 28 July 2021.

8 Anees, Mariyam Suleman, 'How realistic are China's plans to expand the CPEC to Afghanistan?', *The Diplomat*, 15 December 2022.

9 Noorzai, Roshan, 'What will it take for the Taliban to gain recognition from China, others?', *Voice of America*, 10 December 2023; Leslie, Adam, 'China's recognition of the Taliban sets a dangerous precedent', *The Strategist*, 7 February 2024; Raby, Geoff, 'With Russia distracted, China makes its move in Central Asia', *Australian Financial Review*, 22 March 2024.

10 Raby, Geoff, *China's Grand Strategy and Australia's Future in the New Global Order*, Melbourne University Publishing, Carlton, 2020, pp. 35–6.

11 Umarov, Temur, 'Russia and Central Asia: never closer, or drifting apart?', Carnegie Endowment for International Peace, 23 December 2022.

12 Raby, Geoff, 'Ukraine fallout: Australia and the new world disorder', *Australian Foreign Affairs*, issue 16, October 2022, pp. 6–20.

13 Stent, Angela, 'The Putin Doctrine', *Foreign Affairs*, 27 January 2022; Reuters, 5 September 2022; Umarov, loc. cit.

14 Raby, 'Ukraine fallout …', loc. cit.

15 Ibid.

16 Dubnov, Arkady, 'Reflecting on a quarter century of Russia's relations with Central Asia', Carnegie Endowment for International Peace, 19 April 2018.

17 See note 3 for an explanation of 'Core Eurasia'.

18 Lin, Bonny and Jude Blanchette, 'China on the offensive: how the Ukraine War has changed Beijing's strategy', *Foreign Affairs*, 1 August 2022.

19 Raby, 'Ukraine fallout …', loc. cit.

20 Raby, Geoff, 'China's elites gag on "Vlad the Toxic"', *Australian Financial Review*, 18 March 2022.

21 Loc. cit.

22 'The new world order and the rise of the middle powers', *Financial Times*, editorial, 28 December 2022.

23 Thubron, Colin, *The Amur River: between Russia and China*, Vintage, London, 2022.

24 Raby, 'With Russia distracted …', loc. cit.

25 Raby, *China's Grand Strategy* …, loc. cit.

26 Barber, Tony, 'Central Asia emerges gingerly from the shadow of Russia', *Financial Times*, 28 December 2022.

27 Mackinder, Halford John, 'The geographical pivot of history', *Geographical Journal*, vol. 23, no. 4, 1904, p. 436.

28 Kaplan, Robert D, *The Revenge of Geography: what the map tells us about coming conflicts and the battle against fate*, Random House, New York, 2012; Kaplan, Robert D, *The Return of Marco Polo's World: war, strategy, and American interests in the twenty-first century*, Random House, New York, 2018; Sempa, Francis P, 'China and the World-Island', *The Diplomat*, 26 January 2019; Sempa, Francis P, 'Struggle for the World-Island', *Best Defence*, 7 October 2023; Yu, Shirley, 'The Belt and Road initiative: modernity, geopolitics, and the developing global order', *Asian Affairs*, vol. 50, no. 2, 2019, pp. 187–201.

29 Caddis, John Lewis, *On Grand Strategy*, Allen Lane, London, 2018, pp. 259–60.

30 Spykman, Nicholas John, *America's Strategy in World Politics: the United States and the balance of power*, Routledge, London, 2017 (1st ed. 1942).

31 Mahan, AT, *The Influence of Sea Power on History, 1660–1783*, Little, Brown & Co., New York, 1890; Sumida, Jon, 'New insights from old books: the case of Alfred Thayer Mahan', *Naval War College Review*, vol. 54, no. 3, summer 2001, pp. 100–11.

32 Lasserre, Frederic, 'Mackinder, models, and the New Silk Road: a deceiving tool?', Network for Strategic Analysis, Policy Reports, 27 August 2020.

33 Holmila, Antero, 'Re-thinking Nicholas J Spykman: from historical sociology to balance of power', *International History Review*, vol. 42, no. 5, 2020.

34 Soliman, Mohammed, 'A new Asian order takes shape', *The Strategist*, ASPI, 11 April 2023.

35 Mackinder, Halford John, 'The geographical pivot of history', *Geographical Journal*, vol. 23, no. 4, p. 436; Yu, op. cit, pp. 182–9.

36 Brzezinski, Zbigniew, *The Grand Chessboard: American primacy and its geostrategic imperatives*, Basic Books, New York, 1997, pp. 40–7.

37 Ibid., pp. 21–5.

38 Raby, *China's Grand Strategy* …, op. cit., p. 50, passim.

39 Perdue, Peter, *China Marches West: the Qing conquest of Central Asia*, Harvard University Press, Cambridge, 2005, p. 336.

40 Khan, Sulmaan Wasif, *Haunted by Chaos: China's grand strategy from Mao Zedong to Xi Jinping*, Harvard University Press, Cambridge, 2018, p. 236.

41 Pantucci, Raffaello and Alexandros Petersen, *Sinostan: China's inadvertent empire*, Oxford University Press, Oxford, 2022, p. 21; Putz, Catherine, interview with Raffaello Pantucci, *The Diplomat*, 19 April 2022.

## Chapter 2    Original Great Game

1 Weller, Dr R Charles, *Review of The Great Game, 1856–1907: Russo-British relations in Central and East Asia* (review no. 1611), *Reviews in History*, https://reviews.history.ac.uk/review/1611.

2 Kipling, Rudyard, *Kim*, Penguin Classics, London, 1901.

3 Morrison, Alexander, *The Russian Conquest of Central Asia: a study of imperial expansion, 1814–1914*, Cambridge University Press, Cambridge, 2021, pp. 10–11.

4 Kaplan, Robert D, *The Return of Marco Polo's World: war, strategy and American interests in the twenty-first century*, Random House, New York, 2018, p. 260.

5 Hopkirk, Peter, *The Great Game: on secret service in high Asia*, John Murray, London, 1990, pp. 348–9.

6 Ibid., p. 351.

7 Loc. cit.

8 Loc. cit.

9 Ibid., p. 352.

10 Loc. cit.

11 Ibid., p. 353.

12 Ibid., pp. 435–7.

13 Raby, Geoff, 'Why I rate Ladakh the new Tibet', *Australian Financial Review*, 17 November 2023.

14 Hopkirk, op. cit., p. 436.

15 Ibid., p. 463; Everest-Phillips, Max, 'British consuls in Kashgar', *Asian Affairs*, 22:1, 1991, pp. 20–34.

16 Review article, Charles Weller, The Great Game ... *Reviews in History*, review 1611.

17 Hopkirk, op. cit., pp. 1–2.

18 Morrison, op. cit., p. 12.

19 Loc. cit.

20 Hiro, Dilip, *Inside Central Asia*, HarperCollins, India, 2010, p. 25.

21 Sergeev, Evengy, *The Great Game, 1856–1907: Russo-British relations in Central and East Asia*, Johns Hopkins University Press, Baltimore, 2013.

22 Morisson, op. cit., p. 12.

23 Weller, loc. cit.

24 Morrison, op. cit., p. 10.

25 Hopkirk, op. cit., p. 437.

26 Smith, Mark, *The Russia Anxiety: and how history can resolve it*, Allen Lane, 2019, pp. 16–17.

27 Loc. cit.

28 Loc. cit.

29 The Russia Anxiety in the second half of the nineteenth century stretched not only to Australia but as far as the isolated British Dominion of New Zealand. Smith, op. cit., p. 21.

30 Manaev, Georgy, 'How Australia prepared for a war with Russia', *Russia Beyond*, 29 April 2019.

31 Loc. cit.

32 Fitzhardinge, Verity, 'Russian naval visitors to Australia, 1862–1888', *Journal of the Royal Australian Historical Society*, vol. 52, part 2, June 1966, p. 154.

33 Loc. cit.

34 Loc. cit.

35 In 1935, the Melbourne *Age* carried a curious report about a Major-General Milward, who 'Since 1900 has served on the North-West Frontier ... where active service is the order of the day – every day.' *The Age*, 16 May 1935.

36 Boyce, Dean, 'Defending colonial Sydney', *The Dictionary of Sydney*, Sydney, State Library of NSW, 2021.

37 Ibid., pp. 449–50.

38 Ibid., pp. 5–6

39 Hopkirk, op. cit., p. 362.

40 Ibid., pp. 210–13.

41 Hiro, loc. cit.

42 Evengy, op. cit., pp. 125, 135–42.

43 Hopkirk, op. cit., pp. 351–2.

44 Loc. cit.

45 Evengy, op. cit., pp. 209, 237.

46 Weller, op. cit. passim.

47 Everill, Bronwen, 'When economic and great-power foreign policy collide', Review of Dale C Copeland, *A World Safe for Commerce: American foreign policy from the revolution to the rise of China*, Princeton University Press, Princeton, 2024, *Foreign Policy*, 17 February 2024.

**Chapter 3    Graveyard of Empires**

1 Mariani, Scott, *Graveyard of Empires*, Harper North, London, 2022.

2 Personal communication.

3 Raby, Geoff, 'Race across the Stans', *Australian Financial Review*, April 2018.

4 'Countries with the highest number of landmines', *World Atlas*, 17 September 2019, www.worlddata.com.

5 Hiro, Dilip, *Inside Central Asia*, HarperCollins, India, 2009, pp. 128–9.

6 Smith, Mark B, *The Russia Anxiety: and how history can resolve it*, Allen Lane, London, 2019, p. 217.

7 Dilip, op. cit., pp. 129–30.

8 'Fraser condemns Soviet Invasion of Afghanistan', 1 January 1980, *From the Archives*, *The Age*, 30 December 2020.

9 Hon. John Dawkins, 'Response to Soviet Invasion of Afghanistan', 27 February 1980, *Hansard*, House of Representatives.

10 *The Age*, 1 January 1980.

11 Fraser, Malcolm, 'Afghanistan: the challenges and the lessons', 15 June 1980, *Hansard*, PM Transcripts, Department of Prime Minister and Cabinet, Australian Government.

12 Dawkins, loc. cit.

13 Leader of the Opposition, Office of National Assessments Ministerial Statement, *Hansard*, 19 August 1980.

14 Crile, George, *Charlie Wilson's War: the extraordinary story of the largest covert operation in history*, Atlantic Monthly Press, New York, 2003.

15 During this period, China managed to have the US treasury department designate Xinjiang's East Turkestan independence movement as a 'terrorist organisation'. This was subsequently reversed after 2017, following Beijing's harsh campaign against the Uyghurs in Xinjiang. Hua, Sha, 'China irate after US removes "terrorist" label from separatist group', *Wall Street Journal*, 6 November 2020.

16 Ala, Mamtimin and Salih Hudayar, 'Independence is the only way forward for East Turkestan', *Foreign Policy*, 11 August 2021.

17 Panda, Ankit, 'Road to quadrilateral peace talks uncertain as Taliban refuses to participate', *The Diplomat*, 7 March 2016; Kashgarian, Asim, 'With US away, China gets friendly with Afghanistan's Taliban', *Voice of America*, 1 February 2022.

18 Riedel, Bruce, 'Pakistan, Taliban and the Afghan quagmire', *Brookings*, 24 August 2013.

19 Ankit, loc. cit.

20 Pantucci, Raffaello, 'Inheriting the storm: Beijing's difficult new relationship with Kabul', *The Diplomat*, 2 December 2022.

21 Ministry of Foreign Affairs, People's Republic of China, Regular Press Conference, 31 January 2024. Foreign media commentary has exhibited confusion as to whether China has accorded diplomatic recognition to the Taliban interim government in Kabul, but de facto, if not de jure, it has done.

22 Rehman, Zia Ur, 'Security concerns bring China closer to the Taliban', *Voice of America*, 11 August 2022; Kuo, Mercy A, 'China in Afghanistan: how Beijing engages the Taliban', *The Diplomat*, 25 December 2021.

23 Rehman, ibid.

24 Kuo, loc. cit.

25 Gul, Ayaz, 'China gives new trade concessions to Afghanistan', *Voice of America*, 29 July 2022.

26 Ibid.

27 Raby, Geoff, 'With Russia distracted, China makes its move in Central Asia', *Australian Financial Review*, 22 March 2024; Jalalzai, Freshta, 'China welcomes Taliban Ambassador to Beijing', *The Diplomat*, 1 February 2024; Dawi, Akmal, 'China's president accepts credentials from Afghan representative', *Voice of America*, 30 January 2024.

28 Roberts, Sean R, *The War on the Uyghurs: China's campaign against Xinjiang's Muslims*, Manchester University Press, Manchester, 2020, pp. 63–95.

29 Rehman, loc. cit.

30 Ibid.

31 Kelemen, Barbara, 'China's non-leadership in the Taliban's Afghanistan', *The Diplomat*, 27 June 2022.

32 Ibid.

33 Ibid.

34 Raby, Geoff, *China's Grand Strategy and Australia's Future in the New Global Order*, Melbourne University Publishing, Carlton, 2020, pp. 24–8.

35 Asim, Kashgarian, 'How Uyghurs and Taliban view each other – and why it matters', *Voice of America*, 13 September 2021.

36 Ibid.

37 Blumenthal, Lily, Caitlin Purdy and Victoria Bassetti, 'Chinese investment in Afghanistan's lithium sector: a long shot in the short term', *Brookings*, 3 August 2022.

38 Kullab, Samya, 'China eyes investment in Afghanistan's Mes Aynak mines', *The Diplomat*, 28 March 2022.

39 Yi En, Chia Claudia, 'Russia and Afghanistan's partnership of convenience', *East Asia Forum*, 3 November 2022.

40 Ramani, Samuel, 'Russia and the Taliban: prospective partners?', RUSI, 14 September 2021.

41 Yi En, loc. cit.

42 Ramani, loc. cit.

43 Yi En, loc. cit.

44 Webber, Lucas, 'The Islamic State versus Russia in Afghanistan', *The Diplomat*, 9 September 2022.

45 Umarov, Temur, 'Moscow terror attack spotlights Russia–Tajikistan ties', *Politika*, Carnegie Endowment for International Peace, 28 March 2024.

46 Loc. cit.

47 Worden, Scott, 'Russian invasion of Ukraine helps the Taliban but makes Afghanistan worse off', *United States Institute of Peace*, 16 March 2022.

48 Loc. cit.

49 Loc. cit.

50 Sheik, Salman Rafi, 'Afghan–Pakistan border tensions grow', *Asia Sentinel*, 17 December 2022.

## Chapter 4   Fragile Frontier

1 Starr, S Frederick (ed.), *Xinjiang: China's Muslim borderland*, Routledge, London, 2004, p. 19.

2 This section on Tibet follows Keay, John, *Himalaya: exploring the roof of the world*, Bloomsbury, London, 2022; also Peter Hopkirk, *Trespassers on the Roof of the World: the race for Lhasa*, Oxford University Press, Oxford, 1982; Peter Fleming, *Bayonets to Lhasa*, Oxford University Press, Oxford, 1984 (1st ed. 1961).

3 Keay, ibid., pp. xxiv–vii.

4 Keay, loc. cit.

5 Maillart, Ella K, *Forbidden Journey, from Peking to Kashmir*, William Heinemann, London, 1937.

6 Fleming's trip was in part retraced by Stuart Stevens but his, like mine, involved the northern arm of the Taklamakan Desert, whereas Fleming and Maillart travelled the southern arm. Stevens, Stuart, *Night Train to Turkistan: modern adventure along China's ancient Silk Road*, Atlantic Monthly Press, New York, 1988.

7 Zhu Ying, 'The inside story of when China's state-run television criticised the party', *The Atlantic*, 12 June 2012.

8 Theroux, Paul, *Riding the Iron Rooster*, Hamish Hamilton, London, 1988.

9 Khalid, Adeeb, *Central Asia: a new history from the imperial conquests to the present*, Princeton University Press, Princeton and Oxford, 2021, p. 10.

10 Oka, Takashi, 'Takashita on the road to boost China ties', *Christian Science Monitor*, 25 August 1988.

11 Hopkirk, Peter, *Foreign Devils on the Silk Road: the search for the lost treasures of Central Asia*, John Murray, London, 1980, pp. 156–76.

12 Loc. cit.

13 Hopkirk, op. cit., p. 169.

14 China has a single time zone based on Beijing. Urumqi in the west uses official time and local time. The latter is three hours behind Beijing time. So, breakfast at 7 a.m. is at 10 a.m. official time.

15 Hansen, Valerie, *The Open Empire: a history of China to 1800*, W.W. Norton, New York, 2015, pp. 42–3.

16 Hansen, ibid., p. 149.

17 Ibid., pp. 173–4; the quote, ibid., p. 199.

18 Ibid., p. 78.

19 Ibid., p. xvi and p. 77.

20 The concept of 'shadow empire' is from Barfield, Thomas J, *'Shadow Empires': an alternative imperial history*, Princeton University Press, Princeton, 2017.

21 Ibid., p. 399; Bovingdon, Gardner, 'Contested Histories', in Starr, S Frederick (ed.), *Xinjiang: China's Muslim borderland*, Routledge, New York, 2004, pp. 353–74.

22 Millward, James A, *Eurasian Crossroads: a history of Xinjiang*, Columbia University Press, New York, 2022, p. 95.

23  Ibid., p. 178.

24  Hansen, op. cit., p. 401.

25  Perdue, Peter, *China marches west: the Qing Conquest of Central Asia*, Harvard University Press, Cambridge, 2005, p. 13.

26  Brophy, David, *Uyghur Nation: reform and revolution on the Russia–China frontier*, Harvard University Press, Cambridge, 2016, pp. 6–7.

27  Millward, op. cit., p. 79.

28  Ibid., p. 7.

29  Hansen, op. cit., p. 387.

30  Eimer, David, *The Emperor Far Away: travels at the edge of China*, Bloomsbury, London, 2014, p. 6.

31  Loc. cit.

32  Ibid., p. 96.

33  Loc. cit.

34  Ibid., p. 105.

35  Ibid., p. 113.

36  Platt, Stephen R, *Autumn in the Heavenly Kingdom: China, the West and the epic story of the Taiping Civil War*, Vintage, London, 2012.

37  Loc. cit.

38  Millward, op. cit., p. 114.

39  The Khanate of Khoqand was in the Fergana Valley. Today, its territories are in Uzbekistan, Tajikistan and Kirghizstan; ibid., pp. 116–17. Unless otherwise indicated, this section follows Millward (2022), who in turn follows Kim, Hodong, *Holy War in China: the Muslim rebellion and state in Chinese Central Asia, 1864–77*, Stanford University Press, Redwood City, 2004.

40  Skrine, CP, *Chinese Central Asia*, Indus Publishing, Karachi, 1998, p. 4.

41  Khalid, Adeeb, *Central Asia: a new history from the imperial conquests to the present*, Princeton University Press, Princeton and Oxford, 2021, p. 89.

42  Brophy, op. cit., p. 56. Curiously, Brophy asserts that Beg had 'failed to ingratiate' himself with the British or Russians, but this seems hardly to be the case, not least because Beg's relationship with the British was such that when the Qing reconquest commenced, he sent an envoy to London to have the British negotiate a peace settlement with Qing representatives; Khalid, op. cit, pp. 89 and 92.

43  Millward, op. cit., pp. 120–1.

44  Khalid, op. cit, p. 90.

45  Millward, op. cit., p. 123.

46  Khalid, op. cit., pp. 90–1.

47  Milward, op. cit, p. 125.

48  Zuo Zongtang, quoted in Khalid, op. cit, p. 91.

49  Loc. cit.

50  Milward, loc. cit.

51  Brophy, op. cit, pp. 10–13; Khalid, Adeeb, 'Jadidism in Central Asia: origins, development, and fate under the Soviets', Al Mesbar Studies and Research Center, 10 April 2018.

52  Westad, Odd Arne, *Restless Empire: China and the world since 1750*, Basic Books, New York, 2012, p. 84.

53  Millward, op. cit, p. 134.

54  Ibid., p. 136.

55 Ibid., pp. 146–56.

56 Brophy, op. cit, pp. 9–12.

57 Millward, James A, *Violent Separatism in Xinjiang: a critical assessment*, Policy Studies 6, East–West Center, Hawaii, 2004, p. 4.

58 Brophy, op. cit., pp. 10–13, pp. 16–21.

59 Bovington, Gardner, *The Uyghurs: strangers in their own land*, Columbia University Press, New York, 2010, pp. 11–12.

60 Ibid., p. 13.

61 Brophy, op. cit., pp. 274–5.

62 Millward, James A and Nabijan Tursun, 'Political history and strategies of control, 1884–1974', in Starr, op. cit., p. 70.

63 Ibid., pp. 67–77.

64 Maillart, op. cit., pp. 205–52.

65 Millward and Tursun, op. cit, p. 79.

66 Ibid., p. 80.

67 Loc. cit.

68 Ibid., p. 81.

69 Ibid., p. 83.

70 Millward, op. cit, p. 230; Brophy questions whether the elimination of the ETR leadership would have been necessary, as the 'Sino-Soviet deal on Xinjiang … deviated little from Moscow's instructions up to this point.' Brophy, op. cit., p. 271.

71 Millward and Tursun, op. cit, pp. 87–8.

72 Loc. cit.

73 Millward, op. cit., p. 102.

74 Quoted in ibid., p. 247.

75 Toops, Stanley W, 'The demography of Xinjiang', in Starr, S Frederick (ed.), op. cit., pp. 245–6; Eimer, David, op. cit., pp. 83–4.

76 Millward, James A and Nabijan Tursun, 'Political history and strategies of control, 1884–1978', in Starr, S Frederick (ed.), op. cit., p. 90.

77 Millward, op. cit., pp. 254–7.

78 Ibid., p. 259.

79 Loc. cit.

80 Ibid., p. 263. This section on the Cultural Revolution in Xinjiang follows Millward, unless otherwise stated.

81 Quoted in Millward, loc. cit.

82 Millward, ibid., pp. 254–63, passim.

83 'China's efforts to lift the Xinjiang economy may smother it', *Economist*, 5 August 2021.

84 Qobil, Rustam, 'Dreaming of Uighuristan', BBC, 16 April 2015, https://www.bbc.com/news/magazine-32337643.

85 Roberts, Sean R, *The War on the Uyghurs: China's campaign against Xinjiang's Muslims*, Manchester University Press, Manchester, 2020, pp. 164–5.

86 Xu, Beina, Holly Fletcher and Jayshree Bajoria, 'The East Turkestan Islamic Movement', Council on Foreign Relations, 4 September 2014; Botobekov, Uran, 'Understanding the Turkistan Islamic Party: from global jihad to local anti-Chinese resistance', *Homeland Security*, 28 November 2022.

87 Julienne, Marc, Meritz Rudolf and Johannes Buckow, 'The terrorist threat in China', *The Diplomat*, 26 May 2015.

88  Roberts, op. cit., pp.162–3.
89  Ibid., p. 163.
90  Ibid., p. 165.
91  Ibid., pp. 240–2.
92  Ibid., p. 241.
93  Ibid., p. xviii.
94  Ibid., p. xv.
95  Wan, Adrian, 'Pro-government Kashgar Iman assassinated by "religious extremists"',
    *South China Morning Post*, 31 July 2014.

**Chapter 5  'Russia Ends Nowhere'**

 1  Putin, Vladimir, 'Russia's border "doesn't end anywhere"', *BBC News*, 24 November
    2016; Yudon, Grigory, 'Russia ends nowhere', *Meduza*, 25 February 2023.
 2  Raby, Geoff, *China's Grand Strategy and Australia's Future in the New Global Order*,
    Melbourne University Press, Melbourne, 2020, pp. 165–8; Gyngell quotes foreign
    minister Gareth Evans at the time saying the US secretary of state, James Baker,
    'laid the real mark of Zorro on me, slash, slash, slash' when meeting Evans over
    Australia not including the US in the intial APEC group, nor consulting the US on
    its formation. Gyngell, Alan, *Fear of Abandonment: Australia in the world since 1942*,
    La Trobe University Press, Melbourne, 2017, p. 176; Zoellick, Robert, 'A tribute to
    Dick Woolcott', *Asia Society*, 14 July 2010.
 3  Kissinger, Henry, *World Order: reflections on the character of nations and the course of
    history*, Allen Lane, London, 2014, p. 52.
 4  Loc. cit.
 5  Ibid., p. 53.
 6  Reid, Anna, *A Nasty Little War: the West's war to end the Russian revolution*, John
    Murray Press, London, 2023.
 7  Hopkirk, Peter, *Setting the East Ablaze: Lenin's dream of an Empire in Asia*, John
    Murray Press, London, 1984.
 8  Kissinger, op. cit., p. 52; Paine, SCM, *Imperial Rivals: China, Russia and their disputed
    frontier*, Routledge, London, 1996, pp. 50–64, discusses imperial Chinese conduct of
    international relations based on the tribute system and especially the consequences
    for China–Russia relations.
 9  Kissinger, op. cit., p. 58.
10  Ibid., pp. 214–15; Kissinger's interpretation of the 'Great Wall' is in the tradition of
    the romantic narrative about it. The narrative serves the purpose of portraying the
    Chinese people as essentially settled, peaceful and non-aggressive, despite examples
    to the contrary, such as the mid-eighteenth century genocide of the Zunghars in
    western Mongolia. Lovell has challenged the traditional interpretation, highlighting
    that there was not ever a single 'Great Wall', and that the multiplicity of walls served
    defence and offensive purposes, as well as being symbols of internal control and
    oppression. Lovell, Julia, *The Great Wall: China against the world, 1000BC–AD 2000*,
    Atlantic Books, London, 2006, pp. 20–2.
11  Kissinger, op. cit, p. 216.
12  Perdue, Peter, *China Marches West: the Qing conquest of Central Asia*, Harvard
    University Press, Cambridge, 2010, p. 10.
13  Westad, Odd Arne, *Restless Empire: China and the world since 1750*, Basic Books,
    New York, 2012, p. 11.

14  Paine, op. cit., pp. 53–4.

15  Snow, Philip, *China and Russia: four centuries of conflict and concord*, Yale University Press, New Haven, 2023, p. 71.

16  Kilpatrick, Ryan Ho, 'On national humiliation, don't mention the Russians', *China Media Project*, 24 March 2023.

17  Snow, op. cit, p. 37.

18  Millward, James A, *Eurasian Crossroads: a history of Xinjiang*, Columbia University Press, New York, 2022, p. 94.

19  Snow, op. cit, p. 34, pp. 38–9.

20  Westad, op. cit, p. 33.

21  Kilpatrick, loc. cit.

22  Ibid., pp. 34–5.

23  Platt, Stephen R, *Autumn in the Heavenly Kingdom: China, the West and the epic story of the Taiping Civil War*, Vintage, London, 2012.

24  The Convention of Peking is alternatively referred to as the Treaty of Peking, in which, in 1860, the Qing ceded territory east of the Ussuri River to Russia. Here, 'Convention' is mainly used but on occasions when the Treaty of Aigun (1858) and Convention of Peking are discussed together, 'treaties' is used for both, for stylistic reasons.

25  Westad, op. cit., pp. 56–7.

26  Westad, op. cit., pp. 117–18.

27  Raby, Geoff, 'The conflict that shocked and changed the world', *Australian Financial Review*, 26 November 2021.

28  Loc. cit.

29  Loc. cit.

30  Loc. cit.

31  Westad, op. cit., pp. 252–3.

32  Raby, loc. cit.; Hopkirk, Peter, *Foreign Devils on the Silk Road: the search for the lost treasures of Central Asia*, John Murray, London, 1980, pp. 190–208. At the end of his book, Hopkirk is left to speculate on what happened to Otani's collection at Lushun. He quotes a European expert who postulates that the items were removed to the Soviet Union when it took back control of the area. When Hopkirk was writing—and, indeed, up to the mid 2000s—Lushun was closed to foreigners, as it was the base for the Chinese military fleet. It turns out, then, that Otani's collection has been there all along!

33  Chen, Stephen, 'Chinese archaeologists uncover World War II "horror bunker" …', *South China Morning Post,* 23 May 2023.

34  Quoted in Westad, op. cit., pp. 280–1.

35  Ibid., pp. 288–9.

36  Ibid., p. 290.

37  Smith, Mark B, *The Russia Anxiety: and how history can resolve it*, Allen Lane, London, 2019, pp. 220–1.

38  Harl, Kenneth W, *Empires of the Steppes: the nomadic tribes who shaped civilisation*, London, Bloomsbury, 2023, pp. 323–3.

39  Snow, op. cit., p. 2.

40  Harl, loc. cit.

41  Milward, op. cit., p. 60; Westad, op. cit., p. 33.

42  Ibid., pp. 146–8.

43 Snow, op. cit., p. 180.
44 Ibid., pp. 176–7.
45 Ibid., pp. 179–81.
46 Westad, op. cit., p. 146.
47 Snow, op. cit., p. 181.
48 Westad, op. cit., p. 258.
49 Roberts, Sean R, 'A "land of border lands"', in Starr, S Frederick (ed.), op. cit., p. 217.
50 Millward, op. cit., pp. 196–7.
51 Chiang Kai-shek moved the Nationalist government to Nanjing in 1928 because of Japan's occupation of Manchukuo; thus began the 'Nanjing Decade'. Retreating from the Japanese, the Nationalist government moved again, to Chongqing, in 1938.
52 Ibid., p. 203.
53 Ibid., p. 207.
54 Ibid., pp. 207–8; Snow, op. cit., pp. 304–6.
55 Ibid., pp. 313–14.
56 Ibid., pp. 319–21, 329–30.
57 Ibid., pp. 336.
58 Shichor, Yitzak, 'The Great Wall of Steel: military and strategy in Xinjiang', in Starr, op. cit., pp. 137–9.

## Chapter 6  The Other Cold War

1 Westad, Odd Arne, *Restless Empire: China and the world since 1750*, Basic Books, New York, 2012, p. 345.
2 Shen Jiawei, *Standing Guard for Our Great Motherland*, 15 May 1974, 42nd Regiment, 4th Division, Heilongjiang Construction Corps; *Asia Society*, http://sites.asiasociety.org/chinarevo/?p=20; 'Shen Jiawei', 20 March 2015, *Week in China*; private conversations with the artist.
3 Snow, Philip, *China and Russia: four centuries of conflict and concord*, Yale University Press, New Haven and London, 2023, op. cit., p. 352.
4 Westad, op. cit., pp. 292–3.
5 Snow, op. cit., p. 359.
6 Ibid., p. 362.
7 Westad, op. cit., p. 305.
8 Ibid., pp. 304–5.
9 Snow, op. cit., p. 391.
10 Ibid., pp. 393–5.
11 Ibid., p. 394.
12 Ibid., p. 400 and pp. 399–406.
13 Loc. cit.
14 Ibid., p. 410.
15 Maxwell, Neville, *India's China War*, Jaico Publishing House, Bombay, 1970, p. 273.
16 Ibid., pp. 276–7.
17 Ibid., p. 277.
18 Ibid., p. 279.
19 Snow, op. cit., pp. 419–20.
20 Ibid., p. 429.
21 Ibid., p. 432.

22  Westad, op. cit., pp. 343–5, Mao quoted ibid., p. 345.

23  Shichor, Yitzak, 'The Great Wall of Steel: military and strategy in Xinjian', in S Frederick Starr (ed.), *Xinjiang: China's Muslim Borderland*, Routledge, London, 2004, p. 138–9.

24  Snow, op. cit., pp. 430–1.

25  Shichor, op. cit., p. 138.

26  Ibid., pp. 138–9.

27  Snow, op. cit., pp. 439–42.

28  Yitzak, op. cit, pp. 139–40.

29  Jian, Chen, *Zhou Enlai: a life*, Belknap Press of Harvard University Press, Cambridge, 2024, pp. 620–3.

30  Snow, op. cit., p. 493.

31  Jian, op. cit., p. 624.

32  Snow, loc. cit.

33  Jian, op. cit., p. 620.

34  Westad, op. cit., pp. 360–1; Snow, op. cit., p. 450.

35  Jian, op. cit., p. 622.

36  Snow, op. cit., p. 451.

37  Shichor, op. cit., p. 140.

38  Snow, op. cit., p. 461.

39  Perlez, Jane and Grace Tatter, 'Shared secrets: how the US and China worked together to spy on the Soviet Union', *The Great Wager*, National Public Radio podcast, 18 February 2022, https://www.wbur.org/hereandnow/2022/02/18/great-wager-spy-soviet-union.

40  James Curran makes the point that Kissinger and Nixon too had 'Europeanised' American foreign policy, eschewing notions of exceptionalism and manifest destiny. Private correspondence (February 2024).

41  Perlez and Tatter, loc. cit.

42  *Spyscape* 2023, https://spyscape.com/article/project-chestnut-the-us-secretly-gave-china-a-spy-tour-of-cia-hq; Swami, Praveen, 'How CIA and Chinese PLA joined hands in secret Cold War op to snoop on Soviet Union nukes', *The Print*, 24 February 2022, https://theprint.in/world/how-cia-chinese-pla-joined-hands-in-secret-cold-war-op-to-snoop-on-soviet-union-nukes/844469/.

43  Quang, Nguyen Minh, 'The bitter legacy of the China–Vietnam War', *The Diplomat*, 23 February 2017.

44  Snow, op. cit., pp. 478–9.

45  Ibid., p. 482.

46  Ibid., p. 485.

47  Ibid., p. 489.

48  Ibid., pp. 489–91.

49  Ibid., p. 493.

50  Agreement between Russia, Kazakhstan, Krygyzstan, Tajikistan and China on Confidence Building in the Military Field in the Border Area, UN Peacemaker, htts://peacemaker.un. org; Federation of American Scientists, 'Mutual Reduction of Military Forces in the Border Area', nuke.fas.org/control/mrmfba/index.html.

51  Treaty of Good Neighborliness and Friendly Co-operation Between the People's Republic of China and the Russian Federation, 16 July 2001, Peace Agreements Database, https://www.peaceagreements.org.

52 Chen, Qingqing and Liu Xin, 'China and Russia agree to extend good neighborliness treaty …', *Global Times*, 28 June 2021.

53 Rozoff, Rick, 'The Shanghai Cooperation Organization: the prospects for a multipolar world', Centre for Global Research, Canada, 22 May 2009; Stuenkel, Oliver, *Post Western World: how emerging powers are remaking global order*, Polity Press, Cambridge, UK, 2016, pp. 10–11. The SCO was announced in 2001, its charter signed in 2002, and it came into force in 2003.

54 Lei, Yu, 'China–Russia military cooperation in the context of Sino-Russian strategic partnership', *Asia Europe Journal,* 8 July 2019; Kashin, Vasily, 'Russia and China take military partnership to a new level', *Moscow Times*, 23 October 2019.

55 Connolly, Richard, 'Russia's economic pivot to Asia in a shifting regional environment', *Emerging Insights*, RUSI, London, September 2021.

56 Lanteigne, Marc, 'Russia, China and the Shanghai Cooperation Organisation: diverging security interests and the "Crimea Effect"', in Blakkisrud, Heige and Elana Wilson (eds), *Russia's Turn to the East*, Springer, London, 2018.

57 Snow, op. cit., pp. 493–5; Fong, Clara and Lindsay Maizland, 'China and Russia: exploring ties between two authoritarian powers', *Backgrounder*, US Council on Foreign Relations, 20 March 2024.

58 Lo, Bobo, 'Russia, China and the Georgia dimensions', *Bulletin*, Centre for European Reform, 1 October 2008.

**Chapter 7   Concert of Convenience**

 1 Richardson, Jon, 'Putin's war or proxy war', *Pearls and Irritations*, 19 July 2023.

 2 Thubron, Colin, *The Amur River: between Russia and China*, Vintage, London, 2022, p. 185.

 3 Ibid., pp. 132–3.

 4 Galambos, Imre, 'The Blagoveshchensk massacre of July 1990: translation from A. Vereshchagin's account of his journey down the Amur', *Sinologiai Szemble*, 2009/1; Thubron, op. cit., pp. 131–3.

 5 Vereshchagin, in Galambos, loc. cit.

 6 Snow, Philip, *China and Russia: four centuries of conflict and concord*, Yale University Press, New Haven and London, 2023, p. 132.

 7 Galambos, loc. cit.

 8 Higgins, Andrew, 'On Russia–China border, selective memory of massacre works for both sides', *New York Times*, 26 March 2020.

 9 Cockerell, Simon, 'Around China: Aihui History Museum—Russians are not allowed', Koryo Group, August 2021.

10 Fu, Ying, 'How China sees Russia: Beijing and Moscow are close but not allies', *Foreign Affairs*, January/February 2016.

11 Thubron, op. cit., p. 157.

12 Ibid., p. 158.

13 Sharma, Madhur, 'Why has Russia rejected China's new map …', *Outlook India*, 4 September 2023.

14 Thurbron, op. cit., pp. 131–2.

15 Loc. cit.

16 Siow, Maria, 'Could Russia side with the US and India against China?', *South China Morning Post*, 22 August 2020; Skarzynski, Stanislaw and Daniel Wong, 'Is Putin seeking a new balance between China and the West?', *The Diplomat*, 28 August 2020.

17 Made, Jan van der, 'Territorial dispute between China and Russia risks clouding friendly future', RFI (Radio France International), 21 March 2023; Smith-Peter, Susan, 'Dreams of a "broken up" Russia might turn into a nightmare for the West—and an opportunity for China', *The Conversation*, 14 November 2023.

18 Sharma, loc. cit.

19 Kilpatrick, Ryan Ho, 'On national humiliation, don't mention the Russians', *China Media Project*, 24 March 2023.

20 BBC, 22 March 2013.

21 Made, Jan van der, 'Ticking timebomb as Russia continues to occupy swathes of Chinese territory', RFI, 15 September 2022; Jian, Chen, *Zhou Enlai: a life*, Belknap Press of Harvard University, Cambridge, 2024, p. 296.

22 Smith-Peter, loc. cit. The exact territory varies in sources from 600,000 to 1.5 million square kilometres. The discrepancy arises from what is being measured—whether it is just the area north of the Amur lost in the Treaty of Aigun (1858) or also in the Convention of Peking (1860). Khrushchev was reportedly shocked when he saw that the Soviet Union had robbed China of Mongolia and annexed territories 'east of Lake Baikal, including Khabarovsk, Vladivostok, and the Kamchatka Peninsula'. Radchenko, Sergey, *To Run the World: the Kremlin's Cold War bid for global power*, Cambridge University Press, Cambridge, 2024, p. 334.

23 *South China Morning Post*, 2 July 2020.

24 Thubron, op. cit, p. 62.

25 Ibid., p. 107.

26 Tselichtchev, Ivan, 'Chinese in the Russian Far East: a geopolitical time bomb', *South China Morning Post*, 8 July 2017; Thubron, op. cit., pp. 124–5.

27 McCarthy, Simone, 'China and Russia are building bridges: the symbolism is intentional', CNN, 15 June 2022.

28 Thubron, op. cit., p. 97.

29 Ibid., p. 104.

30 Ibid., pp. 109 and 116.

31 Ibid., pp. 126–7.

32 Ibid., p. 61.

33 Ibid., p. 195.

34 MacFarquahar, Neil, 'As Chinese flock to Lake Baikal, local Russians growl', *New York Times*, 2 May 2019; Clover, Charles, 'Chinese land grab on Lake Baikal raises Russian ire', *Financial Times*, 4 January 2018; France 24, 'Russia rules China-backed bottling plant "illegal"', 27 March 2019; China Power Team, 'What are the weaknesses of the China–Russia relationship?', *ChinaPower*, 29 June 2022, updated 9 November 2023.

35 Lemaitre, Frederic and Benoit Vitkine, 'Beijing greenlit to use Russia port of Vladivostok …', *Le Monde* (English online), 26 May 2023; Kallberg, Jan, 'Goodbye Vladivostock, hello Haishenwai!', CEPA (Centre for European Policy and Analysis), Washington, 12 July 2022.

36 Chaudhury, Dipanjan Roy, 'Russia keen for India's expanding presence in Vladivostock …', Russian International Affairs Council, 3 July 2023.

37 Raby, Geoff, 'On any measure, India has disappointed', *Australian Financial Review*, 9 July 2024.

## Chapter 8   Chussia's Feet of Clay

1 Quoted in Liik, Kadri, 'It's complicated: Russia's tricky relationship with China', *Policy Brief*, European Council on Foreign Relations, ecfr.eu, 17 December 2021.

2 Lo, Bobo, 'Turning point? Putin, Xi and the Russian invasion of Ukraine', *Analyses*, Lowy Institute, 25 May 2022.

3 Soliman, Mohammed, 'The folly of merging the Indo-Pacific and Europe', National Security Program, Foreign Policy Research Institute, 24 August 2023; Curran, James, 'Why are we talking ourselves into Armageddon?', *Australian Financial Review*, 16 February 2024.

4 McGregor, Richard, *Xi Jinping: the backlash*, Lowry Institute, Penguin Books, 2019, passim; Raby, Geoff, 'Chairman of Everything: understanding Xi Jinping', *Australian Book Review*, May 2024, p. 14.

5 Raby, Geoff, *China's Grand Strategy and Australia's Future in the New Global Order*, Melbourne University Publishing, Carlton, 2020, pp. 110–13.

6 Laub, Zachary, 'The Group of Eight (G8) industrialized nations', US Council on Foreign Relations, 3 March 2014.

7 Fantappie, Maria and Vali Nasr, 'A new order in the Middle East?', *Foreign Affairs*, 22 April 2023.

8 Chang, Gordon G, 'China deliberately spread the coronavirus: what are the strategic consequences?', *Strategika*, Hoover Institute, 9 December 2020.

9 *BBC News*, 7 November 2019.

10 Private conversations, June–September 2022.

11 Wu, Guoguang, 'Interpreting Xi Jinping's shifting strategy on the Russia–Ukraine war', Asia Society Policy Institute, October 2023.

12 Carpenter, Ted Galen, 'Did Putin's 2007 Munich speech predict the Ukraine crisis?', CATO Institute, 24 January 2022.

13 Smith, Mark B, *The Russia Anxiety: and how history can resolve it*, Allen Lane, London, 2019, p. 287.

14 Wong, Edward and Julian E Barnes, 'China asked Russia to delay Ukraine War until after the Olympics', *New York Times*, 2 March 2022; Westad, Odd Arne, 'The next Sino-Russian split', *Foreign Affairs*, 5 April 2022; Lo, Bobo, 'Turning point? Putin, Xi and the Russian invasion of Ukraine', *Analyses*, Lowy Institute, 25 May 2022.

15 Wested, loc. cit.

16 Gabuev, Alexander, 'China's new vassal: how war in Ukraine turned Moscow into Beijing's junior partner', *Foreign Affairs*, 9 August 2022.

17 Wong, Edward and Julian E Barnes, 'China asked Russia to delay Ukraine war until after Olympics, US officials say', *New York Times*, 2 March 2022.

18 Raby, Geoff, 'The return of the West, Australia and the new world disorder', *Australian Foreign Affairs*, 16 October 2022, p. 1, passim.

19 Raby, *Grand Strategy …*, op. cit., p. 94.

20 Gertz, Bill, 'Putin's war tests China's nuclear security pact with Ukraine', *Washington Times*, 28 November 2022.

21 Walsh and Davey-Attlee, loc. cit.

22 Raby, Geoff, 'On any measure, India has disappointed', *Australian Financial Review*, 9 July 2024.

23 Soldatkin, Vladimir and Olesya Astakhova, 'Russia exports almost all its oil to China and India', Reuters, 27 December 2023.

24 Murray, Brendan, 'China's closer bond with Russia reshapes trade flows', Bloomberg, 25 October 2023; Watanabe, Shin, 'China border city thrives as trade with Russia booms', Nikkei Asia, 4 October 2023; Kawate, Iori, 'China–Russia trade tops $200 billion a year ahead of schedule', Nikkei Asia, 3 December 2023.

25 Global Times, 'China–Russia trade hits $218b in Jan–Nov, exceeding $200b target early: customs', 7 December 2023; The State Council, 'China vows to enhance high-quality energy cooperation with Russia', Xinhua, 16 December 2023, https://english,www.gov.cn/news.

26 Reuters, 'Russia–China energy cooperation in focus as Putin visits Xi', 15 October 2023; Reuters, 'Beijing ready to expand energy cooperation with Russia—Chinese envoy to Moscow', 20 December 2023.

27 Raby, Geoff, 'China and Russia have one bed but different dreams', Australian Financial Review, 21 May 2024.

28 NATO–India engagement has been more low key than others, but began with bilateral discussions from 2019 and continues. Dutta, Anisha, 'Off public glare, India held first round of talks with NATO, agreed to keep dialogue going', Indian Express, 21 August 2022.

29 Psaledakis, Daphne and David Brunnstrom, 'NATO Summit: key points from the Washington Declaration', Reuters, 11 July 2024.

30 Duben, Bjorn Alexander, 'What conclusions is China drawing from the Wagner revolt in Russia?', The Diplomat, 7 July 2023.

31 Lo, 25 May 2022, op. cit.

32 Duben, loc. cit.

33 Kim, Patricia M, 'The limits of the no-limits partnership: China and Russia can't be split, but they can be thwarted', Foreign Affairs, March/April 2023.

34 Fu Ying, 'How China sees Russia: Beijing and Moscow are close, but not allies', Foreign Affairs, January/February 2016.

35 Wachtmeister, Henrik, Russia–China Energy Relations since 24 February: consequences and options for Europe, Stockholm, Swedish National China Centre and SCEECUS (Stockholm Centre for Eastern European Studies), report no.1, 2023; Seddon, Max and Joe Leahy, 'Vladimir Putin visits Beijing for first time since Russia's invasion of Ukraine', Financial Times, 17 October 2023; Wilson, Tom and Chris Crook, 'US aims to halve Russia's energy revenues by 2030', Financial Times, 1 December 2023.

36 Lee, Jong Min, 'What South Korea needs post-Russia–North Korea mutual defence treaty', The Diplomat, 24 June 2024; Wyatt, Austin, 'The fallout of Russia's veto and Putin's North Korea visit', The Diplomat, 8 July 2024.

37 Brzezinski, Zbigniew, The Grand Chessboard: American primacy and its geostrategic imperatives, Basic Books, New York, 2016 (1st ed. 1997), p. 46.

38 Snow, Philip, China and Russia: four centuries of conflict and concord, Yale University Press, New Haven, 2023.

39 Fu, Ying, 'How China sees Russia: Beijing and Moscow are close, but not allies', Foreign Affairs, January/February 2016.

40 Westad, Odd Arne, 'The next Sino-Russian split', Foreign Affairs, 5 April 2022.

41 Lo, Bobo, loc. cit.

## Chapter 9    Sovietstan to Sinostan

1 Fatland, Erika, *Sovietstan: a journey through Turkmenistan, Kazakhstan, Tajikistan, Kyrgyzstan, and Uzbekistan*, MacLehose Press, London, 2014 (reprinted 2019). Pantucci, Raffaelo and Alexandros Peterson, *Sinostan: China's inadvertent empire*, Oxford University Press, Oxford, 2022 (the title is, of course, a cheeky play on 'Sovietstan' coined by Fatland).

2 Altynbayev, Kanat, 'Rahmon's rebuke of Putin stemmed from years of Russian indifference', *Caravanserai*, 20 October 2022.

3 The 'Stans'—Turkmenistan, Kazakhstan, Uzbekistan, Kyrgyzstan and Tajikistan— comprise Central Asia but subsets may also, for brevity, be referred to as the 'Stans'. My trip on this occasion was from the far west of Uzbekistan, to Tajikistan, and through Kyrgyzstan, and on into Xinjiang, China.

4 Chatwin, Bruce, 'Introduction', Robert Byron, *The Road to Oxiana*, Pimlico edn., 2004.

5 Raby, Geoff, 'One road, no frills: Geoff Raby's race along the new silk road', *Australian Financial Review*, 29 March 2018.

6 Loc. cit.

7 Pantucci and Peterson ask, 'Does the south London junkie know that his or her fix came through such spectacular scenery?', op. cit., p. 3.

8 Pannier, Bruce, 'Central Asia in focus: Kyrgyzstan falling deeper in debt to China', Radio Free Europe, 31 October 2023.

9 Hillman, Jonathan E, *The Emperor's New Road: China and the project of the century*, Yale University Press, New Haven, 2020. Hillman refers to seven border crossings when he made the same journey five months earlier than I, in May 2017, p. vii.

10 Morrison, Alexander, *The Russian Conquest of Central Asia: a study of imperial conquest, 1814–1914*, Cambridge University Press, Cambridge, 2020, p. 1.

11 Ibid., p. 24.

12 Ibid., p. 2.

13 Ibid., p. 8.

14 Ibid., pp. 282–7.

15 Ibid., p. 4.

16 Loc. cit.

17 Marat, Erica, 'Central Asia comes out of the Russian shadow', *The Diplomat*, issue 105, August 2023.

18 Walker, Joshua W, 'China's role in Central Asia and the Middle East: geographical vacuum pragmatist or new international order creator?', in David B Denoon (ed.), *China's Grand Strategy: a roadmap to global power?*, New York Press, New York, 2021, pp. 177–8.

19 Pomfret, loc. cit.

20 Pomfret, Richard, 'Central Asian economies: 30 years after the dissolution of the Soviet Union', *Comparative Economic Studies*, vol. 63, 30 August 2021, pp. 537–56.

21 Amanov, Merdan, 'Will Turkmenistan join the WTO?', *The Diplomat*, 2 June 2022.

22 Balci, Bayram, *Islam in Central Asia and the Caucasus since the Fall of the Soviet Union*, Hurst, London, October 2018.

23 'Russian direct investment in Central Asia reached $3.6 billion in 2022', *Central Asia News*, 15 March 2023.

24 World Bank, World Integrated Trade Solutions, wits.worldbank.org. countrysnapshot/en/ECS/textview.

25 European Commission, *EU Trade Relations with Central Asia*, April 2023.
26 Oztarsu, Mehmet Fatih, 'Central Asia: a lucrative back door to Russia', CEPA, 2 January 2024; Mirzakhmedova, Dilfuza, Shakhriyor Ismailkhodjaev and Kamila Fayzieva, 'Following China's export for sanctioned goods through Central Asia to Russia', *The Diplomat*, 9 January 2024.
27 'China has replaced Russia as major source of FDI', *Eurasianet*, 5 April 2024.
28 'Chinese investment in Central Asia', *Eurasianet*, 11 March 2024.
29 Mukhammadsodik, Donaev, 'The EU risks losing the contest for influence in Central Asia', *East Asia Forum*, 23 February 2023.
30 Nelson, Haley, '2022 FDI in the Caspian Region', Caspian Policy Center, 18 April 2023.
31 Loc. cit.; Abbbasoua, Vusala, *Caspian News*, 6 March 2024.
32 Buchholz, Katharina, 'Countries most in debt to China', *Statista*, 29 March 2023; Nelson, Haley, 'Russia's Central Asia decline', Caspian Policy Center, 2 March 2023.
33 OECD, *Weathering Economic Storms in Central Asia: initial impacts of the war in Ukraine*, Paris, 2023.
34 Wani, Ayjaz, 'Amid Russia–Ukraine conflict: advantage China in Central Asia', Observer Research Foundation, 23 November 2023.
35 Chaudhury, Dipanjan Roy, 'China's grand designs in resource rich Central Asia face local ire', *Economic Times*, 16 April 2023; Euroasianet, 21 July 2022.
36 Thornton, Susan A, 'China in Central Asia: Is China winning the new Great Game?', *Brookings*, June 2020.
37 Kubicek, Paul, 'The Commonwealth of Independent States: an example of failed regionalism?', *Review of International Studies*, vol. 35, 2009, pp. 237–56; Mickovic, Nikola, 'What is the future of the Commonwealth of Independent States?', *Global Community*, 31 October 2023.
38 Loc. cit.
39 Mickovic, Nikola, 'How Russia loses allies amid war in Ukraine', *The Diplomat*, 27 January 2023.
40 Stoll, Hunter, 'A case for greater US engagement in Central Asia', Commentary, RAND, 11 September 2023.
41 Barber, Tony, 'Central Asia emerges gingerly from the shadow of Russia', *Financial Times*, 28 December 2022; Courtney, William, 'Russia's appetite may extend beyond Ukraine', Commentary, RAND, 17 February 2023.
42 Alderkhanova, Elvira, 'Why is the Eurasian Economic Union broken?', *The Diplomat*, 23 November 2023.
43 Eurasian Development Bank website, www.eabr.org.
44 Loc. cit.
45 Ruehl, Henry, 'Khorgos: built, financed, owned and operated by Kazakhstan', *The Diplomat*, 27 September 2019.
46 *Global Times*, 11 March 2024.
47 Raby, Geoff, *China's Grand Strategy and Australia's Future in the New Global Order*, Melbourne University Publishing, Carlton, 2020, p. 34.
48 Raby, loc. cit.
49 US Energy Information Administration, 'World oil transit chokepoints', 25 July 2017, p. 6.
50 Strange, Austin, *Chinese Global Infrastructure*, Cambridge University Press, Cambridge, 2024.

51 Yu, Shirley, 'The Belt and Road initiative: modernity, geopolitics, and the developing global order', *Asian Affairs*, vol. 50, no. 2, 2019, p. 47.

52 State Council of the People's Republic of China, Xinhua, 18 October 2023, english.gov.au.

53 Marat, Erica, 'Central Asia comes out of the Russian shadow', *The Diplomat*, issue 105, August 2023.

54 Loc. cit.

55 Loc. cit.

56 Putz, Catherine, 'Before and after the Crocus City Hall attack: Tajik migrants in Russia', *The Diplomat*, 14 April 2024.

57 'Russian direct investment in Central Asia exceeds $3.6 billion in 2022', *Central Asian News*, 15 March 2023.

58 Stoll, loc. cit.

59 'The economic impact of the Russian invasion of Ukraine on the Caucuses and Central Asia', Asian Development Bank, April 2023.

60 Sharifli, Yunis, 'China's dominance in Central Asia: myth or reality?', RUSI, 18 January 2023.

61 'EU sanctions on Russia "massively circumvented" via third countries, study finds', *European Business Review*, 27 February 2024.

62 Wilson, Jeanne L, 'The Russian pursuit of regional hegemony', *Rising Powers Quarterly*, vol. 2, issue 1, 2017, pp. 7–25.

63 Wilson, Jeanne L, 'Russia and China in Central Asia: deepening tensions in the relationship', *Acta Via Serica*, vol. 6, no. 1, June 2021, p. 90.

64 *Moscow Times*, 8 April 2024.

65 Scepanovic, Janko, 'The sheriff and the banker? Russia and China in Central Asia', *The National Security Review*, 13 June 2023.

66 Loc. cit.

67 Larson, Deborah Welch, 'An equal partnership of unequals: China and Russia's new status relationship', *International Relations*, vol. 57, 21 August 2019; Scepanovic, loc. cit.

68 Ibid.

69 Scepanovic, loc. cit.

70 Altynbayev, Kanat, 'Rahmon's rebuke of Putin stemmed from years of Russian indifference', *Caravanserai*, 20 October 2022.

71 Yuan, Jiang, 'Russia's strategy in Central Asia: inviting India to balance China', *The Diplomat*, 23 January 2020.

72 Wani, Ayjaz, 'C+C5 Summit: Beijing's increasing shadow over Central Asia', Observer Research Foundation, 29 May 2023; Scepanovic, loc. cit.

73 Pantucci and Peterson, loc. cit.

74 Wang Yi meets with Sergei Lavrov, Ministry of Foreign Affairs, PRC, 22 February 2023; this is elaborated on in Fu Ying, 'How China sees Russia: Beijing and Moscow are close, but not allies', *Foreign Affairs*, January/February 2016.

75 Shih, Chienyu, quoted in Joe Leahy, 'Xi Jinping courts Central Asia as Russian influence weakens', *Financial Times*, 18 May 2023.

76 Ministry of Foreign Affairs, People's Republic of China, Regular Press Conference, 19 May 2023; Wani, Ayjaz, 'C+C5 summit: Beijing's increasing shadow over Central Asia', Observer Research Foundation.

77 Sharifli, Yunis, 'Growing importance of Uzbekistan for China', *Geopolitical Monitor*, 4 October 2022.

78 Shakil, FM, 'Spoilers and stakeholders in the Trans-Afghan railway saga', *The Cradle*, 4 September 2023; Nina Burna-Asefi, Sophia, 'After temporary suspension, what is next for the Trans-Afghan railway?', *The Diplomat*, 17 February 2023.

79 Avdalani, Emil, 'China uses crises to build Central Asian influence', CEPA, 20 February 2024.

80 Bhat, Vinayak, 'China has built a second military base near key Afghan corridor—just north of PCK', *The Print*, 22 February 2019.

81 Jardine, Bradley and Edward Lemon, 'In post–American Central Asia, Russia and China are tightening their grip', *Texas National Security Review*, 7 October 2021; Scepanovic, loc. cit.

82 Markusen, Max, 'A stealth industry: the quiet expansion of Chinese private security companies', CSIS Briefs, January 2022.

83 Wani, loc. cit.

84 Barber, Tony, 'Central Asia emerges gingerly from the shadow of Russia', *Financial Times*, 28 December 2022.

85 European Commission, news announcement, 30 January 2024.

86 Marat, loc. cit.

87 Advalani, loc. cit.

88 Fatland, op. cit., pp. 462–3.

## Chapter 10   Next Great Game

1 Raby, Geoff, *China's Grand Strategy and Australia's Future in the New Global Order*, Melbourne University Publishing, Carlton, 2020. I wrote: 'The old order shaped by the US is over. The historic moment in the post–Cold War era, of a unipolar order in which the US pursued a liberal internationalist agenda, is already a fading memory.' Ibid., p. 10.

2 Jacobson, Gavin, 'The tragedy of John Mearsheimer: how the American realist became the world's most hated thinker', *New Statesman*, 27 September 2023.

3 Leonard, Mark, 'The decline and fall of Davos Man', *The Strategist*, ASPI, 31 May 2022.

4 Mearsheimer, John, 'Bound to fail: the rise and fall of the liberal international order', *International Security*, vol. 43, no. 4, 2019.

5 Stuenkel, Oliver, *Post Western World: how emerging powers are remaking global order*, Polity Press, Cambridge, 2016, p. 11.

6 European Parliament, Think Tank, 'Expansion of BRICS: a quest for greater global influence', 15 March 2024.

7 Goh, Norman, 'Malaysia asks China to support its bid to join BRICS', *Nikkei Asia*, 19 June 2024.

8 Wirjawan, Gita, interview with John Mearsheimer, 'John Mearsheimer: Is China the real winner of Ukraine War?', *Endgame* no. 136 (Luminaries), YouTube; Mearsheimer, John, *The Tragedy of Great Power Politics*, WW Norton, New York, 2001.

9 Raby, op. cit., pp. 10–11.

10 Economy, Elizabeth, 'China's alternative order and what America should learn from it', *Foreign Affairs*, May/June 2024.

11 Loc. cit.

12 Costigan, Johanna M, 'China's vision of world order', *China File*, 7 December 2023; Wolff, Stefan, 'China's new world order: looking for clues from Xi's recent meetings with foreign leaders', *The Conversation*, 19 April 2024.

13 Raby, op. cit., p. 8, and passim.

14 Khan, Sulman Wasif, *Haunted by Chaos: China's grand strategy from Mao Zedong to Xi Jinping*, Harvard University Press, Cambridge, 2018, p. 246.

15 Quoted in Lasserre, 'Mackinder, models, and the New Silk Road: a deceiving tool', *Network Strategic Analysis*, Policy Paper Report, 27 August 2020.

16 Quoted in Holmila, Antero, 'Re-thinking Nicholast J Spykman: from historical sociology to balance of power', *International History Review*, vol. 42, no. 5, 2020.

17 Walker, Joshua, 'China's role in Central Asia and the Middle East', in David BH Denoon, *China's Grand Strategy: a roadmap to global power*, New York University Press, New York, 2021, pp. 176–7.

18 *Economist*, 'China has became a scientific superpower', 13 June 2024.

19 Beng, Ooi Kee, *The Eurasian Core and its Edges: dialogues with Wang Gungwu on the history of the world*, ISEAS, Singapore, 2015, pp. 7–8, 17–19.

20 European Commission, 'EU–China—a strategic outlook', EU Brussels, 12 March 2019; Chen, Dingding and Junyang Hu, 'Are the European Union and China systemic rivals?', *The Diplomat*, 8 April 2019; Berkofsky, Axel, 'China and the EU: "strategic partners" no more', Institute for Security and Development Policy, 4 December 2019.

21 Etkind, Alexander, 'Putin is opening a door for China', *Noema*, Berggruen Institute, 20 April 2013.

22 Nakazawa, Katsuji, 'Xi–Putin honeymoon at risk as Chinese flood into Russia', *Nikkei Asia*, 21 March 2024.

23 Brzezinski, op. cit., p. 41.

24 The treatment of Xinjiang here as a entity ethnically, culturally, linguistically, spiritually and historically distinct from core China and its Han civilisation is the same as that adopted, and for the same reasons, by Adeeb Khalid in his recent history of Central Asia: *Central Asia: a new history from the imperial conquests to the present*, Princeton University Press, Princeton and Oxford, 2021, pp. 8–9. Of course, large-scale Han migration to Xinjiang over the past four decades has substantially altered its ethnic composition to be predominately Han Chinese.

25 Rollo, Stuart, *Terminus: westward expansion, China, and the end of American empire*, Johns Hopkins University Press, Baltimore, 2023, p. 24.

26 Raby, op. cit., p. 49, passim.

27 Ibid., p. 97.

28 Raby, Geoff, 'Sightseeing at the border of two simmering nuclear powers', *Australian Financial Review*, 10 February 2023.

29 Ministry of External Affairs, India, 'India–Kazakhstan relations: bilateral brief', www.mea.gov.in.

30 Pradhan, SD, 'Second India–Central Asia NSAs meet', *Times of India*, 23 October 2023.

31 Sachdeva, Gulshan, 'India's Central Asia challenge', *East Asia Forum*, 14 April 2022.

32 Shulz, Dante, 'How India can broaden its relationship with Central Asia', *The Diplomat*, 10 December 2022.

33 Gyngell, Allan, *Fear of Abandonment: Australia in the World since 1942*, La Trobe University Press, Melbourne, 2017.

34 Chalmers, Jim, 'Economic security and the Australian opportunity in a world of churn and change', Address to the Lowry Institute, Treasury, 1 May 2024.

35 Curran, James, 'It's time Wong squarely confronted Australia's foreign policy dilemma', *Australian Financial Review*, 17 March 2024.

36 Nicholson, Brenda, 'Australia must avoid war in the region says Penny Wong', *The Strategist*, ASPI, 17 April 2023.

37 Goh, Evelyn, 'Australia's search for strategic equilibrium in Southeast Asia', *ANU Reporter*, 1 May 2023.

38 Stromseth, Jonathan, 'Don't make us choose: Southeast Asia in the throes of US–China rivalry', *Brookings Research*, October 2019.

39 Suruga, Tsubasa, 'Majority of ASEAN people favour China over US', *Nikkei Asia*, 2 Aprill 2024.

40 Curran, James, 'It's a mistake to think about ASEAN in binary terms', *Australian Financial Review*, 3 March 2024.

41 Strangio, Sebastian, 'Malaysia's Anwar warns US that containing China will "accentuate" its grievances', *The Diplomat*, 8 March 2024; Ihsan, Ili Shazwani, 'Malaysian PM defends China again …', Radio Free Asia, 7 March 2023.

42 The concept is from the classical Greek historian Thucydides's *History of the Peloponnesian War* (431–404 BC) between Greece and Athens, when a rising Sparta challenged Athens' dominance of the ancient Greek world.

43 MacMillan, Margaret, *The War that Ended Peace: the road to 1914*, Random House, New York, 2015.

44 Allison, Graham, *Destined for War: China, America, and the Thucydides Trap*, Harcourt, Boston, 2017, p. xvi.

45 Stuenkel, op. cit., p. 8.

46 Shifrinson, Joshua R Itzkowitz, *Rising Titans, Falling Giants: how great powers exploit power shifts*, Cornell University Press, Ithaca, 2018, pp. 160–74.

47 Pottinger, Matt and Mike Gallagher, 'No substitute for victory: American competition with China must be won, not managed', *Foreign Affairs*, May/June 2024.

48 Medeiros, Evan, 'The delusion of peak China: America can't wish away its toughest challenge', *Foreign Affairs*, May/June 2024.

49 Curran, James, 'France grapples with cold, hard truths of its place in the world', *Australian Financial Review*, 22 May 2024.

50 Franko, Blake, 'The "Reverse Kissinger"', *The American Conservative*, 10 January 2017; Kupchan, Charles A, 'The right way to split China and Russia', *Foreign Affairs*, 4 August 2021.

51 Gabuev, Alexander, 'Putin and Xi's unholy alliance', *Foreign Affairs*, 9 April 2024.

52 Giles, Keir, 'Ukraine isn't Putin's war—it's Russia's war', *Foreign Policy*, 21 February 2024.

53 Brzezinski, Zbigniew, *The Grand Chessboard: American primacy and its geostrategic imperatives*, Basic Books, New York, 1997, revised edition with Epilogue, 2016, pp. 40–8.

54 Rollo, op. cit, pp. 65–9.

# BIBLIOGRAPHY

Abbasova, Vusala, *Caspian News*, 6 March 2024.

Agreement between Russia, Kazakhstan, Krygyzstan, Tajikistan and China on Confidence Building in the Military Field in the Border Area, UN Peacemaker, htts://peacemaker.un. org.

Ala, Mamtimin and Salih Hudayar, 'Independence is the only way forward for East Turkestan', *Foreign Policy*, 11 August 2021.

Aidarkhanova, Elvira, 'Why is the Eurasian Economic Union broken?', *The Diplomat*, 23 November 2023.

Allison, Graham, *Destined for War: China, America, and the Thucydides Trap*, Harcourt, Boston, 2017.

Altynbayev, Kanat, 'Rahmon's rebuke of Putin stemmed from years of Russian indifference', *Caravanserai*, 20 October 2022.

Amanov, Merdan, 'Will Turkmenistan join the WTO?', *The Diplomat*, 2 June 2022.

Anees, Mariyam Suleman, 'How realistic are China's plans to expand the CPEC to Afghanistan?', *The Diplomat*, 15 December 2022.

Asim, Kashgarian, 'How Uyghurs and Taliban view each other—and why it matters', *Voice of America*, 13 September 2021.

Avdalani, Emil, 'China uses crises to build Central Asian influence', CEPA, 20 February 2024.

Barber, Tony, 'Central Asia emerges gingerly from the shadow of Russia', *Financial Times*, 28 December 2022.

Balci, Bayram, *Islam in Central Asia and the Caucasus since the Fall of the Soviet Union*, Hurst, London, October 2018.

Barfield, Thomas J, *'Shadow Empires': an alternative imperial history*, Princeton University Press, Princeton, 2017.

Beng, Ooi Kee, *The Eurasian Core and its Edges: Dialogues with Wang Gungwu on the history of the world*, ISEAS, Singapore, 2015.

Berkofsky, Axel, 'China and the EU: "strategic partners" no more', Institute for Security and Development Policy, 4 December 2019.

Bhat, Vinayak, 'China has built a second military base near key Afghan corridor—just north of PCK', *The Print*, 22 February 2019.

Blumenthal, Lily, Caitlin Purdy and Victoria Bassetti, 'Chinese investment in Afghanistan's lithium sector: a long shot in the short term', *Brookings*, 3 August 2022.

Botobekov, Uran, 'Understanding the Turkistan Islamic Party: from global jihad to local anti-Chinese resistance', *Homeland Security*, 28 November 2022.

Bovington, Gardner, *The Uyghurs: strangers in their own land*, Columbia University Press, New York, 2010.

Boyce, Dean, 'Defending colonial Sydney', *The Dictionary of Sydney*, Sydney, State Library of NSW, 2021.

Brophy, David, *Uyghur Nation: reform and revolution on the Russia–China frontier*, Harvard University Press, Cambridge, 2016.

Brzezinski, Zbigniew, *The Grand Chessboard: American primacy and its geostrategic imperatives*, Basic Books, New York, 2016.

Buchholz, Katharina, 'Countries most in debt to China', *Statista*, 29 March 2023.

Caddis, John Lewis, *On Grand Strategy*, Allen Lane, London, 2018.

Carpenter, Ted Galen, 'Did Putin's 2007 Munich speech predict the Ukraine crisis?', CATO Institute, 24 January 2022, https://www.cato.org/commentary/did-putins-2007-munich-speech-predict-ukraine-crisis.

Chalmers, Jim, 'Economic security and the Australian opportunity in a world of churn and change', Address to the Lowry Institute, Treasury, 1 May 2024.

Chang, Gordon G, 'China deliberately spread the coronavirus: what are the strategic consequences?', *Strategika*, Hoover Institute, 9 December 2020.

Chatwin, Bruce, 'Introduction', Robert Byron, *The Road to Oxiana*, Pimlico edn., 2004.

Chaudhury, Dipanjan Roy, 'China's grand designs in resource rich Central Asia face local ire', *Economic Times*, 16 April 2023.

—— 'Russia keen for India's expanding presence in Vladivostock …', Russian International Affairs Council, 3 July 2023.

Chen, Dingding and Junyang Hu, 'Are the European Union and China systemic rivals?', *The Diplomat*, 8 April 2019.

Chen, Qingqing and Liu Xi, 'China and Russia agree to extend good neighborliness treaty …', *Global Times*, 28 June 2021.

Chen, Stephen, 'Chinese archaeologists uncover World War II "horror bunker" …', *South China Morning Post*, 23 May 2023.

'China has replaced Russia as major source of FDI', *Eurasianet*, 5 April 2024.

'China's efforts to lift the Xinjiang economy may smother it', *Economist*, 5 August 2021.

'Chinese investment in Central Asia', *Eurasianet*, 11 March 2024.

China Power Team, 'What are the weaknesses of the China–Russia relationship?', *ChinaPower*, 29 June 2022, updated 9 November 2023.

Clover, Charles, 'Chinese land grab on Lake Baikal raises Russian ire', *Financial Times*, 4 January 2018.

Cockerell, Simon, 'Around China: Aihui History Museum—Russians are not allowed', Koryo Group, August 2021.

Connolly, Richard, 'Russia's economic pivot to Asia in a shifting regional environment', *Emerging Insights*, RUSI, London, September 2021.

Costigan, Johanna M, 'China's vision of World Order', *China File*, 7 December 2023.

'Countries with the highest number of landmines', *World Atlas*, 17 September 2019, www.worlddata.com.

Courtney, William, 'Russia's appetite may extend beyond Ukraine', Commentary, RAND, 17 February 2023.

Crile, George, *Charlie Wilson's War: the extraordinary story of the largest covert operation in history*, Atlantic Monthly Press, New York, 2003.

Curran, James, 'Why are we talking ourselves into Armageddon?', *Australian Financial Review*, 16 February 2024.

—— 'It's a mistake to think about ASEAN in binary terms', *Australian Financial Review*, 3 March 2024.

—— 'It's time Wong squarely confronted Australia's foreign policy dilemma', *Australian Financial Review*, 17 March 2024.

—— 'France grapples with cold, hard truths of its place in the world', *Australian Financial Review*, 22 May 2024.

Dawi, Akmal, 'China's President accepts credentials from Afghan representative', *Voice of America*, 30 January 2024.

Dawkins, John, 'Response to Soviet Invasion of Afghanistan', 27 February 1980, *Hansard*, House of Representatives.

Duben, Bjorn Alexander, 'What conclusions is China drawing from the Wagner revolt in Russia?', *The Diplomat*, 7 July 2023.

Dubnov, Arkady, 'Reflecting on a quarter century of Russia's relations with Central Asia', Carnegie Endowment for International Peace, 19 April 2018.

Dutta, Anisha, 'Off public glare, India held first round of talks with NATO, agreed to keep dialogue going', *Indian Express*, 21 August 2022.

*Economist*, 'China has became a scientific superpower', 13 June 2024.

Economy, Elizabeth, 'China's alternative order and what America should learn from it', *Foreign Affairs*, May/June 2024.

Eimer, David, *The Emperor Far Away: travels at the edge of China*, Bloomsbury, London, 2014.

Etkind, Alexander, 'Putin is opening a door for China', *Noema*, Berggruen Institute, 20 April 2013.

'EU sanctions on Russia "massively circumvented" via third countries, study finds', *European Business Review*, 27 February 2024.

European Commission, 'EU–China: strategic outlook', Brussels, 12 March 2019.

—— *EU Trade Relations with Central Asia*, April 2023.

—— news announcement, 30 January 2024.

European Parliament, Think Tank, 'Expansion of BRICS: A quest for greater global influence', 15 March 2024.

Everest-Phillips, Max, 'British Consuls in Kashgar', *Asian Affairs*, 22:1, 1991.

Everill, Bronwen, 'When economic and great-power foreign policy collide', Review of Dale C Copeland, *A World Safe for Commerce: American foreign policy from the revolution to the rise of China*, Princeton University Press, Princeton, 2024, *Foreign Policy*, 17 February 2024.

Fantappie, Maria and Vali Nasr, 'A new order in the Middle East?', *Foreign Affairs*, 22 April 2023.

Fatland, Erika, *Sovietstan: a journey through Turkmenistan, Kazakhstan, Tajikistan, Kyrgyzstan, and Uzbekistan*, MacLehose Press, London, 2014 (rept. 2019).

Federation of American Scientists, 'Mutual reduction of military forces in the border area', nuke.fas.org/control/mrmfba/index.html. .

Fitzhardinge, Verity, 'Russian naval visitors to Australia, 1862–1888', *Journal of the Royal Australian Historical Society*, vol. 52, part 2, June 1966.

Fleming, Peter, *Bayonets to Lhasa*, Oxford University Press, Oxford, 1961, 1984.

Fong, Clara and Lindsay Maizland, 'China and Russia: exploring ties between two authoritarian powers', *Backgrounder*, US Council on Foreign Relations, 20 March 2024.

France 24, 'Russia rules China-backed bottling plant "illegal"', 27 March 2019.

Franko, Blake, 'The "Reverse Kissinger"', *The American Conservative*, 10 January 2017.

'Fraser condemns Soviet invasion of Afghanistan', 1 January 1980, *From the Archives*, *The Age*, 30 December 2020.

Fraser, Malcolm, 'Afghanistan: the challenges and the lessons', 15 June 1980, *Hansard*, PM Transcripts, Department of Prime Minister and Cabinet, Australian Government.

Fu, Ying, 'How China sees Russia: Beijing and Moscow are close, but not allies', *Foreign Affairs*, January/February 2016.

Gabuev, Alexander, 'China's new vassal: how war in Ukraine turned Moscow into Beijing's junior partner', *Foreign Affairs*, 9 August 2022.

—— 'Putin and Xi's unholy alliance', *Foreign Affairs*, 9 April 2024.

Galambos, Imre, 'The Blagoveshchensk massacre of July 1990: translation from A. Vereshchagin's account of his journey down the Amur', *Sinologiai Szemble*, 2009/1.

Gertz, Bill, 'Putin's war tests China's nuclear security pact with Ukraine', *Washington Times*, 28 November 2022.

Giles, Keir, 'Ukraine isn't Putin's war—it's Russia's war', *Foreign Policy*, 21 February 2024.

*Global Times*, 'China–Russia trade hits $218b in Jan–Nov, exceeding $200b target early: customs', 7 December 2023.

Goh, Evelyn, 'Australia's search for strategic equilibrium in Southeast Asia', *ANU Reporter*, 1 May 2023.

Goh, Norman, 'Malaysia asks China to support its bid to join BRICS', *Nikkei Asia*, 19 June 2024.

Gul, Ayaz, 'China gives new trade concessions to Afghanistan', *Voice of America*, 29 July 2022.

Gyngell, Alan, *Fear of Abandonment: Australia in the world since 1942*, La Trobe University Press, Melbourne, 2017.

Hansen, Valerie, *The Open Empire: a history of China to 1800*, WW Norton, New York, 2015.

Harl, Kenneth W, *Empires of the Steppes: the nomadic tribes who shaped civilisation*, London, Bloomsbury, 2023.

Higgins, Andrew, 'On Russia–China border, selective memory of massacre works for both sides', *New York Times*, 26 March 2020.

Hillman, Jonathan E, *The Emperor's New Road: China and the project of the century*, Yale University Press, New Haven, 2020.

Hiro, Dilip, *Inside Central Asia*, HarperCollins, India, 2009.

Holmila, Antero, 'Re-thinking Nicholas J Spykman: from historical sociology to balance of power', *International History Review*, vol. 42, no. 5, 2020.

Hopkirk, Peter, *Foreign Devils on the Silk Road: the search for the lost treasures of Central Asia*, John Murray, London, 1980.

—— *Trespassers on the Roof of the World: the race for Lhasa*, Oxford University Press, Oxford, 1982.

—— *Setting the East Ablaze: Lenin's dream of an empire in Asia*, John Murray Press, London, 1984.

—— *The Great Game: on secret service in high Asia*, John Murray, London, 1990.

Hua, Sha, 'China irate after US removes "terrorist" label from separatist group', *Wall Street Journal*, 6 November 2020.

Ihsan, Ili Shazwani, 'Malaysian PM defends China again …', Radio Free Asia, 7 March 2023.

Jacobson, Gavin, 'The tragedy of John Mearsheimer: how the American realist became the world's most hated thinker', *New Statesman*, 27 September 2023.

Jalalzai, Freshta, 'China welcomes Taliban ambassador to Beijing', *The Diplomat*, 1 February 2024.

Jardine, Bradley and Edward Lemon, 'In post-America Central Asia, Russia and China are tightening their grip', *Texas National Security Review*, 7 October 2021.

Jian, Chen, *Zhou Enlai: a life*, Belknap Press of Harvard University, Cambridge, 2024.

Julienne, Marc, Meritz Rudolf and Johannes Buckow, 'The terrorist threat in China', *The Diplomat*, 26 May 2015.

Kallberg, Jan, 'Goodbye Vladivostock, hello Haishenwai!', CEPA (Centre for European Policy and Analysis), 12 July 2022.

Kaplan, Robert D, *The Revenge of Geography: what the map tells us about coming conflicts and the battle against fate*, Random House, New York, 2012.

—— *The Return of Marco Polo's World: war, strategy, and American interests in the twenty-first century*, Random House, New York, 2018.

Kashgarian, Asim, 'With US away, China gets friendly with Afghanistan's Taliban', *Voice of America*, 1 February 2022.

Kashin, Vasily, 'Russia and China take military partnership to a new level', *Moscow Times*, 23 October 2019.

Kawate, Iori, 'China–Russia trade tops $200 billion a year ahead of schedule', *Nikkei Asia*, 3 December 2023.

Keay, John, *Himalaya: exploring the roof of the world*, Bloomsbury, London, 2022.

Kelemen, Barbara, 'How the rise of the Islamic State of Khorasan in Afghanistan feeds Uyghur militancy', *The Diplomat*, 17 February 2022.

—— 'China's non-leadership in the Taliban's Afghanistan', *The Diplomat*, 27 June 2022.

Khalid, Adeeb, 'Jadidism in Central Asia: origins, development, and fate under the Soviets', Al Mesbar Studies and Research Center, 10 April 2018.

—— *Central Asia: a new history from the imperial conquests to the present*, Princeton University Press, Princeton and Oxford, 2021.

Khan, Sulmaan Wasif, *Haunted by Chaos: China's grand strategy from Mao Zedong to Xi Jinping*, Harvard University Press, Cambridge, 2018.

Kilpatrick, Ryan Ho, 'On national humiliation, don't mention the Russians', *China Media Project*, 24 March 2023.

Kim, Hodong, *Holy War in China: the Muslim rebellion and state in Chinese Central Asia, 1864–77*, Stanford University Press, Redwood City, 2004.

Kim, Patricia M, 'The limits of the no-limits partnership: China and Russia can't be split, but they can be thwarted', *Foreign Affairs*, March/April 2023.

Kipling, Rudyard, *Kim*, Penguin Classics, London, 1901, 1987.

Kissinger, Henry, *On China*, Penguin Press, London, 2011.

—— *World Order: reflections on the character of nations and the course of history*, Allen Lane, London, 2014.

Kubicek, Paul, 'The Commonwealth of Independent States: an example of failed regionalism?', *Review of International Studies*, vol. 35, 2009.

Kullab, Samya, 'China eyes investment in Afghanistan's Mes Aynak mines', *The Diplomat*, 28 March 2022.

Kuo, Mercy A, 'China in Afghanistan: how Beijing engages the Taliban', *The Diplomat*, 25 December 2021.

Kupchan, Charles A, 'The right way to split China and Russia', *Foreign Affairs*, 4 August 2021.

Lanteigne, Marc, 'Russia, China and the Shanghai Cooperation Organisation: diverging security interests and the "Crimea Effect"', in Blakkisrud, Heige and Elana Wilson (eds), *Russia's Turn to the East*, Springer, London, 2018.

Larson, Deborah Welch, 'An equal partnership of unequals: China and Russia's new status relationship', *International Relations*, vol. 57, 21 August 2019.

Lasserre, Frederic, 'Mackinder, models, and the New Silk Road: a deceiving tool?', *Network for Strategic Analysis*, Policy Reports, 27 August 2020.

Laub, Zachary, 'The Group of Eight (G8) industrialized nations', US Council on Foreign Relations, 3 March 2014.

Leader of the Opposition, Office of National Assessments Ministerial Statement, *Hansard*, 19 August 1980.

Leahy, Joe, 'Xi Jinping courts Central Asia as Russian influence weakens', *Financial Times*, 18 May 2023.

Lee, Jong Min, 'What South Korea needs post-Russia–North Korea mutual defence treaty', *The Diplomat*, 24 June 2024.

Lei, Yu, 'China–Russia military cooperation in the context of Sino-Russian strategic partnership', *Asia Europe Journal,* 8 July 2019.

Lemaitre, Frederic and Benoit Vitkine, 'Beijing greenlit to use Russia port of Vladivostok …', *Le Monde* (English online), 26 May 2023.

Leonard, Mark, 'The decline and fall of Davos Man', *The Strategist*, ASPI, 31 May 2022.

Leslie, Adam, 'China's recognition of the Taliban sets a dangerous precedent', *The Strategist*, 7 February 2024.

Liik, Kadri, 'It's complicated: Russia's tricky relationship with China', *Policy Brief*, European Council on Foreign Relations, ecfr.eu, 17 December 2021.

Lin, Bonny and Jude Blanchette, 'China on the offensive: how the Ukraine War has changed Beijing's strategy', *Foreign Affairs*, 1 August 2022.

Lo, Bobo, 'Russia, China and the Georgia dimensions', *Bulletin*, Centre for European Reform, 1 October 2008.

—— 'Turning point? Putin, Xi and the Russian invasion of Ukraine', *Analyses*, Lowy Institute, 25 May 2022.

Lovell, Julia, *The Great Wall: China against the world, 1000BC–AD 2000*, Atlantic Books, London, 2006.

McCarthy, Simone, 'China and Russia are building bridges: the symbolism is intentional', CNN, 15 June 2022.

MacFarquahar, Neil, 'As Chinese flock to Lake Baikal, local Russians growl', *New York Times*, 2 May 2019.

McGregor, Richard, *Xi Jinping: the backlash*, Lowry Institute, Penguin Books, 2019.

Mackinder, Halford John, 'The geographical pivot of history', *Geographical Journal*, vol. 23, no. 4, 1904.

MacMillan, Margaret, *The War that Ended Peace: the road to 1914*, Random House, New York, 2015.

Made, Jan van de, 'Ticking timebomb as Russia continues to occupy swathes of Chinese territory', RFI (Radio France International), 15 September 2022.

—— 'Territorial dispute between China and Russia risks clouding friendly future', RFI (Radio France International), 21 March 2023.

Mahan, AT, *The Influence of Sea Power on History, 1660–1783*, Little, Brown & Co., New York, 1890.

Maillart, Ella K, *Forbidden Journey, from Peking to Kashmir*, William Heinemann, London, 1937.

Manaev, Georgy, 'How Australia prepared for a war with Russia', *Russia Beyond*, 29 April 2019.

Marat, Erica, 'Central Asia comes out of the Russian shadow', *The Diplomat*, issue 105, August 2023.

Mariani, Scott, *Graveyard of Empires*, Harper North, London, 2022.

Markusen, Max, 'A stealth industry: the quiet expansion of Chinese private security companies', *CSIS Briefs*, January 2022.

Maxwell, Neville, *India's China War*, Jaico Publishing House, Bombay, 1970.

Mearsheimer, John, *The Tragedy of Great Power Politics*, WW Norton, New York, 2001.

—— 'Bound to fail: the rise and fall of the liberal international order', *International Security*, vol. 43, no. 4, 2019.

Mederios, Evan, 'The delusion of peak China: America can't wish away its toughest challenge', *Foreign Affairs*, May/June 2024.

Mickovic, Nikola, 'How Russia loses allies amid war in Ukraine', *The Diplomat*, 27 January 2023.

—— 'What is the future of the Commonwealth of Independent States?', *Global Community*, 31 October 2023.

Millward, James A, *Violent Separatism in Xinjiang: a critical assessment*, Policy Studies 6, East–West Center, Hawaii, 2004.

—— *Eurasian Crossroads: a history of Xinjiang*, Columbia University Press, New York, 2022.

Ministry of External Affairs, India, 'India–Kazakhstan relations: bilateral brief', www.mea.gov.in.

Ministry of Foreign Affairs, People's Republic of China, 'Wang Yi meets head of the Afghan Taliban Political Commission Mullah Abdul Ghani Baradar', 28 July 2021.

—— 'Wang Yi meets with Sergei Lavrov', 22 February 2023.

—— Regular Press Conference, 19 May 2023.

—— Regular Press Conference, 31 January 2024.

Mirzakhmedova, Dilfuza, Shakhriyor Ismailkhodjaev and Kamila Fayzieva, 'Following China's export for sanctioned goods through Central Asia to Russia', *The Diplomat*, 9 January 2024.

Morrison, Alexander, *The Russian Conquest of Central Asia: a study of imperial conquest, 1814–1914*, Cambridge University Press, Cambridge, 2020.

*Moscow Times*, 8 April 2024.

Mukhammadsodik, Donaev, 'The EU risks losing the contest for influence in Central Asia', *East Asia Forum*, 23 February 2023.

Murray, Brendan, 'China's closer bond with Russia reshapes trade flows', Bloomberg, 25 October 2023.

Nakazawa, Katsuji, 'Xi–Putin honeymoon at risk as Chinese flood into Russia', *Nikkei Asia*, 21 March 2024.

Nelson, Haley, 'Russia's Central Asia decline', Caspian Policy Center, 2 March 2023.

—— '2022 FDI in the Caspian Region', Caspian Policy Center, 18 April 2023.

Nicholson, Brenda, 'Australia must avoid war in the region says Penny Wong', *The Strategist*, ASPI, 17 April 2023.

Nina Burna-Asefi, Sophia, 'After temporary suspension, what is next for the Trans-Afghan railway?', *The Diplomat*, 17 February 2023.

Noorzai, Roshan, 'What will it take for the Taliban to gain recognition from China, others?', *Voice of America*, 10 December 2023.

OECD, *Weathering Economic Storms in Central Asia: initial impacts of the war in Ukraine*, Paris, 2023.

Oka, Takashi, 'Takashita on the road to boost China ties', *Christian Science Monitor*, 25 August 1988.

Oztarsu, Mehmet Fatih, 'Central Asia: a lucrative back door to Russia', CEPA, 2 January 2024.

Paine, SCM, *Imperial Rivals: China, Russia and their disputed frontier*, Routledge, London, 1996.

Panda, Ankit, 'Road to quadrilateral peace talks uncertain as Taliban refuses to participate', *The Diplomat*, 7 March 2016.

Pannier, Bruce, 'Central Asia in focus: Kyrgyzstan falling deeper in debt to China', Radio Free Europe, 31 October 2023.

Pantucci, Raffaello, 'Inheriting the storm: Beijing's difficult new relationship with Kabul', *The Diplomat*, 2 December 2022.

—— and Alexandros Peterson, *Sinostan: China's inadvertent empire*, Oxford University Press, Oxford, 2022.

Perdue, Peter C, *China Marches West: the Qing conquest of Central Asia*, Harvard University Press, Cambridge, 2005 and 2010.

Perlez, Jane and Grace Tatter, 'Shared secrets: how the US and China worked together to spy on the Soviet Union', *The Great Wager*, National Public Radio podcast, 18 February 2022.

Platt, Stephen R, *Autumn in the Heavenly Kingdom: China, the West and the epic story of the Taiping Civil War*, Vintage, London, 2012.

Pomfret, Richard, 'Central Asian economies: 30 years after the dissolution of the Soviet Union', *Comparative Economic Studies*, vol. 63, 30 August 2021.

Pottinger, Matt and Mike Gallagher, 'No substitute for victory: American competition with China must be won, not managed', *Foreign Affairs*, May/June 2024.

Pradhan, SD, 'Second India–Central Asia NSAs meet', *Times of India*, 23 October 2023.

Psaledakis, Daphne and David Brunnstrom, 'NATO Summit: key points from the Washington Declaration', Reuters, 11 July 2024.

Putin, Vladimir, 'Russia's border "doesn't end anywhere"', *BBC News*, 24 November 2016.

Putz, Catherine, 'Before and after the Crocus City Hall attack: Tajik migrants in Russia', *The Diplomat*, 14 April 2024.

Putz, Catherine, interview with Raffaello Pantucci, *The Diplomat*, 19 April 2022.

Qobil, Rustam, 'Dreaming of Uighuristan', BBC, 16 April 2015.

Quang, Nguyen Minh, 'The bitter legacy of the China–Vietnam War', *The Diplomat*, 23 February 2017.

Raby, Geoff, 'One road, no frills: Geoff Raby's race along the new silk road', *Australian Financial Review*, 29 March 2018.

—— *China's Grand Strategy and Australia's Future in the New Global Order*, Melbourne University Publishing, Melbourne, 2020.

—— 'The conflict that shocked and changed the world', *Australian Financial Review*, 26 November 2021.

—— 'China's elites gag on "Vlad the Toxic"', *Australian Financial Review*, 18 March 2022.

—— 'The return of the West: Australia and the new world disorder', *Australian Foreign Affairs*, 16 October 2022.

—— 'Sightseeing at the border of two simmering nuclear powers', *Australian Financial Review*, 10 February 2023.

—— 'Why I rate Ladakh the new Tibet', *Australian Financial Review*, 17 November 2023.

—— 'With Russia distracted, China makes its move in Central Asia', *Australian Financial Review*, 22 March 2024.

—— 'Chairman of Everything: understanding Xi Jinping', *Australian Book Review*, May 2024.

—— 'China and Russia have one bed but different dreams', *Australian Financial Review*, 21 May 2024.

—— 'On any measure, India has disappointed', *Australian Financial Review*, 9 July 2024.

Radchenko, Sergey, *To Run the World: the Kremlin's Cold War bid for global power*, Cambridge University Press, Cambridge, 2024.

Ramani, Samuel, 'Russia and the Taliban: prospective partners?', RUSI, 14 September 2021.

Rehman, Zia Ur, 'Security concerns bring China closer to the Taliban', *Voice of America*, 11 August 2022.

Reid, Anna, *A Nasty Little War: the West's war to end the Russian revolution*, John Murray Press, London, 2023.

Reuters, 'Russia–China energy cooperation in focus as Putin visits Xi', 15 October 2023.

—— 'Beijing ready to expand energy cooperation with Russia—Chinese envoy to Moscow', 20 December 2023.

Richardson, Jon, 'Putin's war or proxy war', *Pearls and Irritations*, 19 July 2023.

Riedel, Bruce, 'Pakistan, Taliban and the Afghan quagmire', *Brookings*, 24 August 2013.

Roberts, Sean R, *The War on the Uyghurs: China's campaign against Xinjiang's Muslims*, Manchester University Press, Manchester, 2020.

Rollo, Stuart, *Terminus: westward expansion, China, and the end of American empire*, Johns Hopkins University Press, Baltimore, 2023.

Rozoff, Rick, 'The Shanghai Cooperation Organization: the prospects for a multipolar world', Centre for Global Research, Canada, 22 May 2009.

Ruehl, Henry, 'Khorgos: built, financed, owned and operated by Kazakhstan', *The Diplomat*, 27 September 2019.

'Russian direct investment in Central Asia reached $3.6 billion in 2022', *Central Asia News*, 15 March 2023.

Sachdeva, Gulshan, 'India's Central Asia challenge', *East Asia Forum*, 14 April 2022.

Scepanovic, Janko, 'The sheriff and the banker? Russia and China in Central Asia', *The National Security Review*, 13 June 2023.

Seddon, Max and Joe Leahy, 'Vladimir Putin visits Beijing for first time since Russia's invasion of Ukraine', *Financial Times*, 17 October 2023.

Sempa, Francis P, 'China and the World-Island', *The Diplomat*, 26 January 2019.

—— 'Struggle for the World-Island', *Best Defence*, 7 October 2023.

Sergeev, Evengy, *The Great Game, 1856–1907: Russo-British Relations in Central and East Asia*, Johns Hopkins University Press, Baltimore, 2013.

—— 'Spoilers and stakeholders in the Trans-Afghan railway saga', *The Cradle*, 4 September 2023.

Sharifli, Yunis, 'China's dominance in Central Asia: myth or reality?', RUSI, 18 January 2023.

—— 'Growing importance of Uzbekistan for China', *Geopolitical Monitor*, 4 October 2022.

Sharma, Madhur, 'Why has Russia rejected China's new map …', *Outlook India*, 4 September 2023.

Sheik, Salman Rafi, 'Afghan–Pakistan border tensions grow', *Asia Sentinel*, 17 December 2022.

'Shen Jiawei', 20 March 2015, *Week in China*.

Shifrinson, Joshua R Itzkowitz, *Rising Titans, Falling Giants: how great powers exploit power shifts*, Cornell University Press, Ithaca, 2018.

Shulz, Dante, 'How India can broaden its relationship with Central Asia', *The Diplomat*, 10 December 2022.

Siow, Maria, 'Could Russia side with the US and India against China?', *South China Morning Post*, 22 August 2020.

Skarzynski, Stanislaw and Daniel Wong, 'Is Putin seeking a new balance between China and the West?', *The Diplomat*, 28 August 2020.

Skrine, CP, *Chinese Central Asia*, Indus Publishing, Karachi, 1998.

Smith, Mark B, *The Russia Anxiety: and how history can resolve it*, Allen Lane, London, 2019.

Smith-Peter, Susan, 'Dreams of a "broken up" Russia might turn into a nightmare for the West—and an opportunity for China', *The Conversation*, 14 November 2023.

Snow, Philip, *China and Russia: four centuries of conflict and concord*, Yale University Press, New Haven and London, 2023.

Soldatkin, Vladimir and Olesya Astakhova, 'Russia exports almost all its oil to China and India', Reuters, 27 December 2023.

Soliman, Mohammed, 'A new Asian order takes shape', *The Strategist*, ASPI, 11 April 2023.

—— 'The folly of merging the Indo-Pacific and Europe', *National Security Program*, Foreign Policy Research Institute, 24 August 2023.

Spykman, Nicholas John, *America's Strategy in World Politics: the United States and the balance of power*, Routledge, London, 2017 (1st pub. 1942).

*Spyscape* 2023, https://spyscape.com/article/project-chestnut-the-us-secretly-gave-china-a-spy-tour-of-cia-hq.

Starr, S Frederick (ed.), *Xinjiang: China's Muslim borderland*, Routledge, London, 2004.

Stent, Angela, 'The Putin doctrine', *Foreign Affairs*, 27 January 2022.

Stevens, Stuart, *Night Train to Turkistan: modern adventure along China's ancient Silk Road*, Atlantic Monthly Press, New York, 1988.

Stoll, Hunter, 'A case for greater U.S. engagement in Central Asia', Commentary, RAND, 11 September 2023.

Strange, Austin, *Chinese Global Infrastructure*, Cambridge University Press, Cambridge, 2024.

Strangio, Sebastian, 'Malaysia's Anwar warns US that containing China will "accentuate" its grievances', *The Diplomat*, 8 March 2024.

Stromseth, Jonathan, 'Don't make us choose: Southeast Asia in the throes of US–China rivalry', *Brookings Research*, October 2019.

Stuenkel, Oliver, *Post Western World: how emerging powers are remaking global order*, Polity Press, Cambridge, UK, 2016.

Sumida, Jon, 'New insights from old books: the case of Alfred Thayer Mahan', *Naval War College Review*, vol. 54, no. 3, summer 2001.

Suruga, Tsubasa, 'Majority of ASEAN people favour China over US', *Nikkei Asia*, 2 April 2024.

Swami, Praveen, 'How CIA and Chinese PLA joined hands in secret Cold War op to snoop on Soviet Union nukes', *The Print*, 24 February 2022.

'The economic impact of the Russian invasion of Ukraine on the Caucuses and Central Asia', Asian Development Bank, April 2023.

'The new world order and the rise of the middle powers', *Financial Times*, editorial, 28 December 2022.

Theroux, Paul, *Riding the Iron Rooster*, Hamish Hamilton, London, 1988.

Thornton, Susan A, 'China in Central Asia: Is China winning the new Great Game?', *Brookings*, June 2020.

Thubron, Colin, *The Amur River: between Russia and China*, Vintage, London, 2022.

Treaty of Good Neighborliness and Friendly Co-operation Between the People's Republic of China and the Russian Federation, 16 July 2001, Peace Agreements Database, https://www.peaceagreements.org.

Tselichtchev, Ivan, 'Chinese in the Russian Far East: a geopolitical time bomb', *South China Morning Post*, 8 July 2017.

US Energy Information Administration, 'World oil transit chokepoints', 25 July 2017.

Umarov, Temur, 'Moscow terror attack spotlights Russia–Tajikistan ties', *Politika*, Carnegie Endowment for International Peace, 28 March 2024.

—— 'Russia and Central Asia: never closer, or drifting apart?', Carnegie Endowment for International Peace, 23 December 2022.

Wachtmeister, Henrik, *Russia–China energy relations since 24 February: consequences and options for Europe*, Stockholm, Swedish National China Centre and SCEECUS (Stockholm Centre for Eastern European Studies), report no.1, 2023.

Walker, Joshua W, 'China's role in Central Asia and the Middle East: geographical vacuum pragmatist or new international order creator?', in David B Denoon (ed.), *China's Grand Strategy: a roadmap to global power?*, New York Press, New York, 2021.

Wan, Adrian, 'Pro-government Kashgar Iman assassinated by "religious extremists"', *South China Morning Post*, 31 July 2014.

Wani, Ayjaz, 'C+C5 Summit: Beijing's increasing shadow over Central Asia', Observer Research Foundation, 29 May 2023.

—— 'Amid Russia–Ukraine conflict: advantage China in Central Asia', Observer Research Foundation, 23 November 2023.

Watanabe, Shin, 'China border city thrives as trade with Russia booms', *Nikkei Asia*, 4 October 2023.

Webber, Lucas, 'The Islamic State versus Russia in Afghanistan', *The Diplomat*, 9 September 2022.

Weller, Dr R Charles, *Review of The Great Game, 1856–1907: Russo-British relations in Central and East Asia* (review no. 1611), *Reviews in History* 26 June 2014.

Westad, Odd Arne, 'The next Sino-Russian split', *Foreign Affairs*, 5 April 2022.

—— *Restless Empire: China and the world since 1750*, Basic Books, New York, 2012.

Wilson, Jeanne L, 'The Russian pursuit of regional hegemony', *Rising Powers Quarterly*, vol. 2, issue 1, 2017.

—— 'Russia and China in Central Asia: deepening tensions in the relationship', *Acta Via Serica*, vol. 6, no. 1, June 2021.

Wilson, Tom and Chris Crook, 'US aims to halve Russia's energy revenues by 2030', *Financial Times*, 1 December 2023.

Wirjawan, Gita, interview with John Mearsheimer, 'John Mearsheimer: Is China the real winner of Ukraine War?', *Endgame*, no. 136 (Luminaries), YouTube.

Wolff, Stefan, 'China's new world order: looking for clues from Xi's recent meetings with foreign leaders', *The Conversation*, 19 April 2024.

Wong, Edward and Julian E Barnes, 'China asked Russia to delay Ukraine War until after the Olympics', *New York Times*, 2 March 2022.

Worden, Scott, 'Russian invasion of Ukraine helps the Taliban but makes Afghanistan worse off', United States Institute of Peace, 16 March 2022.

World Bank, World Integrated Trade Solutions, wits.worldbank.org.countrysnapshot/en/ECS/textview.

Wu, Guoguang, 'Interpreting Xi Jinping's shifting strategy on the Russia–Ukraine war', Asia Society Policy Institute, October 2023.

Wyatt, Austin, 'The fallout of Russia's veto and Putin's North Korea visit', *The Diplomat*, 8 July 2024.

Xinhua, 'China vows to enhance high-quality energy cooperation with Russia', Xinhua, 16 December 2023, https://english,www.gov.cn/news.

Xu, Beina, Holly Fletcher and Jayshree Bajoria, 'The East Turkestan Islamic Movement', Council on Foreign Relations, 4 September 2014.

Yi En, Chia Claudia, 'Russia and Afghanistan's partnership of convenience', *East Asia Forum*, 3 November 2022.

Yu, Shirley, 'The Belt and Road Initiative: modernity, geopolitics, and the developing global order', *Asian Affairs*, vol. 50, no. 2, 2019.

Yuan, Jiang, 'Russia's strategy in Central Asia: inviting India to balance China', *The Diplomat*, 23 January 2020.

Yudin, Grigory, 'Russia ends nowhere', *Meduza*, 25 February 2023.

Zhu Ying, 'The inside story of when China's state-run television criticised the party', *The Atlantic*, 12 June 2012.

Zoellick, Robert, 'A tribute to Dick Woolcott', *Asia Society*, 14 July 2010.

# INDEX